THE GREEN BRIDGE
STORIES FROM WALES

Edited by John Davies

Seren is the book imprint of Poetry Wales Press Ltd
Nolton Street, Bridgend, Wales

www.serenbooks.com
facebook.com/SerenBooks
Twitter: @SerenBooks

First published in 1988
Reprinted 2003, 2020

ISBN 0987907476948

A CIP record for this title is available from the British Library.

The publisher works with the financial assistance of the Books Council of
Wales

Cover painting: 'The Road to Gower' by John Elwyn
Printed by Gwasg Gomer, Llandysul

~~823 - 914 DAV~~

The item should be returned or renewed by the last date stamped below.

Dylid dychwelyd neu adnewyddu'r eitem erbyn y dyddiad olaf sydd wedi'i stampio isod.

Newport
CITY COUNCIL
CYNGOR DINAS
Casnewydd

To renew visit / Adnewyddwch ar
www.newport.gov.uk/libraries

Seren Classics

CONTENTS

INTRODUCTION

There is no such thing as a short story entire of itself but the illusion that there is has prompted one of the most dynamic forms language has taken. A good story offers a past and future that aren't there, a suggestiveness with particular resonance for a small country prone to self-questioning. Nor is there, was there – such are the sleights of mind from which art makes its realities – a Wales as it exists in most fiction. It is not social realism that has stimulated the best Anglo-Welsh short stories. From Caradoc Evans, Dylan Thomas and Gwyn Thomas to Leslie Norris, Alun Richards and Ron Berry, they have invariably been mythopoetic, lighting our dream life, its longings, fears. Our mythology is our lasting consensus, an alternative and often buoyant reality. And a means perhaps of reconciling the irreconcilable.

There have been a number of short story anthologies containing translations from the Welsh. Following *The Shining Pyramid and Other Stories*, edited by Roland Mathias and Sam Adams, this is the second anthology devoted solely to the Anglo-Welsh short story. Its development Glyn Jones in *The Dragon Has Two Tongues* and Roland Mathias in *Anglo-Welsh Literature: An Illustrated History* have charted in sufficient detail to make further summary here unnecessary. But it is a reflection of the vigorous talents of the nineteen-thirties and forties that, whereas in Gwyn Jones' 1940 anthology there were only three Anglo-Welsh writers over fifty years of age, by 1976 Alun Richards' anthology included just three such writers *under* fifty. The special social circumstances generating such talents are one factor. Others are the declining status of the short story in English generally during the past thirty years and the fact that poetry was a more inviting vehicle for the sharply political expressions of national consciousness characteristic of the nineteen-sixties and seventies. As for the present, the quality of the fiction in the resurgent *Planet* has been heartening; so too the work in particular of some younger writers willing to resist the datedly pedestrian, responsive to the challenge of developments elsewhere. In America especially, the short story has changed more than any other genre, becoming increasingly elliptical and suggestive, wary of explication in its focus on interior lives.

Another challenge is the theory that Anglo-Welsh literature itself is a shrinking entity, that if the Welsh language declines further so too will identifiable Welshness. It may be so. The possibility has contributed to the tension in contemporary poetry. Alongside the myth (in the creative sense) of the organic community, that nostalgia for the rural past analysed by Raymond Williams in *Culture and Society* – "if there is one thing certain about the organic community it is that it has always gone" – might be ranked the myth of the disappearing Wales. The myth will endure, it cannot be otherwise. But there is evidence, on this edge of the nineteen-nineties, that a certain period of romanticism is over. Increasingly the Welsh language has become one of several metaphors for a complex of values not solely reliant on those metaphors. There has been a widening of focus which itself has become harder-edged. An exploration of place as a microcosm, the possibilities of Anglo-Welsh writing signalled by Gwyn Williams, Raymond Williams and others are continually evolving. To locate the universal in the particular in a manner that resists the charge of regionalism – often the complaint of the larger region against the smaller – is to refine that search for immediacy which is the essence not just of literature.

An increasing diversity has prompted broadening outlooks. Several stories here remind one that Anglo-Welsh literature has not simply strummed on the theme of hearth and home. Whether younger writers though will manifest the kind of rooted cosmopolitanism embodied in Leslie Norris' work at its best remains to be seen. "The Wales I walk is a green bridge," he says in his poem 'The Green Bridge':

> On which I am not lonely;
> But journey on, thinking of

The dead Irish; hearing, far off,
The owners of Africa calling for freedom.

The journey goes on, its story will need telling. Expressing as a historian what might serve equally as a comment on literature, in When Was Wales? Gwyn Williams has written: "The Welsh as a people have lived by making and remaking themselves generation after generation, usually against the odds... Wales is an artefact which the Welsh produce. If they want to." As always it is a matter, difficult as it is necessary, of fusing the two known places, the actual and the dreamscape – both blurred by having been built over physically, psychically – to rediscover rooted things not easily blown away. Whatever else Anglo-Welsh writers may lack in these spinning times, they need not lack a function.

JOHN DAVIES, 1988

IFAN PUGHE

The Wild Horses and Fair Maidens of Llanganoch

I took up the scythe and left my father's house and walked away towards the mountain. There I would find a stone upon which to sharpen my scythe, and as I carried it on my shoulder it seemed heavy, but the blade shone in the morning light, and once I felt the beautiful cool of it against my face, and it was so cool it was like the slated floor in the outer kitchen where I had taken meal and bread and strong tea that morning. "With the sky looking as blue as Our Lady's mantle," my father said, "it should be a splendid day for the corn." I said nothing to that for I am not one to doubt his word. I would go ahead first, he following with the other men. It would be hot to-day. Of that I was certain. Already I could glimpse the far-off haze drawing nearer and nearer like the most delicate veil, and the heat was already coming towards me from all that mass of quivering life which my cold scythe would cut down to-day. But I was not thinking upon that, only upon certain young pines and firs so I rose again and climbed higher. At last. I was stood underneath my pines and firs. I looked at them as they swayed in the wind. I shut my eyes and thought how Mari was just as these young trees, waving first this way, then that, bowing low, then tossing their heads at me. "Perhaps my father is wrong," I was saying to myself, and the cracked weather-glass full of deceit, for up here the wind is rising and after all it might blow the whole day. The corn would dance fickle and unthinking as Mari, and the living field as it moved with the press of wind would not be so easy, the dancing corn would not lie easily enough for the swing of the scythes. When I opened my eyes the wind was stronger and there were my pines and firs like mad children racing towards the blue skies, racing like wild and helpless ships towards some distant horizon, a horizon that was like Mari too, for she had the essence of deceit in her blood also. I looked at "my children". Alive, dancing, and full of song. Waving, waving, bowing, lashing this way and that, heads down, unthrust under the belly of wind. "Blow, blow," I shouted, and my voice was wizened down to a little squeak as the wind whipped up my words. "Blow, blow." Tall young pines, tall young firs, graceful with the grace of blue sky above them and the dark strong earth beneath them. Lovely as the heads of all the young maidens in Llanganoch. Heads thrusting themselves to the sky. "Higher, higher," I cried, and my voice was melting upon air quicker than the thought in my head. "Dance, dance," I said, and the heads swayed this way and that, and the long bodies swayed too, and the grace and strength of wild horses was in them and I knew the sap was rising and the richness about them was in essence of air and riot of colour all about and the deep strong smell of air, and just below them all the witches of nettles that grow about these parts. I looked at my trees a long time and all joy was in looking at them, I could see them growing taller and taller, stronger and stronger, so one day their combined strength would hold the wind back from rushing to the valley below. I had planted them, they were mine. "Goodbye," I cried to them as I picked up my scythe and walked down towards the field. Already I could hear their loud voices, and as I came clear of the wood I saw the bright flash of their knives in the sunlight and one with bent back had a white and blue kerchief about his neck and I knew it was my father. So I hurried to him and I said, "Which end shall I go, father?" He raised himself, wiping black sweat from his face, saying it was hot below here and that I would go to the east end of the field and work towards him. I knew then that his anger had not cooled. He had carried the dead foal to this cornfield and it would be a burden on him all that day, and the air would hold it for us all. "Yes, father," I said, and walked off to the east corner. I ran my hand along the blade and I knew it was ripe for the touch, so bending I began to work. As I swung I thought of the wounds between which I was now standing, and it seemed in my mind as though this mass of corn, this swaying trembling, living corn was a vast desert, obstacle between me and my own happiness. If, I thought, if I mow this field clean I will have made a road nearer to my happiness, yet curiously my heart was heavy as the blade swung and cut down the golden dancing ears of wheat, and more. This waving corn was the waving hair of a young girl, not Mari, but a young girl whom I had never seen in my whole life. Once I paused, my knife in air, thinking of this. Perhaps there was a young girl somewhere, and her young head was covered with hair like the colour of the corn. My heart felt suddenly lightened then and my fancy was in a moment carefree and joyous. So I swung again. Towards eleven we stopped work and stood in our different corners and drank our tea, and wiped sweat from our faces. Whilst I was stood there I looked towards the mountain again and there were my pines and firs doing the maddest dance I have ever seen and I wondered at that for below here the air was quiet and the heat burdensome to one. My father shouted to us then to begin again. Before I began I felt my blade and all its coolness had gone. It was warm, and along its surface glistened its own strange sweat, and I was curious as to this, for the like had not happened to me before. The scythe like me had worked hard that morning, but now I did not like its touch. I saw out of the corner of my eye my father watching me, and such was his mood that day that I had no mind to work more that morning. Again I felt the blade and the sweat of it was upon my fingers. A strange thing it seemed, but a strange day, for the trees above seemed like many young girls to me, and the corn before me like the matted tresses of them all. I was suddenly sad. I threw down my scythe and walked towards the gate, and I heard my father call. I heard him halloo through his cupped hands, and the other men shouted too, loud and long that my father said I was to come back but I walked on, never turning my head until I had reached the wood. My steps were heavy, for all the time Mari was in my head and I felt sick and unable to do anything then for love of her. I lay down underneath my trees and closed my eyes and thought of her. The weather-glass had lied, the foal tricked my father and Mari, but then my thoughts ceased altogether and as I wiped my face it was the sweat of this wound that came from it, for I was crying to myself yet did not know it. To-morrow I was resolved to be up early, to take my scythe and my bundle and leave my father's house for ever.

DOROTHY EDWARDS

The Conquered

Last summer, just before my proper holiday, I went to stay with an aunt who lives on the borders of Wales, where there are so many orchards. I must say I went there simply as a duty, because I used to stay a lot with her when I was a boy, and she was, in those days, very good to me. However, I took plenty of books down so that it should not be a waste of time.

Of course, when I got there it was really not so bad. They made a great fuss of me. My aunt was as tolerant as she used to be in the old days, leaving me to do exactly as I liked. My cousin Jessica, who is just my age, had hardly changed at all, though they both looked different with their hair up; but my younger cousin Ruth, who used to be very lively and something of a tomboy, had altered quite a lot. She had become very quiet; at least, on the day I arrived she was lively enough, and talked about the fun we used to have there, but afterwards she became more quiet every day, or perhaps it was that I noticed it more. She remembered far more about what we used to do than I did; but I suppose that is only natural, since she had been there all the time in between, and I do not suppose anything very exciting had happened to her, whereas I have been nearly everywhere.

But what I wanted to say is, that not far from my aunt's house, on the top of a little slope, on which there was an apple orchard, was a house with French windows and a large green lawn in front, and in this lived a very charming Welsh lady whom my cousins knew. Her grandfather had the house built, and it was his own design. It is said that he had been quite a friend of the Prince Consort, who once, I believe, actually stayed there for a night.

I knew the house very well, but I had never met any of the family,

14

because they had not always occupied it, and, in any case, they would have been away at the times that I went to my aunt for holidays. Now only this one granddaughter was left of the family; her father and mother were dead, and she had just come back to live there. I found out all this at breakfast the morning after I came, when Jessica said, "Ruthie, we must take Frederick to see Gwyneth."

"Oh yes," said Ruthie. "Let's go to-day."

"And who is Gwyneth?"

Jessica laughed. "You will be most impressed. Won't he, mother?"

"Yes," said my aunt, categorically.

However, we did not call on her that afternoon, because it poured with rain all day, and it did not seem worth while, though Ruthie appeared in her macintosh and galoshes ready to go, and Jessica and I had some difficulty in dissuading her.

I did not think it was necessary to do any reading the first day, so I just sat and talked to the girls, and after tea Jessica and I even played duets on the piano, which had not been tuned lately, while Ruthie turned over the pages.

The next morning, though the grass was wet and every movement of the trees sent down a shower of rain, the sun began to shine brightly through the clouds. I should certainly have been taken to see their wonderful friend in the afternoon, only she herself called in the morning. I was sitting at one end of the dining room, reading Tourguéniev with a dictionary and about three grammars, and I dare say I looked very busy. I do not know where my aunt was when she came, and the girls were upstairs. I heard a most beautiful voice, that was very high-pitched though, not low, say:

"All right, I will wait for them in here," and she came into the room. Of course I had expected her to be nice, because my cousins liked her so much, but still they do not meet many people down there, and I thought they would be impressed with the sort of person I would be quite used to. But she really was charming.

She was not very young – older, I should say, than Jessica. She was very tall, and she had very fair hair. But the chief thing about her was her finely carved features, which gave to her face the coolness of stone and a certain appearance of immobility, though she laughed very often and talked a lot. When she laughed she raised her chin a little, and looked down her nose in a bantering way. And she had a really perfect nose. If I had been a sculptor I should have put it on every one of my statues. When she saw me she laughed and said, "Ah! I am disturbing you," and she sat down, smiling to herself.

I did not have time to say anything to her before my cousins came in. She kissed Jessica and Ruthie, and kept Ruthie by her side.

"This is our cousin Frederick," said Jessica.

"We have told you about him," said Ruthie gravely.

Gwyneth laughed. "Oh, I recognised him, but how could I interrupt so busy a person! Let me tell you what I have come for. Will you come to tea to-morrow and bring Mr Trenier?" She laughed at me again.

We thanked her, and then my aunt came in.

"How do you do, Gwyneth?" she said. "Will you stay to lunch?"

"No, thank you so much, Mrs Haslett," she answered. "I only came to ask Jessica and Ruthie to tea to-morrow, and, of course, to see your wonderful nephew. You will come too, won't you?"

"Yes, thank you," said my aunt. "You and Frederick ought to find many things to talk about together."

Gwyneth looked at me and laughed.

Ruthie went out to make some coffee, and afterwards Gwyneth sat in the window-seat drinking it and talking.

"What were you working at so busily when I came in?" she asked me.

"I was only trying to read Tourguéniev in the original," I said.

"Do you like Tourguéniev very much?" she asked, laughing.

"Yes," I said. "Do you?"

"Oh, I have only read one, *Fumée*."

She stayed for about an hour, laughing and talking all the time. I really found her very charming. She was like a personification, in a restrained manner, of Gaiety. Yes, really, very much like Milton's *L'Allegro*.

The moment she was gone Jessica said excitedly, "Now, Frederick, weren't you impressed?"

And Ruthie looked at me anxiously until I answered, "Yes, I really think I was."

The next day we went there to tea. It was a beautiful warm day, and we took the short cut across the fields and down a road now overgrown with grass to the bottom of the little slope on which her house was built. There is an old Roman road not far from here, and I am not quite sure whether that road is not part of it. We did not go into the house, but were taken at once to the orchard at the back, where she was sitting near a table, and we all sat down with her. The orchard was not very big, and, of course, the trees were no longer in flower, but the fruit on them was just beginning to grow and look like tiny apples and pears. At the other end some white chickens strutted about in the sunlight. We had tea outside.

She talked a lot, but I cannot remember now what she said; when she spoke to me it was nearly always to tell me about her grandfather, and the interesting people who used to come to visit him.

When it began to get cool we went into the house across the flat green lawn and through the French window. We went to a charming room; on the wall above the piano were some Japanese prints on silk, which were really beautiful. Outside it was just beginning to get dark.

She sang to us in a very nice high soprano voice, and she chose always gay, light songs which suited her excellently. She sang that song of Schumann, *Der Nussbaum*; but then it is possible to sing that lightly and happily, though it is more often sung with a trace of sadness in it. Jessica played for her. She is a rather good accompanist. I never could accompany singers. But I played afterwards. I played some Schumann too.

"Has Ruthie told you I am teaching her to sing?" said Gwyneth. "I don't know much about it, and her voice is not like mine, but I remember more or less what my master taught me."

"No," I said, looking at Ruthie. "Sing for us now and let me hear."

"No," said Ruthie, and blushed a little. She never used to be shy.

Gwyneth pulled Ruthie towards her. "Now do sing. The fact is you are ashamed of your teacher."

"No," said Ruthie, "only you know I can't sing your songs."

Gwyneth laughed. "You would hardly believe what a melancholy little creature she is. She won't sing anything that is not tearful."

"But surely," I said, "in the whole of Schubert and Schumann you can find something sad enough for you?"

"No," said Ruthie, looking at the carpet, "I don't know any

Schumann, and Schubert is never sad even in the sad songs. Really I can't sing what Gwyneth sings."

"Then you won't?" I said, feeling rather annoyed with her.

"No," she said, flushing, and she looked out of the window.

Ruthie and Jessica are quite different. Jessica is, of course, like her mother, but Ruthie is like her father, whom I never knew very well.

Next morning, immediately after breakfast, I went for a walk by myself, and though I went by a very roundabout way, I soon found myself near Gwyneth's house, and perhaps that was not very surprising. I came out by a large bush of traveller's-nightshade. I believe that is its name. At least it is called old man's beard too, but that does not describe it when it is in flower at all. You know that it has tiny white waxen flowers, of which the buds look quite different from the open flower, so that it looks as though there are two different kinds of flowers on one stem. But what I wanted to say was, I came out by this bush, and there, below me, was the grass-covered road, with new cartwheel ruts in it, which made two brown lines along the green where the earth showed. Naturally I walked down it, and stood by the fence of the orchard below her house. I looked up between the trees, and there she was coming down towards me.

"Good morning, Mr Trenier," she said, laughing. "Why are you deserting Tourguéniev?"

"It is such a lovely morning," I said, opening the gate for her; "and if I had known I should meet you, I should have felt even less hesitation."

She laughed, and we walked slowly across the grass, which was still wet with dew. It was a perfectly lovely day, with a soft pale blue sky and little white clouds in it, and the grass was wet enough to be bright green.

"Oh, look!" she said suddenly, and pointed to two enormous mushrooms, like dinner-plates, growing at our feet.

"Do you want them?" I asked, stooping to pick them.

"Oh yes," she said, "when they are as big as that they make excellent sauces. Fancy such monsters growing in a night! They were not here yesterday."

"And last week I had not met you," I said, smiling.

She laughed, and took the mushrooms from me.

"Now we must take them to the cook," she said, "and then you shall come for a little walk with me."

As we crossed the lawn to the house she was carrying the pink-lined mushrooms by their little stalks.

"They look like the sunshades of Victorian ladies," I said.

She laughed, and said, "Did you know that Jenny Lind came here once?"

Afterwards we walked along the real Roman road, now only a pathway with grass growing up between the stones, and tall trees overshadowing it. On the right is a hill where the ancient Britons made a great stand against the Romans, and were defeated.

"Did you know this was a Roman road?" she asked. "Just think of the charming Romans who must have walked here! And I expect they developed a taste for apples. Does it shock you to know that I like the Romans better than the Greeks?"

I said "No," but now, when I think of it, I believe I was a little shocked, although, when I think of the Romans as the Silver Age, I see that silver was more appropriate to her than gold.

She was really very beautiful, and it was a great pleasure to be with her, because she walked in such a lovely way. She moved quickly, but she somehow preserved that same immobility which, though she laughed and smiled so often, made her face cool like stone, and calm.

After this we went for many walks and picnics. Sometimes the girls came too, but sometimes we went together. We climbed the old battle hill, and she stood at the top looking all around at the orchards on the plain below.

I had meant to stay only a week, but I decided to stay a little longer, or, rather, I stayed on without thinking about it at all. I had not told my aunt and the girls that I was going at the end of the week, so it did not make any difference, and I knew they would expect me to stay longer. The only difference it made was to my holiday, and, after all, I was going for the holiday to enjoy myself, and I could not have been happier than I was there.

I remember how one night I went out by myself down in the direction of her house, where my steps always seemed to take me. When I reached the traveller's-nightshade it was growing dark. For a moment I looked towards her house and a flood of joy came into my soul, and I began to think how strange it was that, although I have met so many interesting people, I should come there simply by chance and meet her. I walked towards the entrance of a little wood, and, full of a profound joy and happiness, I walked in between the trees. I stayed there for a long time imagining her coming gaily into the wood where the moonlight shone through the branches. And I remember thinking suddenly how we have grown used to believing night to be a sad and melancholy time, not romantic and exciting as it used to be. I kept longing for some miracle to bring her there to me, but she did not come, and I had to go home.

Then, one evening, we all went to her house for music and conversation. On the way there Ruthie came round to my side and said, "Frederick, I have brought with me a song that I can sing, and I will sing this time if you want me to."

"Yes, I certainly want you to," I said, walking on with her. "I want to see how she teaches."

"Yes," said Ruthie. "You do see that I could not sing her songs, don't you?"

In the old days Ruthie and I used to get on very well, better than I got on with Jessica, who was inclined to keep us in order then, and I must say it was very difficult for her to do so.

When we got there, right at the beginning of the evening Gwyneth sang a little Welsh song. And I felt suddenly disappointed. I always thought that the Welsh were melancholy in their music, but if she sang it sadly at all, it was with the gossipy sadness of the tea after a funeral. However, afterwards we talked, and I forgot the momentary impression.

During the evening Ruthie sang. She sang Brahms' *An die Nachtigall*, which was really very foolish of her, because I am sure it is not an easy thing to sing, with its melting softness and its sudden cries of ecstasy and despair. Her voice was very unsteady, of a deeper tone than Gwyneth's, and sometimes it became quite hoarse from nervousness.

Gwyneth drew her down to the sofa beside her. She laughed, "I told you nothing was sad enough for her."

Ruthie was quite pale from the ordeal of singing before us.

"It is rather difficult, isn't it?" I said.

"Yes," said Ruthie, flushing.

"Have you ever heard a nightingale?" asked Gwyneth of me.

"No," I said.

"Why, there is one in the wood across here; I have heard it myself," said Jessica. "On just such a night as this," she added, laughing, and looking out of the window at the darkness coming to lie on the tops of the apple trees beyond the green lawn.

"Ah! You must hear a nightingale as well as read Tourguéniev, you know," said Gwyneth.

I laughed.

But later on in the evening I was sitting near the piano looking over a pile of music by my side. Suddenly I came across Chopin's *Polnische Lieder*. It is not often that one finds them. I looked up in excitement and said, "Oh, do you know the *Polens Grabgesang*? I implore you to sing it."

She laughed a little at my excitement and said, "Yes, I know it. But I can't sing it. It does not suit me at all. Mrs Haslett, your nephew actually wants me to sing a funeral march!"

"Oh, please do sing it!" I said. "I have only heard it once before in my life. Nobody ever sings it. I have been longing to hear it again."

"It does not belong to me, you know," she said. "I found it here; it must have belonged to my father." She smiled at me over the edge of some music she was putting on the piano. "No, I can't sing it. That is really decisive."

I was so much excited about the song, because I shall never forget the occasion on which I first heard it. I have a great friend, a very wonderful man, a perfect genius, in fact, and a very strong personality, and we have evenings at his house, and we talk about nearly everything, and have music too, sometimes. Often, when I used to go, there was a woman there, who never spoke much but always sat near my friend. She was not particularly beautiful and had a rather unhappy face, but one evening my friend turned to her suddenly and put his hand on her shoulder and said, "Sing for us."

She obeyed without a word. Everybody obeys him at once. And she sang this song. I shall never forget all the sorrow and pity for the sorrows of Poland that she put into it. And the song, too, is wonderful.

I do not think I have ever heard in my life anything so terribly moving as the part, 'O Polen, mein Polen', which is repeated several times. Everyone in the room was stirred, and, after she had sung it, we talked about nothing but politics and the Revolution for the whole of the evening. I do not think she was Polish either. After a few more times she did not come to the evenings any more, and I have never had the opportunity of asking him about her. And although, as I said, she was not beautiful, when I looked at Gwyneth again it seemed to me that some of her beauty had gone, and I thought to myself quite angrily, "No, of course she could not sing that song. She would have been on the side of the conquerors!"

And I felt like this all the evening until we began to walk home. Before we had gone far Jessica said, "Wouldn't you like to stay and listen for the nightingale, Frederick? We can find our way home without you."

"Yes," I said. "Where can I hear her?"

"The best place," said Jessica, "is to sit on the fallen tree – that is where I heard it. Go into the wood by the wild-rose bush with pink roses on it. Do you know it?"

"Yes."

"Don't be very late," said my aunt.

"No," I answered, and left them.

I went into the little wood and sat down on the fallen tree looking up and waiting, but there was no sound. I felt that there was nothing I wanted so much as to hear her sad notes. I remember thinking how Nietzsche said that Brahms' melancholy was the melancholy of impotence, not of power, and I remember feeling that there was much truth in it when I thought of his *Nachtigall* and then of Keats. And I sat and waited for the song that came to

> ... the sad heart of Ruth, when, sick for home,
> She stood in tears amid the alien corn.

Suddenly I heard a sound, and, looking round, I saw Gwyneth through the trees. She caught sight of me and laughed.

"You are here too," she said. "I came to hear Jessica's nightingale."

"So did I," I said, "but I do not think she will sing tonight."

"It is a beautiful night," she said. "Anybody should want to sing on such a lovely night."

I took her back to her gate, and I said goodnight and closed the gate behind her. But, all the same, I shall remember always how beautiful she looked standing under the apple trees by the gate in the moonlight, her smile resting like the reflection of light on her carved face. Then, however, I walked home, feeling angry and annoyed with her; but of course that was foolish. Because it seems to me now that the world is made up of gay people and sad people, and however charming and beautiful the gay people are, their souls can never really meet the souls of those who are born for suffering and melancholy, simply because they are made in a different mould. Of course I see that this is a sort of dualism, but still it seems to me to be the truth, and I believe my friend, of whom I spoke, is a dualist too, in some things.

I did not stay more than a day or two after this, though my aunt and the girls begged me to do so. I did not see Gwyneth again, only something took place which was a little ridiculous in the circumstances.

The evening before I went Ruthie came and said, half in an anxious whisper, "Frederick, will you do something very important for me?"

"Yes, if I can," I said. "What is it?"

"Well, it is Gwyneth's birthday to-morrow, and she is so rich it is hard to think of something to give her."

"Yes," I said, without much interest.

"But do you know what I thought of? I have bought an almond tree – the man just left it out in the shed – and I am going to plant it at the edge of the lawn so that she will see it to-morrow morning. So it will have to be planted in the middle of the night, and I wondered if you would come and help me."

"But is it the right time of the year to plant an almond tree – in August?"

"I don't know," said Ruthie, "but surely the man in the nursery would have said if it were not. You can sleep in the train, you know. You used always to do things with me."

"All right, I will," I said, "only we need not go in the middle of the night – early in the morning will do, before it is quite light."

"Oh, thank you so much," said Ruthie, trembling with gratitude and excitement. "But don't tell anyone, will you – not even Jessica?"

"No," I said.

Exceedingly early in the morning, long before it was light, Ruthie came into my room in her dressing-gown to wake me, looking exactly as she used to do. We went quietly downstairs and through the wet grass to Gwyneth's house, Ruthie carrying the spade and I the tree. It was still rather dark when we reached there, but Ruthie had planned the exact place before.

We hurried with the work. I did the digging, and Ruthie stood with the tree in her hand looking up at the house. We hardly spoke.

Ruthie whispered, "We must be quiet. That is her window. She will be able to see it as soon as she looks out. She is asleep now."

"Look here," I said, "don't tell her that I planted it, because it may not grow. I can't see very well."

"Oh, but she must never know that either of us did it."

"But are you going to give her a present and never let her know who it is from?"

"Yes," said Ruthie.

"I think that is rather silly," I said.

Ruthie turned away.

We put the tree in. I have never heard whether it grew or not. Just as the sun was rising we walked back, and that morning I went away.

NIGEL HESELTINE

Gothic Halls

In the gothic halls of Rhiwsaeson there was a blast from the ancestral trumpets, and the shields shook on the walls and the suits of armour clashed together, for John Belial as to be elected, was to go up to London to sit in the Parliament for the county of Cariad.

Like ferns in their pots his supporters sat about the room of John Belial mopping like ferns at the dew which fell from his decanters. The shields are plaster, bearing the arms of all the families in Wales with which John Belial is unconnected, and they are all the families of Wales; but the armour is good and was bought in Liverpool. Like ferns in their pots his supporters flourish in the halls of this proper Welsh landlord, and the Hon. Mrs Belial ... for John has married among the nobility ... pours out the decanters for them and the hearts of these Welshmen are glad.

With a bushel of true-blue-tory-ribbon in his button-hole, Cam-Vaughan, the rich and unambitious descendant of Welsh kings and chairman of the English Conservative Association in Wales, caught up the threads of discourse, the backbone of argument! "Shall the county be given over to reform?" And from the potted princelings around came shouts of "No!"

"Social reform is for hotheads," said Cam-Vaughan.

Thwaite, who has been driving a car for the Blue Cause and giving lifts to Socialists in secret, took a large glassful from the decanter. It warmed him, it would improve his driving.

Relays of car-owning Conservatives came beaming into the room; others go out to take up the same work.

"Forty people I took to the Poll and beat off the Socialists with a boxspanner! Sixteen miles from the Poll, and they cannot vote now!"

"Ha! ha!" from the assembly.

And in Thwaite's view the bottles which surrounded these landed and landless squires were filled with roses, which sprouting twined in the hair and moustaches of the gentry, and when they spoke their mouths were filled with thorns.

"Distilled from the Roses," Thwaite read aloud from the label of a bottle near, "that grow along the banks of the River of Tongues where languages and speeches are invented among the stones that rumble under the flowing of the stream, and all are washed down to the sea."

"Mark my speech well," Cam-Vaughan was saying. "And do not interrupt me in Welsh." The thorns caught among his teeth. "The agony of the great," he was saying. "We are the great and our agony is greatness."

But other squireens stood up by Cam-Vaughan and they were greater or had more or less money, or longer or shorter family-trees. They stretched up together and when one stretched an inch beyond another, the rest strained up above him until they were thin and drawn-out like dough.

Thwaite watered their feet with whiskey and tied them together with bunches of true-blue-tory-ribbon, exclaiming:

"Grow, squireens, grow up to hell."

And he went out, skating down the encaustic tiles of the passages like a fly on the water.

Cutting their knots and tearing away the clinging roses, the more normal squires embarked in their cars, emblazoned with the blue banners and blue slogans of BELIAL FOR CARIAD, BELIAL'S BETTER WAY TO WISDOM. Thwaite watched them as they hurtled in strange convoy, through a hole in the hedge:

"What is wisdom?" he said to the air, and the echo came back, "What is Belial?"

Belial is in the town of Trallwm which the Lord forgets on election-day, seated in a special room in the hall, a fine post-Victorian baroque, while the sons-of-bitches rave below for a result. The fair-haired girls sat at a green table and the votes rained down on them from cornucopias in the gilded roof: their hands were rough with the toil of counting and the shouting of the porters at the locked doors who bet on the result. And the poets in the streets were shouting their ballads in the ears of the sons-of-bitches: scurrilous lampoons on Belial and others.

The votes are thrown into baskets as they pour down ... Belial's basket and one for the Socialist. In the lanes the squires were dashing in madness in their cars to the town of Trallwm; it seemed that they would kill anything in the road but they did not, for the law rests on squires. And the smoke rising from the sons-of-bitches stained the facade of the hall and suffocated the sparrows that lodge under the eaves. This is the scene.

Flushed with pride and port, Belial strutted the passages like a bull, but there was Cam-Vaughan with thorns in his teeth and blood running from his mouth to his collar.

"The man of agony!" said Belial as a joke, and Cam-Vaughan's face twisted in a smile half-crucified on the wall.

"Think of your arse, man!" cried Belial, clapping him on the shoulder, "Of the power and the glory etc. Smile!"

But Cam-Vaughan had his mouth full of thorns and Belial was menaced by the ticking of the clocks on the wall.

"Ticking," said Cam-Vaughan.

"They want oil," Belial said, and passed on. He cannot enter the room where the fair-haired girls are counting, etiquette forbids him to bet with the shouting porters at the door. He paced the passages in time with the ticking clocks.

We are in the main street awaiting the result. "By damn!" says one, "Old humbug!" another, "Off my foot, now! Will we raise a howl if the old bastard gets in!"

So is the will of the people milling in the main street, some of us drunk, all of us hot and excited. The last lie has been told on the platforms, the last canvassing jiggery-pokery done; now if the fair-haired girls at the green table are honest, there is no help till the result ... and they are too tired to care.

And now a spark from a strictly-forbidden cigarette has fallen among the votes in Belial's basket, and the fire has run into the basket of John Evans, the Socialist, too. All the votes are burned. Dismayed, the girls stamped on the flames lest the smell of the smoke reach the porters shouting outside; then they laughed, for this was the end of their labour.

According to the hallowed and time-honoured tradition no one can go into the room or come out of it, papers must be passed under the door. The girls giggled and made paper darts of the last votes falling through the cornucopias: in the grate they made a pile and called it Belial, they made another and called it John Evans and saw which burned the quickest.

They said, "Who shall we give it to?" and some said John Evans because he had a long moustache, others Belial because he is rich. But the moustache has it, and they write JOHN EVANS upon the sheet of Announcement; this is a pleasant end to all their labour and the girls dance and sing 'Tipperary' when the sheet has gone under the door.

The porter takes the sheet to the Mayor who signs it, to the clerk who stamps it, to the Commissioner who folds it, to the Seasoner who opens it, to the Mayor who cries aloud the result from the balcony. Belial is sweating in his room.

John Evans has it. Boyo! do we shout and run about on each others' feet! Some of us lean in the pub doorways and take in the scene.

And John Evans follows his moustache out on to the balcony above the cheering and tells us how glad he is that the will of the people coincides with his. The girls who did the Will slip away to put their feet in hot water before the dance.

John Belial was dragged out to say that it was a good clean fight and no hard feeling; but his supporters had thorns in their mouths and ears and drank blood, and we sons-of-bitches below, hooted. And the poets were cheering in the streets and giving away free the unsold copies of their scurrilous ballads which were bought for a penny before.

Like bees in a swarm the pricked squires are off in their cars, and Johnny Evans, the Socialist, gives beer to his picked supporters out of party funds.

The fire has spread from the piles of votes to the rest of the building and when the Mayor and his officers have run screaming into the air and fallen on the stretched canvasses of the Fire Brigade below, the flames roar to the sky and the people cheer to see the Town Hall burn.

Back in his grey stuccoed halls, John Belial and the Hon. Mrs drew up bills of sale. The squires had gone home to bleed by their own fires and there was no celebration at Rhiwsaeson that night; the decanters lay stoppered on the sideboard. In Rhiwsaeson (built A.D.1850) there were no ghosts to wail his defeat, nothing but wealth and John Belial.

"Now perhaps we can leave this dreadful place," said the Hon. Mrs. "And you'll get in somewhere else. Barbarous people of Cariad." Such is a wife's comfort.

Such was the sale of Rhiwsaeson in 20 lots, 4 cottages and 15 farms, commodious mansion in the gothic style. Genuine sideboards from the Paris Exhibition, 1859: organ from the Crystal Palace, 1868: 5-ton chandeliers from dismantled Chateau du Bonsoir, France: real marble staircase from dismantled Palazzo della Figa, Italy: coats-of-arms of principal extinct families of Wales: selection of useful armour. Such were the treasures piled in a marquee on the Rhiwsaeson lawns.

And the squires had crept like ants among the throng, and we sons-of-bitches from the Town of Trallwm were there to stare and see if we dared jeer. And we said, "O John Belial will not be at the breaking-up of his home for sentimental reasons"; but he was in a closet at the back of the marquee noting down what it fetched and checking-up.

And the sideboards were shown, twenty feet high and adorned with leaping lions, with angels, and with family trumpets, and genuine beds were shown warranted slept in since 1852, and pillars of statuary in soap-stone and marble, and five-ton chandeliers. But the people muttered and fingered the half-crowns in their pockets. In vain the auctioneer pleaded and put his case, in vain he patted the sideboards, the sons-of-bitches muttered and made no bids.

Stacked piles of 1860 Spode were shown, 197 pieces to a service, and bedroom utensils, and useful cast-iron hatstands; pictures of life and death and resurrection and defeat copied from the best masters.

A parson bought a dictionary but there were no other bids.

John Belial bit his nails at the back of the marquee. He bit his pencil through. The muttering wounded him. The lack of bids pierced his heart.

He came out on to the rostrum, and they were all silent while he made his personal appeal. They saw there, he said, the vestiges of his poor home, the wretched remains which cruel circumstances obliged him to put before them (for everything of value had long been taken to his new house in his new constituency). He knew, he said, that he had not been a success among them (a tear fell from his eye), but he had done his best.

Here Mr Belial was so moved that he was obliged to stand down; there was scarcely a dry eye amongst the audience. Choking with emotion the auctioneer turned his dim eye from sideboard to public.

Some generous spirit offered him a half-a-crown.

It was Thwaite.

For half-a-crown he had a sideboard 20 feet high, he had leaping figures of lions, and angels, and family trumpets.

Cam-Vaughan, generous soul, descendant of Welsh kings and chairman of the English Conservative Association in Wales, bought a chandelier.

"And who will buy Rhiwsaeson Hall, that princely residence?" asked the auctioneer with a reviving voice. An old and bent woman in rough tweed and country boots answered, "I will."

She was John Belial's aunt. She would buy the house of her fathers' since 1851.

"I was sorry to lose the sideboard," said Miss Belial, "But I have the useful armour and the coat-of-arms." Cam-Vaughan, royal and generous soul, presented her with his five-ton chandelier.

Touched by these moving scenes, the squires crept to their cars and drove guiltily away. The sons-of-bitches melted away to Trallwm, for fresh scenes of riot, for girls, for dancing and for drink. Thwaite went apart and sat thinking of his sideboard; the auctioneer had said he could build a yacht out of it.

John Belial sat adding up his figures, and was five pounds to the good. Such was the sale of Rhiwsaeson, commodious mansion in the gothic style.

GERAINT GOODWIN

The Flying Hours are Gone

I remember everything; one cannot help memory. We come back after fifteen years and a great gulf divides us; we have changed and we look at the world, this world, as at a different place. We think that everything has changed with us and then we see a tree just as it had always been, and the old weir with a timber loose and the timber is still loose; an old gnarled branch, black and sodden, had been caught in the mill-race and it is still there!

This plantation – a planting we called it – seems just the same. It covers all the side of the mountain. It was fearful to walk into it; there was no sound to our footsteps and it was always dark. We liked to think – what did we think in those echoless depths – that somewhere always just beyond the reach of vision there were other shapes, moving like shadows, vague and phantasmal; like a dream that remains on the edge of memory, remote and unseizable. And there, too, we felt a strange compelling presence, the presence of the wood, something primitive and elemental. How absurd it all seems now. The wood of course was like any other wood and with that lattice of branches shutting off the sun, with here and there a spike of light descending like a white lustrous rod, the carpet of pine-needles; why, no doubt it would seem strange.

I thought of all this as I sat there and I laughed at these young imaginings. All gone...! That is the heresy of time that one can say with Elijah, "Behold, there is nothing!"

I sat beside the favourite pool and remembered the great fish in its black depths. Perhaps they were still there. I remembered that intangible thrill as one slithered over the mossy stones to cast a fly under the alders, the whole being braced with a quickened consciousness of life. One heard the twenty tiny metallic tinkles of twenty streams breaking over the boulders and there would be just a flash, a sprung crescent of silver and ... I subscribed to a fishing paper for a long time afterwards but as one of the Elizabethans had said, the flying hours are gone. There was no recapturing those early days. By and by I got bored with everything to do with fishing and really I can't tell you where I have put my rod.

People then predicted great things for me; I cannot for the life of me imagine that they had any cause. But my sincerity was a very real thing and it had the power of infecting others. They believed in me because I believed in myself. I was a law student at the National College of Wales at Aberystwyth, but this was but the outward guise that hid the inner aspect. At that time (how very *vieux jeu* it seems now), I believed in a new Wales; I was always speaking about our heritage and I would hint, in a sort of prophetic way, at our future. I must have got all my ideas from Renan, the all-enduring Celt, driven to the promontories of the world and nursing his proud spirit in solitude. I don't think it did me any harm; it is good for one to believe in something when one is young. How arid my degree course would have been without these, well, yes, dreams.

Still all this is neither here nor there. To continue with the story I had put too big a strain on what St Francis called Brother Ass; the body did not rebel for there was no rebellion left; it collapsed. I came here, to that farm on the edge of the planting and I spent a winter there. Every morning I had half a pint of stout, a glass of warm milk straight from the cow and a raw egg, and then I had the same again in the evening. But I did not grow any fatter. I remember I used to weigh myself in the scales in the little station and chalk up my weight on the 'traffic regulations' on the wall. Good lord! perhaps they are there still. The horror of watching the little sliding racket ... I always used to argue that the scales were wrong. I won't go into details but you know how one always looks into one's handkerchief after one has coughed and then one looks into the glass and sees one's jawbones sticking out and tries to arrange one's face differently; but they always stick out. And the despair that welled up in my heart!

I could not have gone through with it but for her. Of course there were times when she could not reach me, those times when the panic fear of death used to encompass me and one would go walking off into the mountains. One would stand still before a larch, all shriven in the winter, and say: "There will be leaves next spring; a few months at most and the buds will burst out like violent flames. I wonder if I shall ever see them." And a collie all blown about by the wind would rush out of a byre, barking, and you would smell the cows and then the twilight would come and there seemed to be a strange and almost fearful light on the mountain where the last of the day remained. At such times the whole landscape would seem to be transformed into something strange and other-wordly.

All this I remember now but, as I have said, only as one remembers a dream. It may have happened, it *did* happen, but it remains just beyond the reaches of the mind: one rakes over the memory but one is only vouchsafed a glimpse like a familiar face one sees in the darkness.

Ah yes, but I remember all about the place, the old oak dresser in the kitchen (it was worth hundreds of pounds I used to tell them) and the brass harness above the fireplace and the blue tea-canister with a picture of the King on it and a picture of General Buller after some battle or another and of course, on the sewing machine in the corner, The Book, from whence issued, like a wraith, the grim colourless God of our fathers.

But these are only the external things. I can't for the life of me remember that something which is all there is to remember. I can't even recall what she looked like though I should surely know her again. She was tall and dark with violet eyes, yes they were violet or a peculiar shade of blue, and they really were the most expressive eyes I have ever seen. It made one sad to look into them – not really sad if you understand but one began to think about life in a vague kind of way. But as I say, I can never quite remember...

On the top of the hill, was an old ring of piled-up stones. Half sunk into the ground and pock-marked with lichen, they reared their arrogant old heads as though defying time. Some said that this was really a 'castle', but they were more likely the remains of a druidic circle; and indeed to come up out of that wood by moonlight, to walk across the sward, was to become aware of something, some knowledge that one could never utter, that....

Well, we went up there for the last time. I was going away on the Monday, back to college, back to work. I was going to face up to the future again. How bright everything seemed. That hideous cloud had lifted at last. I felt like a small boy who has waited and waited for his birthday and then suddenly realizes after the months, the weeks, that it is the day after to-morrow!

I remember that she had put on her Sunday dress.

"What have you done that for?" I said.

"Only because I want to," she answered sadly.

She was sitting on one of the stones, knees bent up, her head on her hands, looking out into the darkness. I suddenly realised that this was all she could do, all she could do to show how sorry she was that I was going. I felt very sad. I felt a sense of compassion that I had never known before nor ever was to know again. That poor little black dress that some dressmaker had run together in the market-town when her mother had died five years before.

She had done this for me, she loved me with all her soul, she had tended me through all the winter, she had seen me, like an arrogant young hawk begin to stretch his wings and venture forth ... and then life would settle down as before, settle down with its awful inevitability and encompass her. Yet she could say nothing.

"Ceri," I said, "Ceri...."

I felt an ominous dread right down to the depths. I felt afraid of myself and of the future and of what the future might do for me. I buried my head on her lap and began to sob. They were the last scalding tears of youth.

"Help me to remember, Ceri, help me to remember..." I said and the words seemed to come from my heart.

She lifted my head between her hands.

But all this was long ago and you can see what might have happened. I had stopped dead on the brink of a chasm; I might have gone plunging down – where, whither? And now, long after, I know that I was right. I could not then have supported myself, I had not even begun a career. The most important thing in life, whatever the sentimentalists say, is to get a roof over one's head. Well, I have a roof over my head, though it is not a very big one, and I have never thought it necessary to marry.

I had taken my degree and had been called at one of the Inns of Court. I had forgotten to talk about a new Wales, for a Welshman in London has enough to live down without all that. I once thought of changing my name – something with a real good Anglo-Saxon flavour to it – but it was not easy. And if I could have changed my profession I would have done so, for the law is one of the most bourgeois of callings and there are more kicks than ha'pence for the son of a road-mender even though his father carried Thucydides (in the original) in the backside of his corduroys. After four years I could point to an acquittal at Nottingham Assizes (under the Poor Persons Act) and a few words of commendation from the judge and that was about all.

And so I drifted into journalism – after all it is only crossing the street – and became leader-writer for a good nonconformist paper and was able to spread myself out on disarmament, free speech and the right of small nations, and all those things which I had at heart. Some day, I said, when I had enough capital, I would go back to the law ... but perhaps if I went back to the law I would say that some day I would go back to journalism....

And once a year I go back to Wales for my summer holidays, but it is never quite the same; one can never recall the past for there is always that gulf, as wide as – how wide? – why as wide as Time!

I can see from where I stand the old stones on the hillside and just the top of the house with its curl of smoke climbing over the trees, I can smell the peat, that smell which is the mountains to us who have been bred there. I can see a man trimming the hedge on the far end of the bye-take; it must be her husband. I can hear the dog barking and the cheep-cheep of the young turkeys and someone stepping across the cobbled yard and then the slamming of a door and then a child crying ... I will go up and see her, I say. She would be glad to welcome me, I know, and I can even picture myself handing round coppers to the children and perhaps the best teapot will come down and the canister with the King's picture on it.

I had half opened the gate in the meadow; I watched the wind blow it shut again. And I was on the outside, standing with the present and the future. And beyond was the past, but a past that had not stood still. Where it had gone to I did not know.

CARADOC EVANS

Three Men from Horeb

While Enoch the Teller of Things was shearing the ends of his beard for the Sabbath, word came to him that his son Ella, who dwelt in Morfa, was dead. On the morrow he bowed his head in Sion until the time came for him to say the orderings of the service, and when he had said all that was to be said, he expressed his grief: "Flown over Jordan in a White Shirt is Ella bach. Bad was his illness. Nasty is old decline. Come you all to his large funeral at Capel Horeb – "

The Respected Bern-Davydd put out his right arm. "Indeed now, Enoch," he said, "wait a bit, man. Why for you say Horeb? In Capel Sion must Ella be buried. Horeb, ach y fi."

"Iss; gate-post is your head, Enoch," cried Amos Penparc. "Have you no pride in the Glory of Sion? More graves there are in Sion than turnips in two rows."

"Go you, then," commanded Bern-Davydd, "and bring the perished corpse to Sion. Bring him before he stinks. In this way says the Big Man, little animals: 'Give to the Capel what belongs to the Capel, and there shall be laughing in the Palace, Bern bach'."

Old Enoch borrowed a hay wagon, the inside of which he furnished with two patchwork quilts and a pillow, and the outside of which with black cloths and strips of black crepe. To Mati, Ella's wife, he said: "You hog, give you me the corpse of my son bach."

Mati answered him: "Lived have I here all my days. My children were born here and they converse with the Big Man in Horeb. In Horeb Ella shall be put into the pit."

Enoch did not heed the words of Mati his daughter-in-law: he went into the parlour and took the body of Ella and put it in his wagon

36

and he covered it with a patchwork quilt; and on the flat road, which brings you back to Sion, he sat on the shaft, his short bandy legs dangling loosely. He wept in the face of passers-by until his eyes were sore: "Man that is perished is in the cart, people bach. He is my son Ella. Wet will be the tears at his funeral. There's a prayer he was! And a big friend of the Little Jesus bach." He also sang: "In the big floods and swells there is none to hold my head, but my beloved husband Jesus, who died upon the Wood."

He brightened the boots which were on Ella's feet and he shaved Ella's face; and he laid the body on a table and put an open Bible on its belly; and at the side of it he placed an empty coffin, the lid of which was ornamented with gold handles and the plate of which was engraved with Ella's name and age – which was forty-seven years – and a good account.

On the Wailing Night old Enoch stayed by his son, howbeit one asked him to sup of buttermilk or tea or to eat of white bread and butter or bread and cheese. As the praying men and singing men and women were mourning Ella in prayers and hymns, Shon Daviss – a high man in Capel Horeb – opened the door and on the threshold he cried solemnly: "Here's horror. Big Man is looking down and weeping. Male of Horeb was Ella. Awful is the cost you will have to pay for this sin."

"Speech you do like a billhook," said Bern-Davydd.

"No, man," replied Shon Daviss; "serious for sure. Come have I to talk that the boy bach be buried in Horeb."

The words angered the congregation. They said. "Scarce are the graves in the new burying land. Respected Bern-Davydd, speak spiteful phrases to the old cat fach."

Bern-Davydd turned his face upon Shon Daviss, rebuking him: "Boy of the Bad Man, be you in a hurry to go in a haste. Jasto now, give him a kick somebody in the backhead."

"Robber of Sion, away, indeed" some of the congregation shouted. "Or much damage we shall do to you."

The man from Horeb ran away from the house; and the next day Old Enoch prepared Ella for burial: he stripped him of his clothes and put on him a White Shirt of the Dead. The material of the garment was flannel made by Ellen Weaver's Widow, and it was marred by neither spot nor blemish. The flannel at the wrists of the garment had been decorated by an embroiderer, and the hem of the skirt had upon it fluffed sheep's wool. Having ended, old Enoch lifted his hairy cheek to God, and opened his lips: "Big Man bach, religious am I. Shall I button the White Shirt?" He waited and God spoke to him privately. "All right, as you speak, Big Man; quickly Ella will become naked when he hears the trumpet. Quicker than any one in Sion."

A sinful thing happened: while Ella's coffin rested on ropes at the edge of the grave three men from Horeb arrived without the gates of Sion, and the leading man, who was Shon Daviss Shop Boots, shouted: "Ho-ho, sinners Capel Sion, Ella must sleep in Horeb. Come we have for the perished corpse."

In their confusion the people – men and women and small children – who were come to weep and mourn, fell apart into a lane, wherewith the three men passed thereupon to the place where the coffin was.

Bern-Davydd's rage kindled. He screamed: "The son of Enoch shall come up from Sion! Foxes of strumpets you are, boys Horeb."

"Ho-ho!" cried Shon Daviss. "Askings we have put to our Respected, and great is his understanding. Divide you, people, and the coffin bach we will take with us."

"Hares of Horeb," said Bern-Davydd, "take off your hands. Stoutish shall the Glory of Sion grow."

"Stealing from Horeb you are a perished corpse," answered Shon Daviss. "We shall take him away. Come, boys bach, let us put him in the cart. Religious was Ella; shall he be buried among calves?"

"Away, turks of mackerel," Old Enoch cried. "Borrowed a gambo I did to bring Ella to Capel Sion."

The three men from Horeb lifted the coffin; and as they were doing so, Enoch struck Shon Daviss with the gravedigger's pickaxe. The coffin dropped upon the ground and the lid of it came asunder. Shon's temper heightened. "Fiery Pool!" he cursed. "Knock you will I this one small minute."

Old Enoch shivered because of the blow delivered upon his forehead by Shon Daviss; and he fell into the grave.

There was much disorder, during which the three men from Horeb raised the body of Ella out of its coffin and ran away with it and put it on the straw that was on the floor of the cart; and one of them said to the mare between the shafts: "Gee-gee, go on."

The people of Sion, awakened to the value of this that was done against their burial ground, chased the men from Horeb, and as they could not overtake them, they climbed over hedges and went across the fields. In that manner the men of Sion came upon the men of Horeb and stopped them; and the battle went hard against Horeb.

The body of Ella was brought back to Sion in the dim light, and the gravedigger, after Bern-Davydd had prayed that the Big Man would regard mercifully the blemishes on Ella's White Shirt, put a ladder down into the grave, saying: "Come you up, now, Enoch, bach."

MARGIAD EVANS

The Old Woman and the Wind

In her grey, blunted garden, with the gutterings of the long slidden turf mounding about her, old Mrs Ashstone was stooping over her broken crocuses.

"Maybe I can rise them up," she was wailing as she touched their bruised cold petals, "maybe. But what's the use when that old wind'll only blow 'em all flat agen?"

They were her only flowers – just the one clump of ochre yellow sheaths growing under the cottage wall as close and thick as if they were in a pot.

And even them the wind had smashed as it had smashed everything else. The porch, the fence.... Mrs Ashstone had nothing pretty or hospitable to look at; nothing but rocks that broke out of the quivering wire grass, and lay about like sheep. Wind! Mrs Ashstone growled, *wind!*

The air was stiff with it – solid and encroaching. Wind more than age was dwindling her sparrow frame. Sometimes it felt as hard and narrow as churchyard mould; others it was like being cuddled by a giant. Wind, always blowing, roaring, pushing at her and her cottage, shoving her out of her place, pouncing on her hair. Cursed wind, too big for the world.

Look how the grass was bending! That melted bank had been a stone wall once. And the stumbling gusts that harshly rocked her tiny body. And the flattened smoke coming down round the chimney's neck in wisps like her own hair. How she hated it, oh how she hated it!

Mrs Ashstone straightened her spine slowly, pushing her knuckles into her knees, her thighs, and then her hips. "Ah! Ah! Ah!" she groaned, "if only I could get away from here I shouldn't get old so fast. A nice soft little place in the village now, like what Mrs Maddocks has. Or Mrs Griffiths."

Mrs Ashstone was seventy-one. She had little to think of after living alone on her hill for twelve years except her own bad luck. She was not stupid, but so ignorant that she imagined 'Mrs' to be a common Christian name and the marriage service a sort of second baptism. She had forgotten that she was called Annie. Mrs Ashstone, Garway Hill, she was, and there she stood with tears in her eyes, stroking her crocuses and wishing for a pathway, box-edged, and a little orchard with a clothes line. It was the hour of evening, which seems made solely for the first slender winter flowers. The shadowless January twilight enclosed and shaped each contour with leaf-like distinctness. The tiny cottage, slapped with limewash, was built under a single flake of rock. Some bloomless gorse bushes and pale bracken patches, that was all. There was no living feeling, but only a heedless and violent solitude.

Under the slurred turf lay half-buried a few heavy stones. Swept and seamed by each gust, the old woman toiled up and down the frail track she had worn from her door to the gap in the mound. Each journey she brought a stone. These she laid round the crocuses lifting their golden pods: "There, now, if the sun shines, they'll open in the morning," she said when it was done. Then she raised her face menacingly and flapped her fist. The gesture seemed not hers but the wind's. "Keep off," she screamed. "Keep off 'em now. You go down there and break off some of they great el'um trees." She went to the step and rested against the door, arranging her dim dress and apron, gripping them down at the knees with fierce self-conscious modesty. She had a little screw of hair on top of her skull, a screw of nose curled upwards like a dead leaf, and small, clutching yellow hands that were always chasing the flying and broken things floating in the wind's wake. Somebody said she looked as if she were forever catching feathers in the air, and it was true that she did.

She turned to face the valley. The soft sound of it was going underground, but up here it was coming a gale. She could feel it in her heart. Every breath seemed too big for her. Her eyes followed the downward path to the village. Ah, it was always still there, always blowing here. Below the oak trees, where the round winds whisked the dead leaves in figure forms, the quietness began. Warmth, sounds, birds' voices. Up here she had to listen through the wind, but after the oak tree was passed things found their own way into her hearing. Voices, footsteps trickling from cottage to cottage through the peaceful lanes....

It had been like that this morning. There she had stood and stroked her hair. She'd lifted her face and smelled the sky as if she were smelling at a flower. A flock of birds as fine as dust she'd seen. Then she had gone on down, cruel rage and cruel envy in her mind, tears in her eyes. Mrs Griffiths' daughter had cancer, they said, but Mrs Griffiths' front path was ruled between primulas and violets. The sunlight touched the dark-green box bush.

"Good morning, good morning," the ninety-year-old woman had nodded cheerfully. Well, Mrs Ashstone wished her no harm, for her son carried the coal up Garway. But, oh, the meadows, the gentle river at her garden side, made tired flesh drag with longing. Old Mrs Ashstone had passed on, not answering the human greeting, but hearing the water's poem, the crow flock's rustling over the elms.

Mrs Maddocks, she was hanging out washing – sheets, Fred's shirts. This time it was Mrs Ashstone who stopped. Under the hedge, wide open in the grass of the bank, a constellation of celandine shone at the sun. Five of them, shaped, she noticed, like the Plough. She put out her torn, black foot. She wanted to kill their beauty. But she closed her eyes. The sunlight was red through the flesh. And then she had a vision. A white willow tree in a red world. It was an effort to raise her tired lids. Mrs Maddocks was slapping each garment out in the air. She was standing aslant, empty wash bath on her hip, the breezeless sheets a white screen for her shadow.

"There 'tis!" she cried in triumph. "But will it dry? Bain't no wind." Would it dry! Mrs Ashstone sneered to herself as she fingered a twig in the hedge. Would it dry and the sun gloating on the orchard! She pressed her lips together and walked on quickly.

When she came out of the shop some impulse took her up the steps to the churchyard gate. She stood there eased of some of her misery, for it relaxed her just not to hear the grind of the wind. She waited for the hatred to return and help her home.

Her feet were on a cracked stone, her hands folded on the dusty gate, when old Captain Ifor and Mr Brewer went by below with their sheepdogs and retrievers, talking.

"Good day, good day," the Captain called. "You down from your eyrie?"

She blinked at them mockingly, fumbling with the old spoon latch, clicking it with her thumb, her face expressing only a kind of humiliating wistfulness. What was an ar-ry – and what had it to do with her hill? So she turned her back on them. "One day I shall lie here, and none to prevent me," she told herself. Up there, where the greyness roamed the bracken, was her home, looking from where she stood, like a white pebble that a boy had flung out of the river. Later on she trod her way upwards with her groceries and a bucket of shallots Mary Maddocks had run out to give her. They were very heavy, but she stopped to gather a handful of bracken, bending the canes over and over to lit her small grate. The climb made her tremble. The wind took her breath and threw it away as if it were nothing. "There's no mercy, no mercy," she began to whimper, feeling her hair blowing awry, and her knees clutched invisibly.

That night old Mrs Ashstone had to bolt her door against the boulders of air the wind rolled against it. The latch and bolt jigged with each solid blast: the glass in the window rustled, a beast roared in the chimney, and a wet black mark like a footprint appeared under the door.

She looked at it. "This is a rare storm that brings me such a visitor," she said.

The rain tumbled down the chimney on the flames.

"My fire's scalded," she said.

She sat down on her fender and began to unravel the shallots. Suddenly, letting her hands fall, she called: "John? John Ashstone?" She thought a voice had spoken to her aloud. She wasn't afraid. She had many voices inside her, but fear had seldom spoken. Her mind turned and talked to her often enough. Yet this had sounded different. It had come in the gale, now all but through the walls, now backing away, moving it seemed with and among the freakish screams, the lumps of wind, and the long dragging sounds that hung back along the earth.

A slate crashed. "Mrs Ashstone, Mrs Ashstone!"

Mrs Ashstone stood up. "Be you my conscience?"

"No."

"Then you be my stomach?"

"No."

"Then you must be the roof going?"

"No. I'm the wind. And you're a witch." And the roaring rose all round the room, like heatless flame.

"You may be the wind, but I'm no witch."

"Yes, you are."

"I'll pummel ye," said she. "Leastways I would if I could see ye. But all I can see is black cobwebs a-shaking in the chimney and soot in the lamp. I never was no witch."

"You've lived alone, and that makes a woman a witch."

"Oh, do it? Well, be that your footmark?"

The wind laughed and the sound was like stones leaping in a quarry. Then it seemed to fade, and when it spoke again there was only a tiny distinct vibration, like embers tinkling and creeping when a fire is left alone.

"Come outside and look at me," said this sequestered voice. The gale at that moment stopped; it was flat calm.

Mrs Ashstone stood on her doorstep, looking to the southwest, where a low black toadstool of cloud gloated over the hollow. She gazed at this evil web in silence, rubbing her little hands. In the doorstone dent lay a handful of starlit rain.

The old woman shook. She waved her fist and shouted: "I don't like you. Get away, wind, ugly thing you be!"

The cloud was nearer. Around it the stars shone as in tender piety. "I cannot abear that thing," the old woman said, and she went in and closed the door. But the voice bent itself round the chink before she could thud the bolt: "Where shall I go, where shall I go?" it uttered shrilly and rapidly.

"Go?" screamed Mrs Ashstone. "Go anywhere. Go down the village and blow down all they great el'ums and rookeries and Captain Ifor's peaches. Haven't them had peace all these years?"

Her words were repeated, but slowly, as a lesson is read, meditatively, engraving the stillness. Then there was silence. She was

44

alone. Her fingers hovered about her ears as if to catch meanings in the lamplight. But she heard nothing except clock, kettle, and mouse. She felt that she lived in these stirrings. Thoughtfully she went to the cupboard, took down the sugar-basin and flipped a mouse-pill out of it with her thumbnail.

When she opened the door again before going to bed she noticed that the darkness had a strange sallow smell. There was a faint wavy noise. She strained to hear. " 'Tis like the weir!" she said staring. On the hill it was as still as mid-summer, with the sheep cropping the hushed mounds. She saw a star sinking slowly as if someone were lowering a candle to the floor. The old woman put out her hand to catch it....

In the morning, looking under the sunrise, she saw the empty floods and the river winding through their vacancy. Red as copper, the dull waters showed seaweed like patches spread upon them. These were ricks of hay and clover and corn which the wind had lifted and carried away and dropped furlongs from their foundations.

Mrs Ashstone dropped her sticks and ran away down to the village without lighting her fire or even so much as lifting the lid off the bread pan. When she was past the oak tree the breeze fluttered like a flag in her face, but it made no sound at all. She ran into the 'Street', holding her left wrist in her right hand, and then she stopped and listened.

Slates were lying on the paths, trees were down, with their roots that had burst the sod, washed bare of earth, and strange sand bars and pearly pebble beaches rippled across the lane.

Most of the doors stood open on the tightly-furnished rooms, but nobody stood looking out. It was so quiet except for the cadaverous murmur of the flood that she could hear the puddings snuffling in the saucepans.

She ran on round the bend. Then what a sight! The river had cut the village in half. It had felled the bridge, and was rushing over the road fifty yards wide, and rough and red as a ploughed field.

On the side where Mrs Ashstone was running the slope was abrupt and the houses stood clear above the torrent. But on the far side old Mrs Griffiths' cottage was four feet deep, with a broken door and the green velvet furniture floating in the garden. In the greatest danger was Mrs Sate, the baker's wife, at her second-floor window with her baby up against her cheek. For the river divided from the flood at the corner of her chimney wall, and with enormous pressure split into two, islanding the cottage, with the cage of its partly-demolished porch clinging to it like rubble.

Mrs Sate was shouting wildly to the people who stood by the water. They did not seem to listen for they were all telling one another the story of their night. They had remote incredulous expressions on their faces because they could not go to work. The children were crawling out as far as they dared along the broken bridge stones. Captain Ifor was there in a mackintosh cape, prodding the water with his stick. And Mrs Maddocks, shouting at him, her white cotton bosom overlapping her folded arms. And many others.

" 'Twere more like sunset than sunrise, so wild and lonely 'twere," Fred was saying.

Then they all turned round, hearing old Mrs Ashstone running. Her footsteps sounded intelligent, as if they brought an explanation. But the old woman was rushing towards the river without any idea, her arms stretched before her as if she wanted to prevent the waters. She ran right up to the end, and then pulled herself up. She put out her foot and gently paddled her shoe in it. Old Captain Ifor cast her a glance, and then once more plunged his stick in it.

"What I do say is it's come to something when your own roofs blown off you and you're the last to know it," Mrs Maddocks was screeching at him: "Sitting there mending Fred's shirt I was, and not a notion in the world what was happening till he comes in. 'Mother,' he says, 'do you know the roof's lifting up and down like a rick-cloth? For God's sake,' he says, 'come out and see'."

Mrs Ashstone looked at her, and angry as she was Mrs Maddocks politely included her. But a voice that might have spoken out of the group itself, so monotonous and undistinguished was it, began to recite:

"Mrs Sate, she be s'ying as she 'ev nowt with 'er for sus-ten-ance but 'alf a pork pie and a crust. And her the baker's wife! Charley, 'e's been at the bake'ouse all night. What ool 'appen I can't think, for 'er can't swim to 'e, and what be good o' 'e swimming to 'er? And there bain't no boats in this village."

"And all the telephone wires are down. I've tried and tried," said the Captain.

Mrs Maddocks raised her stern voice again: "Whose fault is this, I said, when I'd seen. Eh? Who won't do the repairs? Eh? Who? Captain, you can take the key this minute if you're a mind, for I'm not a woman that will live under a roof that's tied on me head with wagon ropes as this one be this minute. All me furniture's out." And she handed the key out from her armpit where she had been hatching it. The Captain took it gingerly. Mrs Ashstone turned her eyes across the water. She stretched out her arms, and it seemed to her she was stroking the faces in the upper windows. She wanted to say something, but the waters and the gossiping stopped her frail words. Her face was beautiful.

Just then, on the other side, a man came running down the slope in a greatcoat. It was Charley Sate. He threw down the coat by the water's edge. He was in vest and pants. Round his waist he wore a scarf, and tucked into it were two bottles of milk.

"Ah, brave fellow, brave fellow," clucked the Captain. "Many waters cannot drown love. Besides they're going down. He'll make it."

Charley thrust out. His jaw was like a knot under his ear. He seemed to look into all their faces and to live in the look. The current knitted itself round his neck and his separated hands, walking, as it were, before those dark and frenzied eyes. He plaited his arms in with the water, weaving all three.

In a few minutes he was safe on the shed roof, lifting up a little window under the chimney. Mrs Sate's face vanished. Everyone shouted and a little boy dropped a flat stone with a ringing splash.

Captain Ifor nodded: "Well done, well done!" He propped his stick against his shaking knees so that he could clap. This made him recognise the key. Mrs Maddocks was crowdedly cheering with the rest, and for the first time the old man saw what was in his hand: "What's this? A key?" His eyes settled on Mrs Ashstone – eyes like smoky glass. "Want it? She doesn't. Mary always makes up her mind by accident, but when it's done it's done. You're more pliable. You have it. Get you down from that eyrie of yours."

Mrs Ashstone was no longer beautiful. Her body had dropped that direct expression. She stood twisted in an attitude of crooked secrecy before the Captain, and between their two silent figures flowed a little eddy of air, as it might between two trees.

She shook herself, as you might shake a clock that is stopping, and the slow tired look of secrecy was gradually transferred from one old face to the other, as though by reflection.

And so Captain Ifor and Mrs Ashstone stared silently at each other.

To him it was suddenly revealed that she was not like other old women. At least when you thought of an old woman you did not think of anybody like this one. Old women in the imagination are all alike. But old Mrs Ashstone was nothing you could imagine. She had a child's distinctness, he thought, yet she looked enfeebled, as though in her old age she saw the world by candlelight.

"Won't you have it?" he said.

She shook her head: "I have a friend up there. One that do know where I was born. To live with me."

"A relation?"

"Nearer than that," she said. And then shyly, and, as it were, *wonderingly*, she took a peppermint like a white button out of her pocket and tossed it in her mouth. She turned away and walked slowly up the road, her feet leaving little quiltings in the thin red mud, where the nails in her soles stuck. Under the oak tree she stumbled over the wind as if it had been a dog asleep. It circled round her, blowing a wren out of a bush.

"Well?" it said out of the grass.

The old woman sat down on a stone.

"If you was a beetle I'ood stamp on you," she scolded.

"Oh!"

"Some of them people have been kind to me."

"Then why didn't you take the key and go and live with them?"

She considered this question as if it lay on her lap with her hands. After a pause she said quickly, "*You* didn't ask me that – I asked myself. I can't hardly sort you out from my thoughts," she said, "even when it's quiet like here. I bain't got the *use* of a lot of people and voices. I bin too long on Garway. Down there I couldn't hardly tell whether I were glad or sorry. I couldn't seem to hear. And that's the reason as I don't want to change my ways now. I do like to hear even the mice in the cupboard, and the cockroaches, I'm that curious and learned. I 'ave got used to them. I've worked with people, not loved them, and now I be done with work I do want to be shut of 'em."

"It can't happen again," said the wind.

"Nor I don't want it should," said she, rising and beginning to bend over the crackling bracken.

GEORGE EWART EVANS

Possessions

A month after my father died they sold up the shop to pay the debts. Our big family and the pit-strikes had knocked the stuffing out of the grocery business and after my father's death it passed out without a whimper. The only bit of stock left after the sell-up was the pony and cart. My mother had held on to the pony by swearing it was hers – down in the books in her name; but even then, if she hadn't been pretty downright with the auctioneer, a big chap with a smooth skin and an expensive, whisky complexion, they'd have put the pony under the hammer as well. They left the cart because it wasn't worth taking away. Ma also clung on to the old piano with the pleated silk front. The auctioneer had walked round it, mumbling that it would fetch a pound or two and ought by right to be sold up with the other things, but Ma had stood her ground over this, too.

Dick, the pony, had been with us for nearly twenty years, and none of us wanted to part with him. He was like one of the family. He was something more than an ordinary pony, too: he had some real blood in him. My uncle bred Welsh cobs and Dick had come from his stable. When he was younger he pulled the grocer's cart as though he was doing us all a big favour. But he had no belly then for this kind of life: there were too many stops in it for his liking, and he waited for the time when he had the light pleasure-trap behind him or our Tom on his back. Then you'd see him prance and tear the road up as you'd expect from a pony whose uncles and cousins had fought in two wars. He stood about thirteen hands, and he could do most things bar talk, and if tossing his head was anything to go by, he'd made a pretty good try at that.

But there was a bit of difference just before the sell-up, when Ma said she was determined to keep the pony. Tom, my eldest brother, tried to reason with her.

"But what are you going to do with the pony, Ma?" he asked.

"What should I be doing with him? Let him rest, of course! He's done his work. Besides, you'll all be growing up before long and going off and getting married and leaving the house. I'd like to have the old pony for a bit of company."

"Talk sense, Ma," Tom said. "Who's talking of leaving you?"

"Well, I'm keeping the pony," Ma said doggedly, "and the piano as well. Gomer's got talent, and we can make do with that old piano for a good while yet."

A short while after the sale Tom had another try to make Ma see reason. The pony was in the stall, just doing nothing except take Gomer and me for a joy-ride in the rickety old cart occasionally.

"We'll have to sell Dick," Tom said one day after he came home from his new job at the pit. "We can't afford to keep him, Ma. We're short of money."

My mother went on with her darning, her spectacles halfway down her nose. Then our Gomer spoke: "Dando Hamer the Ragman has been asking about Dick," he said. "His donkey is failing." But straightaway he wished that he'd not opened his mouth, because he wanted to keep the pony as much as I did.

"Dando Hamer, is it?" Ma said, sitting up. "There's a fine one to get the pony! He'd either work him to death or else freeze him, keeping him standing outside the Greyhound while he gets drunk. And when he'd slaved him until he was a bag of bones, he'd pack him off to the knacker's yard."

"Look, Ma," Tom said persuasively, "why not have a word with Dando Hamer? I'll ask him to call up, and if he offers a fair price, let him have the pony. Better to sell him to Hamer, where we can keep an eye on him, than for him to go goodness knows where, and get the skin tanned off his backside." Then he added quietly: "Don't forget all the oats we'll be having to buy. He's just about through the bin we had left out of the stock."

My mother could see the sense of Tom's arguments, but she pondered for a long time before answering. Then she laid down her darning. "All right, you know best, Tom," she said without looking up. "We'd better see this Dando and have a talk with him. I'll send Gomer or Willy down to ask him to call. I tell you this, though: the family won't be the same without the pony; it will be like losing one of the children." Then as a stubborn afterthought: "But say what you like, I'm going to keep that piano. I saved it from the sale, and I'm going to keep it if it's the last stick of furniture we've got in the house!"

The next morning I walked down to call on Dando the Ragman; and took the first step towards selling the pony. I felt that I was drawing down heavy shutters on the past. There never had been a time when I couldn't remember hearing the strangely comforting clatter of the pony's hoofs on the cobbles in the stable; and the way he gave you a prod with his nose or a playful nip on the arm with his teeth when he wanted something you were a bit slow in getting. Nor could I forget the time when I was very young and the business was roaring ahead like a heath-fire, and Dick the pony was lifting up his knees high enough to make a champion trotter look to his rosettes and his ribbons. At that time, when we had made our last call, usually at the topmost house of the village, halfway up the steep hillside, Tom would sit back on an upturned sugar-box with the reins loose in his hands, and he'd say, "Home, Dick!" and the old pony would go as fast as a baby for his first birthday; his neck arched, his legs working like pistons, and the cart like a flying chariot behind him. I was very sad, and both my feet were on my mother's side in this business of selling the pony. But I could see that the sense was with Tom.

Dando the Ragman lived by himself at the bottom end of the village, in an old stone cottage by the river. When he opened the door to my knock I saw him without his cap for the first time, and I noticed how his hair was all matted and tangled like the inside of an old mattress. His eyes were as red as two plums.

"My mother wants you to call to see the pony," I said.

Dando's lips moved silently before he spoke. A few of the boys were saying that he had given some of his wits away with the balloons and paper windmills that he traded in exchange for rags. But he seemed to have a sure grip on all his wits this morning. "Selling him, she is?" His eyes narrowed as he thrust his bristle-covered face towards me.

"I don't know," I answered cautiously, mistrusting the cunning bloodshot eyes.

He grinned as he thrust a two-inch nail through the top of his trousers to secure one tag of his braces. "That will be all right, boy. Tell her I'll call this morning." And as I walked back towards the village he roared after me in his raucous street-cry: "And if you've got any old rags or jam jars, false teeth or ironwork, turn 'em out, turn 'em out! Dando'll be there!" I hurried off up the road, glad to be away from this apparition who was likely soon to be Dick's new owner.

Dando came up to our house later that morning, just after Gomer and I had got home from school. Gomer was practising on the piano, and Dando stood at the back door looking through to the parlour at him and listening, as though he were in a trance, to the old notes' chiming. Ma paused by the table and watched Dando for a moment. Then she clicked her tongue in disgust and whispered: "Drunk already, at this time of the morning!" Gomer's left hand stuttered a bit and he came to a stop. The spell was broken, and Dando collected himself and nodded at Ma, whom he had noticed now for the first time. Ma told him about the pony.

"But I'm not wanting a pony, Mrs Pritchard," he said, looking sheepishly at her from under his peaked cap. Dando was a bit afraid of Ma's dark eyes and her sharp tongue.

"Well, there's not much use you and me talking by here, is there?" Ma said briskly, taking off her apron. Dando leaned against the jamb of the door and scratched the back of his neck. He watched her fold her apron and place it neatly on the dresser. He was still silent after she had smoothed down her skirt in a last gesture. She repeated: "If you don't want the pony, there's no use our wasting breath, is there now?"

Dando seemed to ponder this. Then he stood up off the door-jamb and scratched his shoulder. He spoke quietly, cautiously, like a pleading child, uncertain of the effect of his words: "Any rags today, Mrs Pritchard, jars, old ironworks, false – "

"No!"

He took off his cap, examined the inside of it carefully, and clapped it back on his head. "How old would your pony be now, Mrs

Pritchard?" he asked casually, as though it was a question he had just read in the dirty lining of his cap.

"Nineteen," Ma answered boldly, waving Gomer and me back to give Dando air to make up his mind.

"A bit old for a horse," he answered with a wary, tentative leer at Ma.

"Old! Nonsense! Be off with you! This pony's father fought in the wars and lived until he was thirty-one. He used to carry a thirteen-stone drunken fanner over the mountains to Pentre until a few years before he died. If you think he's old," she took up the folded apron and held it under Dando's nose, "you try stopping him once he's got his head pointed towards home."

"Can I see the pony, Mrs Pritchard?" Dando asked, very subdued.

"Certainly, if you're thinking of buying him. Otherwise it will be a waste of my time." She pretended to hesitate, then said, "Besides, I've not decided for sure that I'm going to sell him."

But Ma showed him the pony; and Dando was made to feel that he was looking at a prince among horses, a possession without price; and indeed he was, but only to my mother. They manoeuvred and haggled for half an hour, until at last Dando offered a pound less than the eight Ma had asked for him. Ma accepted the offer and the skirmish was over.

Afterwards, Tom said that it was a good price, better than we should have got elsewhere. But she said, "Fair price or no, I wouldn't let him take the pony from the stable until he'd sworn, with his five fingers to the sky, that he'd treat him kindly and never let the knackers get hold of him while he was still living."

After the pony had gone, the empty stall was like a big draughty hole in the side of the house. Dando Hamer had sold his donkey, and Dick was now in the shafts of the rag-and-bone cart, though none of us had seen him yet. Whenever we heard Dando's war-cry bellowing up the street, Gomer and I slunk into the house, not wishing to see Dick heading Dando's sordid turnout.

But we still had the piano; and Ma polished it so often that it shone better than a pulpit; and our Gomer, as he sat by it, could see the top of the garden and the post for the clothes-line reflected in it. Badgered by Ma, Gomer practised night and morning; and at no time was the house free, or so it seemed, from the tinkling chimes of 'The Bells of Aberdovey'.

Within a few weeks, in the press of the new order after the sale, the pony slipped out of my mind. But my mother still had him very much in mind all the time. As soon as she heard the ragman's raucous voice in the street she'd be out on the doorstep to see how the pony was shaping. One day she walked across to him with an apple. Dick knew her as soon as she approached, and he lifted his head and showed a little of his old spirit. Ma was surprised, as we were, when she saw Dick close up – not that there was anything wrong with him, not anything you could put your finger on. Although he was a good deal thinner, he was still in pretty good condition. Yet he seemed to have shrunk into himself; his head had lost its angle and his neck its arch. He reminded you of an old man who had reached the breathing-through-the-mouth stage. Ma's eyes darkened as she drew her hands through the pony's mane. Often when she was moved by some emotion it turned suddenly to anger; and now she looked at Dando and sharpened her tongue: "You want to use the brush and currycomb on this pony a bit more than you're doing!" Harmless words, but spoken in a voice and with a look that accused Dando of a crime no less than the starving of his own children would have been. His bloodshot eyes looked obliquely at her from under the peak of his cap; but that morning he didn't have the spirit in him to say that the pony was no longer hers.

A short while after this a sore developed on one of the pony's legs. Ma spotted it and told Dando that she would report him unless he got the leg attended to. The sore got better, but it was plain that the pony was being neglected. Dando spent all his time in the pubs. He'd start out early on his round, full of good intentions as a new minister; and then he'd stop at the Greyhound, and get himself anchored there for the rest of the day with the old pony drooping his head outside. Tom used to see him there often as he came home from work in the afternoon; but he told Ma nothing.

One evening, however, we could see that something was wrong. It had been a pouring wet day, with a cold wind blowing the weather up the valley. Tom's face was black even after he'd washed all the coal off it. As he was having his meal, he broke a piece of bread

savagely and nodded his head over his shoulder as he blurted out:
"That pony's outside the Greyhound in this rain. Look's as if he's
been there all day."

Ma returned the teapot to the hob and looked at Tom. She took
her apron off and folded it neatly on the dresser. Something was going
to happen.

"Go outside to the stable, Gomer," she ordered. "There's still a
lot of bracken in the loft. Strew it deep in Dick's stall."

"What are you going to do, Ma?" Tom asked.

"We're going to have him back."

"But you can't!"

"Can't we?" she said, looking round for her coat. "We'll see! I'll
go for him myself if no one else will."

"But you can't, Ma! It would be stealing to fetch him back here."

"Who's talking about stealing? He's outside the Greyhound, is
he?"

"Ay, tied to the fence at the side."

"Well, you've only got to loosen him!" Ma said, her dark eyes
dancing with anger, "and I know which home he'll make for!"

It was as simple as that, and none of us had thought about it! Tom
got up from the table and reached for his cap. Ma said: "No, let one
of the boys go, Tom. It won't look so ... downright," she added
cunningly. "You go, Willy," she said, turning to me. "It's still raining
hard, so the streets will be empty. Just untie him and stand back. Here,
take this sugar with you."

I was outside on the pavement in no time, with a pocketful of
lump sugar and my face red with excitement. It was raining sheets of
glass, and the pony was almost frozen when I got down to him. His
head was as low as the ground. The road was a stream and the street
was deserted. As I gave him the sugar, I spoke his name. He nudged
me in his old way, and tried to get his nose into my pocket. "Now
he's alive," I thought, "and now he'll go." I slipped the piece of
orange-box rope off his bit; and the street was still empty as he turned
his head round to the road. Then I said, "Home, Dick!"

The old pony turned his head and looked at me inquiringly. I
repeated the words. His ears went up suddenly – and within a few
seconds the wheels of the rag-cart were turning faster than the wheels

of a pit-cage. And all the rags and cans Dando had collected before he'd gone to earth were strewing themselves about the swimming roadway. Up the street went the pony, the cart flying behind him and fanning out the water like a speedboat. Ma was right: he'd find his way home; and what's more, he'd be there in half of no time. But Gomer and Tom were there waiting for him, and when I got home he was deep and snug in his bracken with a feed of oats in the manger.

After the excitement of the transfer was over we went back to the kitchen. Tom said: "What are we going to do now, Ma? Hamer'll be up as soon as he's sober. What are we going to tell him?"

"Tell him he can't have the pony."

Tom looked worried: "But he bought him, Ma!"

"Ay, but he didn't keep his part of the bargain."

"He won't take that for an answer, daft as he is."

"He needn't. I'm going to buy Dick back from him."

"Buy him! But what are you going to use for money?"

"I'll get the money. We'll sell the piano."

"But what about our Gomer's music lessons?"

"Gomer can learn the flute. Can't you Gomer?" she asked, turning to my youngest brother with persuasion ready on the tip of her tongue. But Gomer nodded: he was easy; he wouldn't pout over the loss of the piano. In any case he'd got no further than 'The Bells of Aberdovey', and his left hand was shaky even with those.

Dando Hamer came up early next morning and Ma was ready for him. Gomer and I were there to see the fun. Dando was very mild and sheepish.

"'Morning, Mrs Pritchard," he said. "Thank you for putting up the pony." Ma looked at him without speaking, and he twirled the peak of his cap uneasily. "It was all a perfect accident," he went on quite animatedly. "I was detained, you see, longer than I expected."

"Dando Hamer," Ma said with all the scorn she could command, "you're not fit to brush out the pony's stall!"

Dando bent his head and acknowledged his failings. "Can I have him now?" he asked after a few long seconds.

Ma quietly folded her apron: "No, you cannot. The pony is staying with me," she said.

Dando stiffened and worked himself into a fury. A flood of words poured out, all in a beery jumble. The word police was mixed up with them.

"Police!" my mother said quietly. "Don't you use that word, Dando. Just you be thinking what you'll say when I've fetched the Cruelty Inspector to see the pony!"

Dando worked his lips in silence. "But how can I go on my round?" he whined.

"Davy Prothero Bonanza Stores has just bought a motor-car, and his horse is spare. Go up and ask him to lend you the horse, and take your old cart away from here. I'll pay back the money you gave me for the pony."

Dando looked narrowly at my mother. He knew that there were no long stockings hidden in our house. "When, Mrs Pritchard?" he asked with a polite leer.

"As soon as I've sold the piano. Be off with you now! I can't waste time talking to no purpose."

But Dando had suddenly brightened up. The word piano had struck a hidden chord somewhere deep inside him. "Is that the piano with the green front?" her asked eagerly. "Wanting to sell it you are?"

"Yes!"

"Can I have a look at it?"

My mother stared at Dando, and then she remembered how he'd stood listening at the back door, to Gomer's playing when first he had come to the house, weeks ago. She motioned him to follow her into the parlour. He stood back from the old piano, his cap in his hand and his little mottled eyes dancing under his untidy mop of grey hair. "Does it still work?" he whispered.

"Of course it works," Ma answered scornfully. "Our Gomer can nearly make it sing!"

She moved her finger across the keys, all yellowed with age, and Dando was plainly moved by the tinkling shower of notes that scattered themselves about the room. He stood before the piano as if it were an altar. The melancholy echo of the notes, filling the room long after they had been sounded, had stirred some long-forgotten memory in him. He was a man transformed: a man who had heard angels. Then he stirred to life and blurted out suddenly: "The pony back, and one pound extra for the piano!"

Ma looked at him and saw his excitement. "Two pounds with the pony," she countered.

Dando glanced at the piano again.

"Go on," Ma encouraged, "take your time. Have a good look at it!"

He stepped forward timidly and ran his hand over the silk front and touched the smooth mahogany with reverence. His fingers hovered above the keys, but he drew back before striking them. Still looking at the piano, he said: "Right you are, Mrs Pritchard. A beautiful instrument! Two pounds and the piano. Fetch it before tea-time. Here's the money to start with." And with one movement he whipped out the two notes from his inside pocket. He placed them on the piano and was away up to Prothero's to get the loan of a horse. Some strange concord of sweet forgotten sounds had moved Dando so that he was already a new man with a shining purpose in life.

Ma smiled as she watched him hurrying away. "And now the Lord preserve us," she cried, shaking her head. "Dando's going to teach himself to play." And later, as she got Gomer and me a meal, she said, "I think you'll do better with the flute, Gomer. That old piano was getting out of tune, anyway. A trouble, too, it was getting to polish it every day."

Dando borrowed Prothero's horse, as Ma had suggested, and fetched the piano that afternoon. And Dick stayed in his old stall and soon had some flesh on his bones again. None of us minded very much about losing the piano. Its tinkling had become as unwelcome as the sound of the school bell; and until Ma could get him a flute Gomer was quite content to play at football. Tom brought home a card-table he'd won in a raffle, and Ma placed it in the parlour to fill up the space; and soon the piano was forgotten.

At least so we thought, until a certain morning when Ma went in to polish what was left of the furniture. It was hard to say just what had reminded her of the piano. Perhaps she had heard, as she bent down to her dusting, an echo of one of its chiming, melancholy notes; or perhaps she had just seen its dark outline on the faded wallpaper. Whatever it was, she stopped and called to Gomer and me in the back kitchen: "I wonder how the piano is getting on. I wonder if that Dando is using it properly. I'll have to take a walk down that way before I'm much older, just to have a look at it. Pity for the damp to get into it and ruin it – a beautiful instrument like that."

And as I looked at Gomer I saw his face beginning to screw itself up dolefully, exactly as it used to do when he struggled to ring those chiming, jangling 'Bells of Aberdovey'.

GWYN JONES

The Pit

A kerman came by the pits just after eight o'clock. There were four of them, and near each a high bank of rock discarded from the ore. These were now thinly grown with silver birches, feathered with young ferns, starred with saxifrage and wild strawberry flowers. The stones were about a foot to eighteen inches wide and thick, many of them embedded in livid moss, and those lying loose nearer the pit edge handsomely weathered. The first pit and the fourth coming from Coed-y-Mister had, said the countryside, been sunk in Roman times to meet the level running in under the hill at the Ystrad, and had been worked off and on through fifteen hundred years. The two middle ones had been cut through the rock by Lewis Tywern the ironmaster in Chartist times, and made him a wealthy miser, and had been abandoned as it grew difficult and expensive to fetch the ore out by basket from the pits or by tram through the level. Around two pits, one Roman, one Lewis Tywern's, there still hung from rotten posts the last rust-riddled strands of wires; the other two were open to the hillside, twenty yards from the disused path. In this path, which led from the Roman Steps to the ruined farmhouse of Coed-y-Mister, there were still visible beautifully smoothed stones grooved by the wire that had pulled the full trams to the shoots above the Ystrad. Because there was no fencing, occasionally a sheep went over and, once only, a dog. The largest pit of all, the one Akerman had visited three or four times, had claimed a child, but that was in the days when it was still being worked.

He went to the edge. From the curtain of trees opposite he heard the complaining of birds at his presence, and smiled. The pit was roughly circular, some eighty feet across. For three parts of its round

61

it went steeply over smooth bluffs of ruddy stone mottled with moss, very warm looking in the apricot coloured light. In four places a tree went out from where its roots knitted frantically into a crevice, and there were tufts of greenery twenty or thirty feet down. On the fourth side there was a convex slope covered with last year's leaves, and then a drop to a ledge that he could just distinguish in the brown darkness which always filled the shaft. Carefully he stretched himself on the grass and worked forward till his face was clear of obstruction. Nothing to see. For as the setting sun slipped from the brow of the hill, it cast solid-seeming shadows into its heart.

Then he shouted. He had barely time to hear his voice die in the pit when with a frantic squawking a flock of jackdaws broke raggedly from the trees where they had been watching him and made uneven flight over the chasm. They wheeled and came back to the trees, but half of them, uneasy still, went off a second time with a loud clapping of wings and much jabber. Getting to his feet, Akerman shouted again just as they settled, whereon out they poured in full flock like a devil's chorus screaming across the pit, so that a ewe with two lambs to Akerman's right ran off all huddled. They swarmed up over his head, cursing and jeering, with a hundred insults telling him to take himself off. "All right," he called to them; "but I'll be back tomorrow. I'm going down that pit." He grinned, reading meanings into their cries. A reprobate with a hanging feather banked within a yard of his face. "Don't worry," he said, "I'm going." The last he heard of them as he set off towards the steps was a tetchy interchange of suspicion and one commanding squall. Hang-Feather was making a speech.

The Roman Steps led from the mouth of the level at the Ystrad to the ancient earthwork at Castell Coch. Much of it above the point where he joined the way was grass-grown, but in places he could see the series of wide flat steps at the sharper ascents, and there were ten-yard stretches of curbing on the model of the Roman roads he had seen in southern Italy. No wagons could have come this way, though; the iron ore must have been slave-carried in baskets. "Seen a bit of misery in its time," he reckoned, wagging his head.

He reached Castell Coch in twenty minutes. The stone house in which he was staying had been built within the earthwork itself. Castell Coch: Red Castle – in the evening one saw why it bore its name. The sun was sinking, and here on the hill top the light was a lovely soft gold, and the stone outcrop seemed flushed with blood under a tough skin. And what a view! To the west he could see the debouchment of three valleys into the open Vale, and far away the oak trees of Coed Duon went in slow successive folds into fairyland. Behind him, when he turned towards the Ystrad, he found the brown dusk stretched up the hillside to the home meadow, but Cader Emrys wore a purple robe and a crown of light. Then, even as he looked, in a minute, the giant drew a dark hood over his head, and the sun left him.

As he stood there, Mrs Bendle came from the house and crossed to the well. She looked towards the red and yellow streamers, shading her eyes, and saw him on the mound. He went down to her, telling himself not to hurry.

He hesitated. "Bendle in?"

She had been treating him this way for a fortnight. "By the fire. He's a terror for being kept warm, is Tom. Winter and summer, day and night."

"Bed and board?" he asked, watching her. She was a fine, sly-faced woman, smooth and supple. Her throat was like milk, her hair raven-black. Akerman's age. As high as his mouth.

"If you say so, sir." Her eyes flashed at him, her mouth drooped humorously, then she had turned to the well again.

"In his place I should want as much," he challenged.

"As much, sir?"

"Cherishing at bed – and board." He leaned over the well beside her. "And don't keep calling me 'sir'."

"But I ought to. It is proper."

"I call you Jane, don't I?"

"Sometimes" – she smothered a laugh – "when my husband can't hear you."

He knew he was colouring, but as the bucket came up he reached for the handle, his grip locked upon hers. "What I ought to do with you – "

"You'll tip the bucket!"

"Never mind about the bucket. There's plenty of water where that came from." Setting his left hand to the bucket he caressed her soft round forearms with his right. "Why didn't you come this afternoon?"

"Why should I – sir?"

"Because you promised you would."

She pushed his hand away. "Oh, no, I didn't!"

"Oh, yes, you did! But never mind now. Will you come tomorrow?" He had forgotten about the pit.

They were walking towards the house. She looked down at her feet. "It's my day for mam and dad tomorrow." She smiled sideways. "And what would Tom say?"

He scowled, knowing himself a fool. "Tom will say nothing – if he knows nothing."

"It's bad you want me to be, I know. And tell my husband lies!"

He could have struck the slut. But she had pushed at the door, calling out: "Tom, here's Mr Akerman," and he could do nothing but follow her inside with the bucket of water. "Put it in the bosh. There's good of you, sir."

Bendle said nothing. He was of middle height, very broad, indeed fattish, none too well shaven. Forty years old. He wore a shepherd's jacket, earthy looking trousers stuffed into short leggings and heavy boots. His red hair was frizzed out at the sides, but the top of his head was quite bald. He was reading a three days' old newspaper, though whether he got anything from it in so bad a light Akerman couldn't know.

"Turns chilly on top here when the sun goes," Akerman suggested, putting his hands towards the small fire.

"It's too late in the year for fires. They make more work," said Mrs Bendle, as she went into the scullery.

Akerman had picked up the poker. "Someone has to make them, I suppose."

Bendle put down his paper. "It's women makes the fire and fools play with it." He got up boorishly and clumped into the scullery after his wife.

Later, they had supper. Akerman's meal would have satisfied the former holders of the earthwork: brown bread, cheese, lettuce and an onion, a pint of milk. The other two drank tea. Only one part of the conversation mattered to Akerman. Mrs Bendle was leaving at half-past seven in the morning to catch the train at Maes-yr-Haf, four miles away. She did not know whether she would be back at eight or

ten o'clock. Bendle could expect her when she came. First, and
foolishly, Akerman thought of slipping out at dawn and waiting for
her on the Steps; then he looked at Bendle. What he had said about
fools playing with fire. Cutting the rind from his cheese, he thought
of Bendle in a rage. Heavy shoulders, thick neck like this rind, bull
head, shag eyebrows, he could see his powerful jaws going like
machines. Awkward to handle if he came at you. He looked full at
Mrs Bendle. No cause for rage – yet.

The two men smoked while Mrs Bendle washed up outside.
Akerman offered his pouch: "Good stuff," he said. "Try some."

"Try some more, you mean."

"You said that, not me." He watched him press the tobacco down
with a stumpy finger. "I may go down one of Lewis Tywern's pits
tomorrow. The big one."

Bendle looked up. "Why?"

"Curiosity. And habit. I've done a lot of cave work. I like it."

"You won't find much to interest you."

"What if I don't? Could you come with me?"

He shook his head. "Got something better to do with my time."
He fell to puffing steadily.

"You've got a rope in the" – he pointed – "the shed there?"

"Ay. I got a rope."

"Long enough, is it?"

"Ay. Plenty of rope." He looked into the bowl. "I'll give it to you."

In the scullery outside his wife had begun to sing. Akerman leaned
back in his chair, listening and thinking. There was no savour to his
pipe. He felt the strong beat of his heart; heard it too. Even her voice
had a sly laugh in it; the lullaby was tender and caressing. He knew
nothing of the Welsh words but found himself nodding as Bendle
with half-shut eyes beat time to her singing with his pipe. "Sing it
again," he called to her when she finished; "Sing it slow." She did so
and Bendle hunched to the fire. "When I was a crwt of a boy, no
heavier than a bag of nails," he said at the end, "I remember my
grannie singing that to my sister who died." He began knocking out
his pipe against the square palm of his hand, and blew as he stood
up. "I must see to that cow before I go to bed. There was a mistake
for you." He lit a lantern. "Ten minutes I'll be." He had hardly gone

from the room with a pan of hot water when his wife came inside.

"It's in her belly, poor creature."

"What is?"

She laughed. "Her calf, what d'you think?" She began to rake out the fire, rounding out her hips as she bent in front of him. "It makes you wonder, don't it?"

"What does?"

"Oh, nothing. Hasn't it been a nice day?"

"It might have been."

She stepped away from him. "It is so nice in the woods at night, lying among the flowers, looking up at the moon."

So fierce a vision possessed him at her words that he had to stand up. "I'm willing to try it," he said, dry-mouthed.

"Only there's no moon!"

"There will be, in an hour. Will you come?"

"What a question – sir! Whatever would my husband say? Oh no, I couldn't do a thing like that, could I?"

"Listen!" He came quickly around the table and moved between her and the scullery door. "Before he comes back – "

"We mustn't forget that he will come back, must we, sir?"

"And if you call me sir once again, I'll do something I'm wanting to do, at once, husband or no husband. Understand?" He thought she would have dared him, but warily she nodded, half-smiling, and rubbed the flats of her fingers across the table top. "Come here," he ordered.

"Why then?"

"Because I don't like you always dodging away from me. Come here!"

Slowly she came a little nearer. "Yes?"

"What time are you coming back tomorrow night?"

She glanced, he thought uneasily, at the door. "Why?"

"Because I'm going to meet you. And bring you home."

"You can't do that," she said. "If I come by the eight train at Maes-yr-Haf I shall walk with the Trefach folk as far as the Ystrad." She looked towards the door.

"Then I'll wait at the mouth of the level. And help you up the Roman Steps."

66

"You mustn't talk such things. If my husband came in and heard you – "

"Who cares?" Her mouth, her throat affected him almost to drunkenness. "To hell with him anyway!"

"No, no!"

Before she could draw back he had her by the shoulders. Their lips met, hers full and wet and soft, his dry and harsh and bruising. For one moment she clung to him hotly, kissing and taking kisses, and then she broke roughly away. "No, no!" It was then they heard the scrape of a bucket on the scullery floor. Without a word, hands to hair, she was through the door that led to the stairs. Akerman, a wave of cold dousing the flame in his veins, turned to the table and was fiddling with the lamp when Bendle came in. "Giving a bit of trouble," he said steadily.

"Your fault, was it?"

Akerman stared at him. "Possibly it was."

"It's best to leave well alone. Where's the wife?"

"Gone to bed, I think." He patted at a yawn. "Not a bad idea, either."

"No."

"How's the patient?"

"She'll manage."

"Then I think I'll have a glass of water and away to go."

In the scullery, pouring water from the jug kept on the drainer, Akerman noticed a strange thing. Part of the plaster had broken away over the bosh that morning and the bit of shaving glass that hung there had been set at an angle against the rack. He saw that it reflected the living-room mirror, and what could be seen in the living-room mirror was the table edge where he and Mrs Bendle had kissed. He managed one gulp of water and poured the rest down the sink, but when he came back into the living-room, Bendle had gone upstairs.

After a minute he followed him, holding his candle well aloft to illuminate every corner of the stairs and landing.

When he came downstairs in the morning, it was to find Bendle about to leave the house and his wife long on the way to Maes-yr-Haf. His breakfast was set ready on the table, the kettle steamed on the oil stove in the scullery. "Good," he said, and smacked his hands together.

Bendle dawdled. "You serious about the pit?"

"I am."

"I'd advise you not." He used last night's phrase. "Leave well alone, that's best."

He seemed troubled. Akerman's anxiety about the scullery mirror grew less. "Don't worry. But I'll borrow your lantern, shall I? I know all there is to know about caves and pits. No nerves to bother me. Start to worry when I don't get back."

"Ah," said Bendle. He pulled at his legging, frowned, then straightened up. "And what time?"

Akerman poured out his tea, "I may go off for the whole day. Expect me when you see me."

"Like the wife, then?" Before Akerman could reply he had gone out, but at once reappeared. "Don't say I haven't warned you." With that he went for good and Akerman finished his breakfast and had a smoke before going to the shed for the rope. It was very strong, and there was plenty of it. Plenty of rope! He screwed up his eyes, remembering Bendle's phrase, remembering other phrases of his. He sat on the back door bench for some time, wondering. Mrs Bendle was a slut and a cheat; so far he had made a fool of himself to no purpose. What was wrong with himself tramping four miles to Maes-yr-Haf and catching a train for a long way off from Wales? But his vanity was against it, and his desire. If he met her tonight at the mouth of the level, he'd fetch her to account before they reached Castell Coch. Then, tomorrow he would be off – not another day here – and so let her know what he thought the worth of her. Nice in the woods, looking up at the moon. He felt again her lips against his, the soft weight of her breasts, her loins under his hands. He would not go away before tomorrow.

He found and opened the lantern. The stub of candle was tilted right over, so he set it straight and went into the house for a better supply. He knew where everything was kept and slipped two candles into his jacket pocket. Then, thinking facetiously and yet with a hint of panic: "I can always eat candles!" he stuffed several more alongside them. He made sure that he had matches, his own beam torch, his penknife, and odds and ends. He put half a loaf and a piece of cheese in his knapsack, and a flask two parts full of whisky. By this time he was growing out of taste with his venture and again sat on the bench out of the sun, wondering.

He'd feel a damned fool if he didn't go. "Worse be one than feel one," he said aloud. Alone as he was, he said other things aloud too, about Mrs Bendle, perversely pleased with himself for doing this. He stood up. He would go just a little way down. No one could say he was afraid.

In twenty minutes he was at the iron pits. It was a little more than ten o'clock. "Hullo there!" he called, and the jackdaws dashed from the trees to revile him. While they swooped and swore he worked out where the level would meet the pit shaft – somewhat to the left of the slope over the first ledge. Best have a look from there, but first he pitched a stone half-way across the crater. Pang! it came off a distant ledge; then pang! again but fainter, and at last a noise like breath sucked in between the teeth as it met water. Five hundred feet? Six? More? And how far down to the level?

With all the care in the world he passed his rope twice around a tree trunk as thick as his own body, growing near the brink, and then knotted it securely to a second tree six feet away. Slowly he paid it out into the pit. "Here goes," he said finally, and began his descent. With only his face above ground level, he hung awhile, staring around. He felt a hundred eyes on him. Climb back up, climb back up!

His feet made untidy tub-like holes in the leaf-laden slope, and then he went down the short drop to the first ledge. It was cooler here, but there was light enough for him to do without his torch. He stood for half a minute, his hand gripping a stout iron bar sunk into the rock, and looked up at the smooth penny of blue sky above him. Nothing would be more natural than that a face should peer over at him. But there was nothing – not even a jackdaw flying across the chasm. He now looked down, but had to wait till the glare left his eyes before he could see much. He fancied the opposite wall slanted towards him as it went farther down. "H'm," he began, and ended – "Jane Bendle!" though she had not been present to his mind when he began to speak. "Well –". He gave his rope a turn around the iron bar, after dragging at it with all his might, and went over on the next stage. He had his torch tied to his button-hole with cord. At once he saw that his own wall was falling away from him and that the shaft was growing narrower. He was glad he had given the rope a turn around the bar; it made him swing that much less. Even so, he would be glad to reach the second ledge. Down another ten, twenty, forty feet – when would it – ah!

The wall of the pit, which had fallen right away from him, suddenly became a wide, flat terrace, on which he landed clumsily, striking his left hip and skinning the knuckles of his right hand. A flash of light rather than an oath went through his head, and then he was moving cautiously towards the back of the shelf. He was not surprised to find right in behind a small level stoutly timbered off. This must be a heading driven from the main road to the Ystrad. The rope secured, he lit his lantern.

There was little to see. The rock was bare as a shin-bone, and as dry. There were many boulders, though none of them, so far as he could judge, had fallen from the roof. From the level he could not even see daylight, and from the front edge of the platform the opening was a thin gash of white. Cloud going over, he judged it, and sat down, frowning into the darkness. He had done enough. He had had enough. He felt very cold, and cursed lumpishly.

Then something happened. He heard a rushing from above, stones and earth began to whang down the pit, the lantern went out as he snatched it up, there was a vicious rustle within a yard of him, and he was knocked a dozen feet as the rope went cracking under his knees. There was a loud groaning of timber from behind him, then silence, except for the clear, plangent notes of the last small stones falling.

For a minute he lay in the darkness, afraid to move lest he go over the edge. He endured a full paralysis of horror before he began to tremble and found his voice. "What is it?" he asked huskily. "What happened? Who is there?" With shaking fingers he struck a match, but it went out with the flare, and he failed three times before remembering his torch. It was still on the cord. "Pray God –" he stammered, and clicked the button. The first thing he saw was his rope running flat and two-fold along the floor, and at sight of it he trembled so violently he could not direct the beam. He began to whimper, then to cry, and then he was shouting and choking and beating his fists on the rock under him. He did this for some time before the sounds brought him to his senses and he lay quiet, he did not know how long, in darkness.

Gradually he found courage. "No good crying," he said calmly. "Light the lantern and see. That's the thing."

He did this. His rope was still fast to the balk, but it had fallen from above and both ends were downwards from the platform. His lantern and knapsack were safe. A bubble of hysteria rose from his stomach to this throat, but he fought it and won. "What – ?" he asked. "What –?"

He went to the entrance to the level. Could he get out that way? He flashed his torch along the timbers, sickened by their size and preservation. He looked inside. The walls so far as he could see were dry, the roof solid, the floor unlittered. The slow travelling light picked out some figures inside the gate, and he steadied it to read: 60 ft. ↓. He looked at this till it shone white on his eyeballs. What could be sixty feet down? "The main level," he said excitedly. He walked to the edge of the platform. Where his rope went over he saw two artificially-made grooves about eighteen inches apart, and a foot back two holes drilled in the rock. Lying flat, he thrust his head as far out as he dared, his torch flashed downwards. In half a minute he rose to his feet, grunting. He had picked out the top of an iron ladder about twenty feet down. Once only he looked up to the top of the shaft, put his broken knuckles to his mouth, and sucked them, and then, having satisfied himself that the rope would hold, lowered himself downwards. He went very slowly, and soon found the ladder. From here progress was easy, and even before he expected it he was on the next ledge. Landing, he gave his rope a tug. No Bendle this time to – but he felt that same bubbling of hysteria at the thought, and to drive it away began to talk about the pit in a loud, determined voice. There were lengths of rail here, very rusted like the ladders, pieces of timber, and the clean and frightening skeleton of a sheep. And at the back he found the mouth of the level.

It had been gated off like the smaller one above. As above, his torch went flashing inside. It was seven or eight feet high at the entrance. "I've got to try it," he said. He had grown very confident and so practical-minded that he pulled a contemptuous face at the notion that he throw a stone into the water at the bottom. "Something else in hand," he said severely. "Get on with it, not mess about." He carried a short length of rail back to the timbered level, tested and pushed and probed. It would be easy. He inserted the rail between the timbers and, using it as a lever, managed to force one of the horizontal pieces off the nails. He could now enter the level – if he wished to. Facing a grim moment, he began to sing: "When the fields are white with daisies I'll be there." I'll be there, Mrs Bendle! But behind all this went images he dared not outface: of himself lost in the level, cut off by a fall of rock, coming out to another pit, plunged into bottomless water, poisoned by bad air, falling and breaking a leg, hunted by Something the black level might contain. So he sang to cheer himself, as he had whistled when a boy on a lonely country road, to keep away this Something.

What was the time? He looked at his watch. It was a quarter-past eleven. He had been down the pit more than an hour.

And now came a second noise from above. First a hissing, then a smash, then a heavier one, and as he crouched to the ground he saw a large, shapeless, whirling body go from the darkness of air to the darkness of water. He had just time to hear the chink and patter of tinier missiles before it struck bottom. The noise of the splash came up in rapidly overtaken waves, as though the water itself was washing upwards from shelf to shelf, tearing the air into gouts, sucking and buffeting like rollers trapped in a gulf. It subsided abruptly, leaving him battered with noise in a painful silence. Raising the lantern he saw a small piece of dark material on the edge of the platform and went towards it. It was his face flannel.

Bendle! The thought he had forced from his mind came back so strongly that he gasped like a swimmer taken with cramp. Bendle had followed him, Bendle had untied the rope, Bendle had gone back home and removed every trace of him, Bendle would tell his wife he had gone away that day. Bendle, Bendle, Bendle! He could see him standing above the leaf-deep slope, his bull neck thrust forward, heavy jaws clenched, listening so intently. He leapt up. "Bendle!" he shouted. "Bendle, Bendle – for God's sake, Bendle!" His voice clattered about the shaft, boomed back into his lungs, suffocating him. "I never touched her, Bendle! I never! I never!" To be up there in the sunshine, under God's blue sky! To be free, free! "I'll go away! I'll do anything! Kill me after, only help me out! Bendle, for Christ's sake, help me out!" He was dancing with terror and hope. "Bendle! Oh, Bendle!" He choked with sobs, his chest split in two. "Oh, oh, oh!"

Through the echoes of his shouting came a roaring from the shaft. A boulder tore down a yard from where he stood, a second smashed itself on the ledge above, the iron ladder clanged under a mighty impact. A multiplied crashing and rumbling filled his ears with the noise of an avalanche. Snatching at the lantern, he ran back to the level and climbed through the timbers, the bombardment growing madder each moment. From inside, the lantern threw gigantic bars of yellow light through the gating, and through these bars boulders and splinters hurtled incessantly. Rocks a foot or more square rebounded from the walls of the shaft, shot from its irregular declivities, playing hell's own tattoo before they thrashed into the water below. Some of them burst like bombs on his own ledge, spraying the sides with shrapnel, lumps of stone singing through the air and thudding against the heavy timber framework which protected him. Something went past him with a sigh, to rattle down the stone tunnel; from below an ocean of watery echoes lashed up at him; and through it all he could hear the tremendous sonorous song of metal struck like a harp. He dared not look out, and what he saw as he pressed himself to the floor and joist was Bendle, in bright day, throwing down the cube-shaped blocks of waste till the shaft reverberated as under a hammer.

The uproar continued for ten minutes, great stones cascading all the while to destruction. On the ledge outside nothing would have saved him. Whether Bendle had calculated as much he did not know, but he himself judged that most of the stones, rolled rather than thrown down the leafy slope, would leap away to strike the far wall level with the first ledge and thence smash off, whole or in jagged pieces, to fall sheer to the ledge he had descended from, or just missing that, to the one behind which he now cowered. At least twenty such crashed within as many feet of him, the last of them bounding, hardly splintered, against the rock face left of his head.

The silence when it came was shocking. His ears went on humming and roaring, and there was a muffled bludgeon beating bad time inside his head. At last he left his shelter. The ledge was screed with rubbish, the timbers sconched, the skeleton hit to pieces. "All right, Bendle," he whispered, actually fearful lest Bendle should hear him. "All right."

He went back into the level and trimmed a new piece of candle. Thank God he had plenty of candle! His hearing became normal again, his head cleared. He had, he reckoned, the third of a mile to go, and with a convulsive effort of mind brought himself to start. He must forget everything else except the will to save himself. "When the fields are white with daisies –" he began, but bit the words off as the roar of falling boulders was renewed behind him. This time he smiled grimly. "Fool," he said, "wasting his time." If he got out soon, to go quickly back through the woods, surprise Bendle as he levered up his ammunition, push the fool over the edge to go bump, bump, bump to the bottom! And Mrs Bendle –. He laughed out loud. Trust him!

He was a fool to laugh in a level. A noise might set up tremors, those tremors strong enough to fetch the roof in. He looked up, very grave now. The height had decreased to little more than five feet already. As he lifted the lantern against the face of the stone, his foot kicked against something, so that he stumbled heavily. He panted, had to set his hand against the cold wall, for there were tramlines running ahead of him. "Oh!" he cried. "Oh!"

Then the roof came down to four feet six, so that he went clumsily doubled. The sides were cut clean and plumb, the floor was flat and worn. The air was fresh and there was a slight draught on his face. Here and there, just as in a coal mine or a railway tunnel, were manholes let into the sides, big enough for a man to shelter in. "In less than an hour," he said exultantly, "in less than an hour I'll be out." That cold air was coming straight from the Ystrad, and he had covered a hundred yards already! Almost as he spoke the tunnel went half right, and on the left he saw the opening of a subsidiary shaft running up and away in the direction he had come from. The level of the second ledge he judged it, and was puzzled by a buzzing in his ears. This grew louder with each step he took, and after twenty yards and a sharp turn became a dull rushing noise shaken intermittently like a pulse. Twenty more and the rock throbbed with it, the gush of a pent-up river seeking low levels seeming to push the air faster along the tunnel. It was on his right, no great distance away, the heavy baritone of fast-moving water. It grew colder, the sound a thunderous bass, and then he saw it. Through a fault in the rock a band of black water stretched foamless and unspilling. He had the fancy that if he advanced his fingers it would break them off like pencils. It had the might of a hundred times the flow in sunlight, the unhurried electric stream sucked into blackness. Alarmed, he hurried away.

After another hundred yards, the roof for a long stretch not more than three feet six, he came into a lofty hall. It went so high that his lantern did nothing to illuminate it, and even his torch could not find the centre of the dome. It was some fifty yards across, and circular, save for a huge bulge on his right. From a floor that grew increasingly irregular towards the rim there reared tremendous round bastions, so symmetrical that they gave the impression of being tooled by men. The light of the lantern fell softly from their brown masses as Akerman moved slowly around. A pantheon given to silence and emptiness, his footfalls the first in fifty years. He tried to imagine it aglow with lamps in its working days, when men no bigger than he trundled the heavy trams of ore and sent the only noises of an aeon around the vast hollows of its ceiling. "We don't know we are alive," he said wonderingly.

It was now, as he came back to the rails and found the other end of the tunnel, that he grew afraid. Bending to enter it he gasped, for he had imagined some huge, shapeless Being of the Hall behind him. He turned, shuddering, and snarled when he found nothing. "Fool!" he grated, and bent again, and once more had to turn, the hair all alive on his neck. In these black antres who knew what might dwell? Shoulder demons, hunters from behind. "Nonsense," he said. "Nonsense!" Men had worked here, crawling about like bees in a hive. Why, look! there was the haft of a mandril. He caught it up, a weapon, rubbed it against his face, careless of the dirt. "Come on!" he said hoarsely, staring about him. "You or Bendle – come on!"

But nothing came. The fist-blows of his heart slackened, "All right," he said, "all right."

Then, in the mouth of the level, a new panic brought him up stock-still. How did he know he was right? Were there other exits from the hall, with rails? Had he taken the right one for the Ystrad? Had he even gone the whole way round and was now retracing his steps towards the pit? This was a hundred times worse than terrors of the dark. Was the air still blowing against his face? With frightful vividness he thought of the piled-up hillside above him. Four hundred feet of unbroken rock under which to creep and creep till your lantern gave out and you were part of the dark for ever. The whole weight of it rested on his shoulders, compressed his chest so that he could not breathe. He drew his hand across his forehead, caved forward, caught at the wall for support. Breathe slowly, he told himself, breathe slowly! He must go back to the hall, work around it to the other mouth of the level and go on until he heard the waterfall. That would settle one doubt. Then he must return to the hall and come around it in the other direction, and if he found no other exit there was nothing to worry about. If there were other exits – . He threw the weight from his back and set off.

He had no fear of a Being of the Hall as he went back, after leaving the mandril haft at the mouth of the level. He came to an opening which he recognised as that he had left and, sure enough, after going some way along it, he heard the roar of the river. Back he came to the hall and around it, to his left this time. "There you are," he said, when he found the mandril haft; "what did I tell you?" He was a fool to have doubted that the air still blew on his face. He went on.

There was an odd feeling in the middle of his body, as though a tennis ball had been stuffed under the V of the breastbone. "Because I'm doubled up," he thought and said, but it was growing bigger and harder. It took him half an hour again to recognise that he was hungry – this where a runnel of clear water was squeezed from under the rock and went gently along with him. He took out the bread and cheese and the flask of whisky, all of which he had forgotten. After eating, he took a couple of mouthfuls of the spirit and felt warm and confident. He was glad the little stream was going his way. It showed he was going downhill, towards the Ystrad. For several minutes after drinking he sat there in a golden tent of light, resting. His watch said half-past two, and at first he could not believe it. He had been down the pit four and a quarter hours.

After attending to his lantern he started off once more. He must be more than half-way. At the slowest reckoning he would be at the Ystrad by four o'clock. And then? It would be barred, he knew that, perhaps locked and double bolted, but once he saw the light of day he'd have no fears. At the worst, he had only to wait until eight o'clock, when Mrs Bendle would come that way from Maes-yr-Haf.

Mrs Bendle! Head bent, going sideways under the low roof, he thought of her till her naked body glowed before him in the darkness, white as bone. So nice in the woods at night, lying among the flowers, looking up at the moon. "All right," he said, "all right." He would be quits with Bendle then. He hissed, changing hands on the lantern, surprised to find himself alone as the vision of her milk-and-raven nakedness faded from in front of him.

Without warning the runnel squeezed back under the right-hand wall. Was he going up a slight incline? Still, there could be only the one way, so he kept on unworried. Easy going, plain sailing, nothing to it. So he thought elatedly, and only superstition prevented him saying so aloud. To match his mood, the floor dipped again on the sharpest gradient he had so far found. His breathing grew deeper and more laboured. Surely this was the last stretch towards the Ystrad. Any moment now he'd see daylight. All right, Bendle. All right, Mrs Bendle. He heard himself panting and forced himself to walk slower.

In less than a minute the tramlines divided at a full set of points and led off at an angle of thirty degrees into two levels of equal size. For a moment he stood gaping, and then examined them carefully. There was nothing to tell him which was the right one. He had his first sensation of panic since leaving the great hall. Left or right? He made a futile attempt to assess the compass, and then felt the need of sitting down. In a very deep voice, which he did not recognise as his own, he began to assure himself that it did not matter which road he took, as both must lead to the same opening. It was now half-past three.

Finally he decided to go right, ridiculously equating left with wrong. After twenty yards there was a new forking off – in impossible directions, so it seemed to Akerman. He retraced his steps and made a sally down the left-hand tunnel. This ran true for forty yards and then, as he was congratulating himself, branched into two. He was very worried now, and had to get a grip on himself before deciding to take the right-hand turn. But in less than five minutes he came to a fall of rock and knew a year would be no better to him there than a day. Without delay he went back into the road to the left. Soon he was climbing again, steeply, and the rails had come to an end. He went on for a couple of hundred yards, twice bearing right, before deciding this would not bring him to the Ystrad. Once more he must go back and take great care with his turnings. But ten minutes later he came unexpectedly into a bigger level with tramlines. This both frightened and comforted him, frightened him because clearly he had failed to keep his bearings, comforted him because the main level to the Ystrad must be tram-bearing. Nor had he any idea whether to go left or right along this roadway. Fatalistically he went right, but before long discovered that he was going back along the level that had brought him so straightforwardly from the pit, so in a cold sweat he turned yet again and after half an hour found himself at the same main fork. He looked at his watch. It was a quarter to five. He had been down the pit six and a half hours.

He was very tired. He sat down and took a drink from his flask. It did him good, for the flutters of panic seemed always to come from his stomach. "Work it out," he said: "Let's work it out." Evidently he must go to the right, unless the roadway blocked by the fall was the proper way to the Ystrad. In that case – he resisted the temptation to drink again, saw to the lantern, and, with his teeth chattering slightly, began to walk. At the parting from which he had already returned once, he decided to go left. He knew that freedom must lie within a hundred yards, perhaps a hundred feet, if only he could get to it. But he covered at least the greater distance before coming into a round clock chamber with a fourfold set of points and three other galleries leading from it. He felt certain as death that one of these was the way he wanted, and that this was a clearing house near the Ystrad end of the level. "Which one then?" he asked, and noticed how shrill his voice was. "Why don't they put directions?" One gallery looked exactly like the others, and all were menacing. Then, leaving this small chamber, he had exactly the feeling that had terrified him in the great hall: that some blacker shape in the darkness stretched out hands after him. "Don't!" he cried. "Don't!" and stood stiff and trembling and telling himself not to be a fool. But he had given the darkness life and a power of listening – listening to his footsteps, listening to his words, listening to the horrors that tightened around his heart. "Don't!" he said a third time, his head on one side, and went blundering down a gallery. In ten minutes he was facing a dead end.

He had just resolution enough to follow the rails back to the rock chamber. From time to time he said in a broken voice: "Must get out. Appointment with Mrs Bendle. Must get out." He went blundering down the next gallery, began to make little runs, bumped against the sides. His forehead was bleeding. "Must get out!" he said, giddy and staggering.

He stood staring stupidly. There was a great yellow lake in front of him, and by holding up the lantern he could not see to the end of it. At his feet the rails dipped gently into it, and so shallow was the water that they travelled several yards before disappearing. "Got to go on," he muttered; and then: "No, got to go back. Yellow water"; and went stumbling away. He was talking all the time now: about getting out, Mrs Bendle, the tramlines, the Being who was Darkness. Several times he nearly fell, and his clothes were badly torn. "Like a rat," he sobbed, "like a rat!" At the rock chamber he ran to the third gallery and went into it headlong. At once he fell sprawling, knocking the wind from his body, and the lantern was jolted from his hand and went out. Strangely, this restored some measure of self-control, and after scrambling for the lantern and lighting it, he sat still for several minutes. It was twenty past six. He was quite certain that if he were not out before darkness fell on the hill, he would not get out at all. This was not because by that time his candles would be at an end, but from the operation of a time limit he had subconsciously come to accept. "Must move," he told himself, and at once was in the rock chamber. "Ah!" He went back into the gallery, walking quickly and at length dazedly. Surely he had been walking like this since he was born! The world above, the sunshine, the rain, the white clouds, these were all dreams of his. All creation centred in his head. But the birds, the little birds that flew and sang – . He began to sob, terrible dry-throated sobs, and then to howl like a dog.

He was at the yellow lake again. He looked at it and ran away. When he came to the rock chamber he entered another gallery at random and ran forward crying till once more he reached the yellow lake. Back he went the third time, and back he came to it. He ran crouching and fell often, and always found and lit the lantern. Several of its panels were now smashed, and its light was much dimmer. Sometimes he was mounting endless stairs, sometimes running from shadows that gambolled noiselessly behind him; sometimes he was tiny as a pinhead, sometimes swollen to the tight verges of the tunnel. Sometimes he saw Mrs Bendle – not the delicious version of her nakedness, but an elongated, swirling, slimy body with green cheese-mould for hair, her breast wet and rotten, the eyes like cockles. Even when he could not see the face, he knew it was Mrs Bendle, no other who waited for him now at this corner, now around that. And wherever he ran, whatever he did, always he came back to the yellow lake.

The sounds he made were now part of the mine. They clashed about him, endlessly repeated, challenging him to cry and howl and whimper. No recognisable word came from him, yet he was never silent. And so long as one throb of strength was in him he would go on running, running, running.

Then the yellow of the lake, the yellow of the lantern swung up in a blinding, golden flame as he struck his forehead full on the rock, and for a long time he knew nothing.

At last he stirred, and in time sat up. There was a clashing of knives in his head; he felt cold as a toad. Through the dullness of his brain regret that he still lived cut like a razor. All his pains seized him together, and he could not light the lantern without crying out. His torch and knapsack were gone; he was down to his last piece of candle. The gentle light fell on the yellow lake, and, sickened, he turned away, resting the lantern on his naked legs, hoping to warm them. Soon he leaned back against the rock, his head nodding, and saw to his left two tiny green points of light. They moved, and he came to know it was a rat watching him. This was the first living thing he had seen since he descended the pit, and he felt a great love for it, and wanted to stroke it and nurse it. But as he moved the lantern it dodged past him into the water, and he saw it swimming ahead in line with the tramrails. His mouth fell open, his eyes glared under the bloody eyebrows, he shook like a mammet. He got up and walked into the yellow lake he had fled from so often. He went very slowly, drawing his foot along the inside of the rail not to miss the way. Now the water was to his knees, now to his thighs, now it set clamps on his belly; but he went on, lifting the lantern higher. Slowly the water rose to his chest. He could not have been colder in a coffin of lead. The roof was slanting steadily towards the water, the floor fell as steadily beneath his feet. The water now came above his armpits. Soon the roof was six inches from his head, the water to his neck; then it was three inches and he had to tilt the lantern. He made six strides in an eternity, and the roof rubbed his hair and the water touched his chin. For one unforgettable fraction of time he saw around him the yellow ochre and a slight swirl as of something swimming ahead, then the lantern went out and he let it fall from his fingers. The water now lapped his mouth, and he tilted his head back so that his nose and forehead scraped along the top. One stride – two – three – the water jolting into his eyes before the roof lifted miraculously from his face. Three strides each a century long, and his mouth was clear. His foot struck the tramline. To his shoulders, his chest, his waist, his knees, his ankles the bitter line sank, and he was slishing forward, his hands before his face lest he dash it against rock again. He fell on his hands and knees to follow the rails and crept on to dry ground, shivering so hard that from time to time he could not proceed. He moved forward with appalling slowness, and it was fifteen minutes later he came to a turn and saw a weak diffusion of light ahead. His tongue came out to lick his lips, but he was now past emotion and continued to crawl. It was not for twenty minutes that he looked up again and saw ahead of him a dull beam of light reddening the rock. He blinked and went on crawling and did not lift his head until he himself was part of that beam. He looked with curiosity at what he did not know were his hands, felt pleased and amused at them. The Ystrad entrance to the level was not ten yards away, and he went crawling towards it. Quite properly there was room for him to squeeze himself past a block of stone, fallen from where it pinned a stout paling, so through he squeezed, leaving half his jacket behind him. For a minute or two he sat playing with the dust, and then with animal patience dragged himself on all fours into the road. He looked up, and then down, and was not surprised to see Mrs Bendle coming up the road from Maes-yr-Haf.

Bendle was with her. For their part they saw something half human flopping along the ground towards them. It was three-parts naked and unutterably filthy. The hair was grey, the face indistinguishable for blood, the hands raw. It had a voice, too, and squeaked as they came up with it: "I came. I said I'd come." Then it looked up at the man, "He did it," it cried. "He made me like this!" It collapsed, sobbing, its face in the dust.

There was a long silence left to two thrushes over the level. Mrs Bendle looked at the thing at her feet, then at her husband. "We never – . We never – ." Her voice guttered out, and she panted for breath. In Bendle's forehead a thick red cord pulsed, and he clenched his right fist. He dropped on his knees. "No," said the broken mouth, "oh, no!" But Bendle's fist unclenched, his thick hand stroked the bloody hair. "Don't be afraid," he whispered. "I won't hurt you, machgen i." Very gently he caught Akerman up in his arms. Then he rose, his burden to his chest, and after one strange glance at his wife set off for the Roman Steps and the house at Castell Coch. She, her face grey and rat-like, her fingers pinching at the buttons of her bodice, followed slowly behind, and it was so they disappeared, all three, into the quiet woods.

GWYN THOMAS

Arrayed Like One of These

I have known little of elegance. South Wales in the twenties was a forest of blue serge and, among the older men, suits of black material hard as teak and meant to outlast the earth. After twenty years or so under a steady fall of rain and sermons the stuff went a deep green, and I have seen many a seatful of deacons that made the preacher look like Robin Hood, a Hood who has chopped down the trees of his paradisal wood to make chapel furniture and plagued by a Marian eternally old and forbidding. It was a material that creaked like armour, and one of my darkest recollections is being shepherded to punishment by a group of elders after some witless antic on the chapel gallery and hearing the distinct deathly rustle of their suits. In that rig people of forty really looked cut off from life.

There was a good deal of amateur dressmaking. Someone would get a very rough pattern from a newspaper and work on it in a kitchen lit for groping only. I recall at the age of about five being in need of a shirt. I had set my mind on something fancy from the shops. There was a girl in the Sunday School on whom I wanted to flash a clear impression. But it was not to be so. Partly to teach me that sex and Sunday School, even at the tentative age of five, do not mix; partly to help a struggling widow, a close neighbour, who had taken up work with the needle, it was decided to place the order for the shirt with the widow.

The material chosen for the shirt was the most earnestly brown stuff I have ever seen. It would have looked well in a tent. It had been bought cheap from a packman who had almost lost his reason lugging this great lump of sad-looking fabric about. My father was so impressed by the melancholy on the packman's face that he bought a thick wad of the cloth, and he was delighted to see what a load he had taken off the packman's mind, even though he was now going to lift it on to mine. When I saw the colour of it I wrote a message on a wall for that girl in the Sunday School telling her that I had gone to India.

My father told me that this was the widow's first job and that we should not be fussy or demanding.

"He's only a kid, Mrs Supple. All a boy of that age needs is a rough covering. Don't bother about finesse or exact measurements. He's a shy boy. He doesn't like to be fiddled with, and I can see by your eye, Mrs Supple, that it can register a clear impression of size. Trust your eye, Mrs Supple. A shirt is a friendly sort of garment. Don't bother about an inch here, an inch there."

Mrs Supple didn't. The finished shirt was brought to us on a Saturday night as I was standing in the bath in front of the kitchen fire. My father brought the garment in to me, looking very pleased and saying that Mrs Supple had more of a gift than even he had imagined. My father slipped the shirt on to me. My brothers stood around staring and I could taste their astonishment. The front of the garment was about the size of a shirt front, a dickie. The back fell right down into the water of the bath and was a good inch longer than I was. I was like some new gruesome type of bird. Mrs Supple had also used all two feet of the neckband she had ordered. My father could have come in with me and we would still have been breathing better than normal.

"It's a fine shirt," said my father. "You couldn't expect anything stodgy, anything the same." He tried to keep his eyes on the enormous drape at the back. "I told her a kid your age grows like magic. She's given you coolness where a man needs it most and warmth where you'll appreciate it best."

I stepped out of the bath. The effect of the shirt was even more striking when one had a full view. My father sat in the corner smiling, praising Mrs Supple and saying that as a boy he had hated always having to wear shirts that were the same distance off the ground all round. As I walked around the kitchen trying to work this new fact into my existence my brothers followed me around as if I were a potentate, and my father said he had never seen any bit of raiment that so brought out the dignity in me.

I wore the shirt for several months. I still haven't quite recovered my sense of balance. And the mound of cloth that accumulated around my middle like a lumpy sash still has people convinced that I was once a cripple healed in the revival of 1921, a splendid year for miracles and early greens.

It was many years later that my father went into action on the clothing front again. We had been discussing a chronically shy neighbour of ours, Aaron Phipps, and his sympathy for this voter had caused an axiom to ripen in his mind. "If you see a man who is failing to look life in the eye," he said, "lay a helping hand on his neck muscles."

He had a tic of compassion that made him find people on every hand who seemed to be dodging life's eye but they usually turned out to be men who were chronically wary and were dodging everything about life, not just the eye. But we went to work on the neck muscles all the same and at the end of each experiment it was our necks that were in need of the sun-lamp.

At that time I was due to take my Final Schools at Oxford. I needed a suit of 'sub-fusc'. I had avoided dark suitings from the age of thirteen when I was thrown down the stairs of the Sunday School by a teacher who had been made distraught by our Darwinian banter and driven by jagged doubts first to quoits and corkwork, then to cheaper drugs. Also in that year, in dark blue serge, I had had the experience, at the funeral of an uncle, of being thrown into an open grave by an elderly cousin demented by grief and ale. So, in 1934, after a fair spell dressed in tweeds, I had to find a suit in the lower chromatic register. The last suit I had bought had been one of bold checks. My father had wanted at least one of the family to look like a bookie although no group of people could have been more remote from horses seen in a sporting light. But the check suit had given my father a lot of pleasure, and often when I had come into the kitchen when my father was exchanging perplexities and roast cheese sandwiches with the lost bewildered preacher, Mr Cornelius, he would add a mile to Mr Cornelius' maze by forsaking theology and asking me if there had been any scratchings and what the future was for the turf.

I could have managed the business of the suit in a few days if left to myself and was making my way to the newly opened branch of a nationally known outfitter when my father stopped me and said:

"You want a new suit?"

"That's it. Dark. Got to be dark. A feudal regulation."

"How would you like to strike a blow for Aaron Phipps?"

I thought at first that my father wanted me to give the money I had set aside for the suit to Phipps and I said no. First the exams I said, then succour Phipps, if need be.

"Oh no," said my father. "I just want you to let Aaron make your suit. He's just made a start with that very sad tailor, Horatio Clemett the Cloth, and it would stiffen Aaron's confidence if you asked him to make you a suit for such an important event as an exam."

My father, true to his basic rhythm of complexity, did not take me at once to the shop of Clemett and let Phipps measure me. He introduced me to Aaron Phipps that night in the coffee tavern of Aldo Nitti. Aaron had thick glasses and the most pointed set of nerves. He had been through a thorough mill of mishaps. He was jumpy and was not improved by my father's way of suddenly bending over him and saying that his day had come. He now looked like a lion tamer who has thrown away his whip and is urging the lions to leap to their last black climax.

"Aaron," said my father, "has got a natural gift of style and he'll be a first-class asset to Clemett the Cloth if he can be nursed back into a belief that things can really fit. His last job was with Tiller's fairground. In charge of various contraptions that go up and around. Swings and roundabouts and articles like that. Aaron gets vertigo. He gets giddy just watching people wheeling around on those painted horses and cockerels that are such a feature of Tiller's merry-go-rounds. And Aaron would have the idea that they were going to fall off. He would leap on to the back of a horse or cockerel and hang on to the customer. Sometimes it was a woman and Aaron got a thrust with hand or shoe for his trouble. This made him giddier and he would rush to the lever or brake and bring the whole contraption to a halt with a jerk that sent voters flying about the fairground like chaff."

Aaron smiled at me and made a gesture of pulling something towards him.

"Too abrupt," he said. "I'd warn them to hang on but there was such a racket of music from the panatrope."

He began to sing 'Let a smile be your umbrella', a popular fairground tune of the day, but Aldo Nitti told him to stop because Aaron's voice was penetrating and caused a pervasive buzz among the taller toffee bottles.

"Well," said my father, "the fairground owner told me that Aaron came within an inch of bringing organised jollity in the zone to a full stop. But now Aaron is going to have a fresh start. It seems that his mother, who died a short while back, was a lover of Clemett the Cloth."

"Very close, let's say," said Aaron, "very close." He blinked.

"The gas meter was in the front room." My father cautioned Aaron with his eyes that he had made another nervous leap ahead of his narrative.

"To get on in tailoring, Aaron," said my father, "you'll have to learn to talk smoothly to the clients. It won't do to make them wonder why your stories sound as if they've been blown up in the middle. If necessary, check the facts of each story on your fingers."

Aaron went back a page.

"I had a penny in my hand to put in the meter. The front room was dark. I fell over Clemett. I lost the penny. Clemett told me not to bother and I could hear my mother, very muffled, seconding him. He has a very harsh voice in the dark, Clemett." By his tone I could sense that Aaron did not take much to Clemett.

"And he's not much better in the light."

"So Aaron's mother made Clemett promise to give Aaron a start in the tailoring trade. But it seems as if Clemett shot his bolt as far as love was concerned with the passing of Mrs Phipps and he's trying to bully Aaron into some other trade. But we'll show Clemett. Aaron's the boy to make your sub-fusc suit for you. Give him a chance."

Aaron fished a book of styles from his pocket. It looked ravelled and years out of date. On its cover was a group of men who had borne off the palm of neatness in the year of the book's publication. I put my finger on one of these and told Aaron I would like to look like Jimmy Walker, the Mayor of New York, a noted dandy, and Aaron said that if he ever set eyes on Walker he would bear this in mind.

My father took me to the shop of Clemett on the afternoon of the next day. It was one of the darkest shops in Meadow Prospect. Some years before Clemett had turned against his own trade and had stated in the Discussion Group of the Christian Men's Guild that, without going all the way with those elements who sat naked around lagoons and one or two local voters he had spotted through gaps in the ferns, humanity would be a lot better off for being less well covered. He had been told off by the Christian men and advised to go and think it over.

Aaron was in the back of the shop, hardly visible and pushing a large, hard bristled brush along the floor.

"A terror for keeping the floors clean, is Clemett," whispered my father. "Dreads the plague and keeps on having his brushes stolen. So he keeps Aaron at it. That way he always knows where the brush is and keeps Aaron frustrated."

Clemett shook us by the hand and apologised for the gloomy atmosphere.

"Many of my clients come to me in a state of grief for funeral suits and they wouldn't want too garish a light."

"I can see that," said my father. "Death leaves the voters in mixed states." And he went on to explain to Clemett about sub-fusc, Oxford and the examination and I could see that he had left Clemett as much in the dark as the shop. Behind me in the shadows the rub of Aaron's brush was like the rustle of doom, putting me on edge and I was wishing myself out in the light and my father through the floor-boards.

Clemett produced one of the thickest books of patterns ever assembled. Sub-fusc was no problem here because among these hundred heavy slabs of cloth, any one of which could have gone straight on to a grave, there was not one tint that rose above a blackish grey. It was clear that Clemett had long been seeing humanity as a kind of cortege. I picked one out at random. I could not go wrong in that clamp of shadows. But my father told me not to take it. He had been fingering his way through the samples and he had come up with one which, on first touch, felt like two-ply sail cloth. My father was most impressed and I could see that Clemett too was keen on this particular fabric.

"That," said my father, "strikes me as a pretty durable weave."

"The average cloth in that book of samples," said Clemett, "would last fifteen years. But that cloth there would see you right for twenty-five."

My father said this was just the thing. He had, he said, seen many people like deacons and merchants wear suits of this material and the fact of having themselves encased in such impenetrable, deathless stuff had given these voters a stern unsensual look which had improved their work with morals and merchandise. For myself I was thinking that when they saw me in this raiment at Oxford they would declare that Roger Bacon the alchemist was back.

Mr Clemett now got a pencil, a book and a tape and told me to take off my jacket.

"If you don't mind, Mr Clemett," said my father, "we've heard a lot about Aaron Phipps' very gifted way with the tape and my boy would like Aaron to handle the order."

Clemett's first impulse was to carry on with his measuring and wait until he had the cash in his hand before telling my father that he was off the hinge. But my father had rushed to the back of the shop, snatched the broom from Aaron's hand and was pushing him towards us. He took the tape off Clemett, not without what looked like a bit of a scuffle and gave it to Aaron.

"Now then, Aaron," he said. "Here's your chance to become the best loved tailor and stylist in the gulch."

"Do your best, Aaron," I said in the softest voice I will ever employ outside dreams. "You know the main points; chest, legs and that."

"Don't you worry," said my father. "Aaron and I have spent hours talking about men's styles in the cafe of Aldo Nitti and by the time he's finished he's going to launch a new race of dandies."

Then began one of the most strenuous ten minutes I shall ever know. Possibly, left alone and helped by drink, Aaron Phipps might have arrived at a series of figures on his pad that would have furnished me with a jacket, a waistcoat and a pair of trousers roughly in touch with my shape.

But he had no chance. First there was the whole phalanx of insecurities that kept the base of him in a fearful throb. Then there was Clemett who was leaning against a shelf, glaring at Phipps and humming a hymn in one of the lowest and most threatening voices west of Chepstow. But the top turn was my father. Every whipstitch he would startle the wits out of Phipps by stepping between us and saying in a voice of real command:

"Plenty of slack there now, Aaron. A tight suit will be no good to my boy when he's working hard and bulging his brain out in that examination." And instantly Aaron would let out so much tape he'd lose the end of it. My father would follow this with a warning to Aaron not to overdo the bagginess and then the tape would come back to around me, constricting as a python. Once my father challenged a measurement and found that Aaron had the tape around himself and me and finding some kind of happiness in the thought of being roped in and safe from Clemett. I told my father to come in and keep us company but he told me that this kind of callow irony might be all right in a place like Oxford but it was not going to do Aaron Phipps a lot of good when he caught the full flavour of it.

Then we came to the trousers.

"Now don't forget, Aaron," said my father. "You'll need some of your most delicate measuring when you come to what they call the fork. The say the whole soul of a suit resides in the way it hangs from the fork."

Aaron was not at all sure about the fork and applied the tape to a point between the shoulder blades. Covertly, not wishing to embarrass Clemett, my father showed Aaron where the fork was. "And don't forget, Aaron, you'll need a firm, precise measurement at the fork. No guesswork there."

Aaron nodded and made a grab at that quarter that left a dark psychotic scar on me for years.

The suit was delivered on the evening before my departure for Oxford. My father watched me put it on. As he saw the monstrous inaccuracies of Aaron Phipps twist my body into the likeness of Quasimodo he did not show any depression. When I pointed out that one sleeve seemed to go out of business at the elbow and the other was waiting for the delivery of another arm before it would show any fingers, all he did was praise the quality of the cloth and he also said cryptically:

"What the artist sees is not always what we see."

I tried on the trousers. At the sight of them even my father fell silent. I could feel my rump aching through the space for the feel of cloth. I felt like Grock. The trousers had a length of fly that would have inhibited Messalina. By the time my father had helped adjust the endless row of buttons I felt like a bond in a safe-deposit box. My father stood back and gave judgement. "It was probably Aaron's first traffic with the fork. And he was flurried. But I see the hand of Clemett in the design of that codpiece. Years ago he swore to make the libido feel like a war-memorial. He's done it."

For the first three days of my Final Schools the ushers let me into the Examination Hall well ahead of the other candidates because I looked so abnormal. During the first four papers everything was sloped at an angle I had never seen before because Aaron's right sleeve forced my fist eastward. On the fourth day I half unpicked the seams and that helped a little.

It worked out not so badly. I wrote an essay on French writers in the modern period whose work was like a howl of pain from a trap of outrage and I could never have got the authenticity into the analysis if it had not been for the tailoring of Aaron Phipps. Those trousers had me right there in the trap and I howled with the best of them.

Aaron went on to a fair success. Now and then his primal terrors would come to fresh bloom and his skill with the tape would go to tatters and for a few months after we would see some voter walking about like Lon Chaney.

But my father remained complacent about it to the very end. He claimed it was my revulsion from the chapel tradition that made my limbs contract or twist at the touch of that heavy sombre material. He saw that I was not accepting this and he went on: "That suit was Aaron's map of his own inner self. And one day he will make you a free new suit, one with matching arms to show that he now feels all his nerves and desires to be right down on the flat sane earth." He became very thoughtful.

"All the same," he said, "he could have brought the seat of those trousers a few feet off the ground. Walking behind you was like following a procession."

GLYN JONES

Jordan

I am worried. Today when I cut my chin with my white-handled razor I didn't bleed. That was the way Danny's shaving went. Danny was my friend. Together we had a spell working the fairs and markets out there in the country where there are nothing but farms and chapels. It was a sort of uncivilized place. I had invented a good line, a special cube guaranteed to keep the flies off the meat, and Danny had his little round boxes of toothpaste. This toothpaste he scraped off a big lump of wet batter, a few pounds of it, greenish in colour and with a bad smell, it stood on a tin plate and sometimes Danny would sell it as corn cure. So as to gather a crowd around his trestle he used to strip down to his black tights and walk about with a fifty-six pound solid iron weight hanging by a short strap from his teeth. This was to show what wonderful teeth you would have if you used Danny's toothpaste. It was only when he was doing this that you ever saw any colour in Danny's face. The colour came because he did the walking about upside down, he was on his hands doing it with his black stockings in the air.

Danny was thin and undersized. If I made a joke about his skinny legs he would lower his lids offended and say, "Don't be so personal." He was very touchy. His tights were corns dyed black and they looked half empty, as though large slices had been cut off from inside them. He had a fine, half-starved face, very thin and leathery, like a sad cow. There was only one thing wrong with his face and that was the ears. Danny's ears were big and yellow, and they stood out at right angles to his head. From the front they looked as though they had been screwed into his skull, and one had been screwed in a lot further than the other. His straight carrot hair was very long and thick and brushed back over his head. When he scuffled about on his bandy arms with that half hundredweight dangling from his teeth, his mop opened downwards off his scalp as though it was on a hinge, and bumped along the cobble-stones. He was very proud of his teeth. He thought so much of them he never showed them to anyone. Nobody ever saw Danny grinning.

My own line was that special cube I had invented to keep the flies off the meat. I used to soften down a few candles and shape the grease into dices with my fingers. Then I put one or two of these white dices on a cut of meat on my trestle in the middle of the market crowds. There were always plenty of fat flies and bluebottles buzzing about in those markets, what with the boiled sweet stalls and the horse-droppings, but you never saw one perching on my meat with the white cubes on it. This wasn't because the flies didn't like candle-grease but because under the meat-plate I had a saucer of paraffin oil.

One night Danny and I were sitting on the bed in our lodging house. The place was filthy and lousy and we were catching bugs on our needles off the walls and roasting them to death one by one in the candle flame. Danny was bitter. The fair had finished but the farmers had kept their hands on their ha'pennies. And the weather was bad, very wet and gusty and cold all the time. Danny said we were pioneers. He said these farmers were savages, they didn't care about having filthy teeth, or eating their food fly-blown. He was very down-hearted. He hadn't had much to eat for a few days and between the noisy bursting of the bugs his empty belly crowed. I was down-hearted too. We had to get money from somewhere to pay for our lodgings and a seat in the horsebrake drawing out of town the next morning. I asked Danny to come out into the town to see what we could pick up but he wouldn't. At first he said it was too cold. Then he said he had got to darn his tights and his stockings. In the end I went by myself.

The town had been newly wetted with another downpour and Danny was right about the cold. As I walked up the dark empty main street I could feel the wind blowing into the holes in my boots. Everywhere was closed up and silent and deserted. I looked in at the Bell and the Feathers and the Glyndwr, but they were all empty. Then from the swing door of the Black Horse I saw inside a big broad-shouldered man sitting down by himself in the bar. Apart from him the bar was deserted. He was by the fire and his back was towards me. I knew bumming a drink out of him would be as easy as putting one hand in the other. I knew this because he had a red wig on coming down over the collar of his coat, and a man who wears a wig is lonely.

On the table in front of the man I could see a glass of whisky and in his hand was a little black book. He was singing a hymn out of it in Welsh. It was sad, a funeral hymn, but very determined. I stood by the door of the empty bar and listened. The Horse was small and gloomy inside. I wondered if I would go in. The man seemed huge in the neck and across the shoulders, and every time he moved all the flesh on him seemed to begin to tremble. If he kept dead still he stopped trembling. I went in past him and stood the other side of the table by the fire.

When I got round to the front of this man something snapped like a carrot inside me. His face was hideous. The flesh of it looked as though it had been torn apart into ribbons and shoved together again anyhow back on to the bones. Long white scars ran glistening through the purple skin like ridges of gristle. Only his nose had escaped. This was huge and dark and full of holes, it curved out like a big black lump of wood with the worm in it. He was swarthy, as though he was sitting in a bar of shadow, and I looked up to see if perhaps a roof-beam had come between him and the hanging oil-lamp lighting the bar. There wasn't a hair on him, no moustache or eyebrows, but his wig was like the bright feathers of a red hen. It started a long way back, halfway up his scalp, and the gristly scars streamed down over his forehead and cheekbones from under it. He had a tidy black suit on and a good thick-soled boot with grease rubbed in. The other leg was what looked like a massive iron pipe blocked up at the end with a solid wooden plug. It came out on to the hearth from the turn-up of his trousers.

It is best to tell the tale when you haven't got any cash to put on the counter. When I began to talk to him by the fire I tucked my feet under the settle and said I was a salesman. Although Danny and I could put all our belongings in a tobacco-box, I soon had a fine range

94

of second-hand goods for sale. The man closed his little book to listen. He told me he was Jordan, man-servant to the old doctor of the town. I took a polished piece of a rabbit's backbone out of my waistcoat pocket and passed it over to him. It looked like a small cow's skull, complete with horns. He examined it slowly, trembling all the time. He had huge soft hands and his finger-nails were as green as grass. I told him he could keep it. He called for whisky for both of us.

As I drank my whisky I enjoyed thinking what I had for sale. I had a little harmonium, portable, very good for Welsh hymns, perfect except for a rip in the bellows; a new invention that would get a cork out of a bottle – like that!; a nice line in leather purses, a free gift presented with each one – a brass watch-key, number eight, or a row of glass-headed pins; a pair of solid leather knee-boots, just the thing for him because they were both for the same leg. The man's eyes were small, they looked half closed up, and he watched me hard without moving them all the time. In the heat of the fire a strong smell came off him. It was a damp clinging smell, clammy, like the mildewed corner of some old church, up there behind the organ where they keep the bier. At last he bent forward and held his smashed face close to mine. I stopped talking. He trembled and said softly, "I am interested in buying only one thing."

Somehow I felt mesmerised, I couldn't say anything. I am not often like that. I lifted my eyebrows.

Jordan didn't answer. His little eyes slid round the empty bar. Then he moved his lips into a word that staggered me. I stared at him. For a minute by the blazing fire I went cold as clay. He nodded his head and made the same mouthing of his smashed face as before. The word he shaped out was, "Corpses".

There was dead silence between us. The clock in the bar echoed loudly, like a long-legged horse trotting down an empty street. But I let my face go into a twist and I squeezed a tear into the end of my eye. I crossed myself and offered the serving man the body of my brother. I had buried him, I remembered, a week ago come tomorrow.

Jordan took his hat and stick out of the corner. The stick was heavy, with a lot of rope wound round it, and the black hat had a wide brim. When he stood up he was like a giant rising above me. He was much bigger even than I thought. He looked down hard at the little bone I had given him and then threw it on the back of the fire. We went out into the street. As we walked along, his iron leg bumped on the pavement and made a click-clicking noise like a carried bucket. He would show me where to bring the corpse and I was to come between midnight and daybreak.

We walked together out of the town into the country. It was pitch dark and soon the way was through wet fields. It was still cold but I didn't feel it any more. Jordan had this peg leg but he was big, and I sweated keeping up with him. He trembled all the time as he walked but his shaking didn't make you think he was weak. He was like a powerful machine going full force and making the whole throbbing engine-house tremble to the foundations with its power. I trotted behind him breathless. He was so busy singing the Welsh burial hymn that he didn't drop a word to me all the way.

At last we came to a gate across the lane we were following. There was a farm-house beyond it, all in darkness. Jordan stopped singing and shouted, twice. There was no reply. He started singing again. He poised himself on his iron leg and his walking stick and gave the gate a great kick with his good foot. It fell flat. We found ourselves going at full speed across a farmyard. A heavy sheepdog ran out of the shadows barking and showing a fringe of teeth. He looked huge and fierce enough to tear us in pieces. Jordan didn't pause and I kept close behind him. The dog changed his gallop into a stiff-legged prowl, and he filled his throat with a terrible snarl. Then suddenly he sprang straight at Jordan's throat. As he rose in the air Jordan hit him a ringing crack on the head with his stick. He used both hands to bring it down. The dog dropped to the pebbles of the yard passing a contented sigh. He didn't move again. Jordan put his good foot on him and brought the stick down on his head again and again. He went on doing this, his sad hymn getting louder and louder, until the dog's brains came out. I went cold in my sweat to hear him. At last he wiped the handle of the stick in the grass of the hedge and went on down the lane, singing.

We came in sight of the lights of a big house. "That's the place," he said. "Bring it round to the back door. Good night."

He went off into the darkness like a giant in his broad-brimmed hat. I wiped the sweat off my head. After he had disappeared I could hear his hymn and his leg clicking for a long time. His hymn was slow and sad, but it didn't make me unhappy at all. It frightened the life out of me.

On the way back to the town, I kicked the dead dog into the ditch.

Danny never let his job slide off his back. As I climbed up the stairs of the lodging house I came face to face with two eyes watching me through the upright bars of the top landing banister. It was Danny dawdling about on his hands, practising. I had a lot of trouble persuading him to be a corpse. All he had to do was pretend to be dead and to let me and the black-man on the landing below carry him out to the doctor's house. Then when we were paid and everybody in the house was asleep he would get out of one of the downstairs windows. We would be waiting for him. We could leave the town by the first brake in the morning. It was safe as houses. Nothing could go wrong. At last Danny agreed.

At midnight the three of us set out for Jordan's house. We were me, Danny and Marky. Marky was a half-caste cheapjack, a long thin shiny man the colour of gunmetal, selling fire-damaged remnants and bankrupt stock and that. He used to dribble and paw you at close quarters but he would do anything you asked him for tuppence or thruppence. We walked through the fields carrying a rolled up sack and my trestle until we came in sight of the house Jordan had shown me. Danny stripped to his coms under a tree and hid his clothes. He put on an old cream-flannel nightgown Marky had brought out of stock. Then we sewed him in the sack and put him on the planks of my trestle. It was pitch dark and cold, with the small rain drizzling down again as fine as pepper.

The doctor's house was all in darkness. We went round to the little pointed wooden door at the back of the garden. I whispered to Danny to ask if he was all right. There were two answers, Danny's teeth chattering and the uproar of dogs howling and barking inside the garden. I had never thought about dogs. What were we going to do?

At once I heard the click of the leg the other side of the wall and Jordan's voice speaking. "Down, Farw. Down, Angau," he growled. The narrow pointed door was thrown open, and suddenly we saw

Jordan. He was stripped naked to the half and he had left off his wig. He looked so huge, so powerful and ugly in the doorway, with his swelling nose and his fleshy body all slashed, I almost let go of our load with fright. And behind him the hounds, three of them, black and shaggy and big as ponies, yelped and bayed and struggled to get past him to attack us. Jordan spoke sharply to them and at last we were able to carry Danny into the garden. He was as light on the boards as a bag of hay. Jordan spoke only to the dogs. He made a sign and led us hobbling along the pebble path across the yard towards some dark out-houses. The three hounds paced whining beside us, sniffing all the time at the sack and spilling their dribble.

The room we went into smelt like a stable. It was dim and empty but there was an oil lamp hanging from a nail in a low beam. We laid Danny across some feed-boxes under this lamp. Jordan stood back by the stable door with the whimpering dogs while we were doing it, watching us all the time. I could feel his eyes burning into my back. His skin was very dark and his chest bulged up into big paps resting above his powerful folded arms. But all his body was torn with terrible wounds like his face. Long shining scars like the glistening veins you see running through the rocks of a cliff-face spread in all directions over his flesh. His bald head had a large dome on it and that was covered with scars too. His whole body gleamed down to his waist, the drizzle had given him a high shine like the gloss of varnish.

We left Danny lying on the boards across the feed-boxes and came back up to the door to ask for our money. Jordan didn't reply. Instead he took a large clasp-knife out of the pocket in the front of his trousers and opened it. Then, ordering the dogs to stay, he went past us and bumped over to where Danny was lying in his sack. He seemed to take a long time to get there. There was dead silence. As he went from us we could see a black hole in his back you could put your fist into. My skin prickled. Marky's eyes rolled with the dogs sniffing him and he began to paw the air. I looked round and saw a hay-fork with a stumpy leg in the corner. Jordan turned round under the lamp and looked back at us. The blade of the open knife trembled in his hand. He turned again and cut open the sewing in the sack above Danny's face. I could hardly breathe. Danny was so white under the hanging lamp I thought he was really dead. My hair stirred. Danny's teeth showed shining in his open mouth, and in the lamplight falling right down upon them the whites of his half-opened eyes glistened. He was pale and stiff, as if he had already begun to rot. Jordan bent over, gazing down at him with the knife in his hand, the lamp spreading a shine over the skin of his wet back. I was frightened, but if Danny's teeth chattered or his belly crowed I was willing to use that pitchfork to get us out. At last Jordan turned. He spoke for the first time.

"He is a good corpse," he said.

"He is my brother," I told him.

"Where did you get him from?"

"I dug him up."

He nodded. He left the knife open on the feed-box and came over to us. Putting his hand again into his front pocket he brought out a large lump of wadding. This he opened and in the middle lay three gold sovereigns. He passed the coins over to me with his huge trembling hands and motioned us out roughly. He went back and blew out the oil-lamp and we left Danny alone there in the darkness. Jordan locked the stable door and the hounds trotted round us growling as we left the garden through the little door.

"Good night," said Jordan.

"Good night, brother," I said.

We walked about in the fields, trying to keep warm, waiting for the time to go back to get Danny out. Marky had gone icy cold. I was worried, especially about those dogs. I wished I had a drop of drink inside me. When we thought everything would be quiet again we went back to see if it was safe to give Danny the whistle. I threw my coat over the bottle-glass stuck on top of the garden wall and climbed up. I could see a candle lit in a downstairs window of the doctor's house and by its light Jordan moved about inside the room in his nightshirt and nightcap. Presently his light disappeared and all was in darkness.

An owl in a tree close by started screeching. Marky was frightened and climbed up on to the garden wall to be near me. There was no sign of Jordan's dogs in the garden. It was bitterly cold up there on top of the wall without our coats on. The wind was lazy, it went right through us instead of going round. It had stopped raining again. There was a moon now but it was small and a long way off, very high up in the sky, and shrunken enough to go into your cap.

We waited a long time shivering and afraid to talk. Marky's eyes were like glass marbles. At last I saw something moving in the shadows by the stable. My heart shot up hot into my throat. Marky caught hold of me trembling like a leaf. A figure in white began to creep along the wall. It was Danny. He must have got out through one of the stable windows. I whistled softly to him and at that there was uproar. The three hounds came bounding across the yard from nowhere, making straight for Danny, baying and snarling like mad. I didn't know what to do for the moment with fright. The dogs were almost on top of him. Danny sprang on to his hands and began trotting towards them. His black legs waved in the air and his nightshirt fell forward and hung down to the ground over his head. The dogs stopped dead when they saw him. Then they turned together and galloped away into the shadows howling with fright. When Danny reached the wall we grabbed him firmly by the ankles and pulled him up out of the garden at one pluck. We were not long getting back to our lodging-house. The next morning we paid our landlord and the brake driver with one of the sovereigns we had had off Jordan.

I didn't have any luck. All the rest of the summer it was still wet and there were hardly any flies. I tried selling elephant charms, very lucky, guaranteed, but the harvest failed and in the end I couldn't even give them away. Danny got thinner and thinner and more quiet. He was like a rush. He had nothing to say. There never was much in his head except the roots of his hair. Having been a corpse was on his mind. And he was like a real corpse to sleep with, as cold as ice and all bones. He lost interest even in standing on his hands.

We visited a lot of the towns that held fairs but without much luck. One market day we were sitting in a coffee tavern. It was a ramshackle place built of wooden planks put up for the market day in a field behind the main street. The floor was only grass and the tables and benches stood on it. You could get a plate of peas and a cup of tea there cheap. Danny didn't care about food now even when we had it. Because it was market day this coffee tavern was crowded. It was very close inside, enough to make you faint, and the wasps were buzzing everywhere. All the people around us were jabbering Welsh and eating food out of newspapers.

Presently, above the noise, I heard a bumping and clicking sound in the passage. I felt as though a bath-full of icy water had shot over me inside my clothes. I looked round but there was no way of escape. Then I heard the funeral hymn. In a minute Jordan was standing in the entrance of the coffee tavern. He was huge, bigger than ever, a doorful. In one hand was his roped-up stick and in the other his black hymn-book. His broad-brimmed hat was on his head, but instead of his wig he had a yellow silk handkerchief under it with the corners knotted. He stopped singing and stood in the doorway looking round for an empty seat. A man from our table just then finished his peas and went out. Jordan saw the empty place and hobbled in. We couldn't escape him. He came clicking through the eating crowd like an earthquake and sat down at our table opposite us.

At first I didn't know what to do. Danny had never seen Jordan and was staring down at the grease floating on his tea. I tried to go on leading the peas up to my mouth on my spoon but I could hardly do it. Jordan was opposite, watching me. He could see I was shaking. I pretended to fight the wasps. I could feel his bright bunged-up eyes on me all the time. He put his arms in a ring on the table and leaned over towards me. I was spilling the peas in my fright. I couldn't go on any longer. I lowered my spoon and looked at him. He was so hideous at close quarters I almost threw up. The big black block of his nose reached out at me, full of worm-holes, and the rest of his face looked as though it had been dragged open with hooks. But he was smiling.

"Jordan," I said, although my tongue was like a lump of cork. "Mr Jordan."

He nodded. "You've come back," he said. "Where have you been keeping?"

The whole coffee tavern seemed to be trembling with his movements. I felt as though I was in the stifling loft of some huge pipe-organ, with the din coming out full blast and all the hot woodwork in a shudder. His questions had me stammering. I told him I had been busy. My business kept me moving, I travelled about a lot. The wooden building around me felt suffocating, airless as a glasshouse. I glanced at Danny. He looked as though he had been tapped and all his blood run off. Even his yellow ears had turned chalky.

Jordan nodded again, grinning his terrible grin. "The chick born in hell returns to the burning," he said. All the time he watched me from under the front knot of his yellow handkerchief. He ignored Danny altogether. His eyes were small, but they looked as though each one had had a good polish before being put into his head.

"Our bargain was a good one," he went on, still smiling. "Very good. It turned out well."

I was afraid he would hear my swallow at work, it sounded loud even above the jabbering. "I am glad," I said, "I did my best. I always do my best."

"My master was pleased," he said. He leaned further forward and beckoned me towards him. I bent my head to listen and his wooden nose was up touching my ear. "A splendid corpse," he whispered. "Inside, a mass of corruption. Tumours and malignant growths. Exactly what my master needed. Cut up beautifully, it did."

There was a loud sigh from Danny. When I turned to look at him he wasn't there. He had gone down off his bench in a heap on the grass. People all round got up from their tables and crowded round. Some of them waved their arms and shouted. "Give him air," they said, "he's fainted. Give him air." For a minute I forgot all about Jordan. I told the people Danny was my friend. They carried him out of the coffee tavern and laid him on the grass at the side of the road. "Loosen his neck," somebody said, and his rubber breast and collar were snatched off showing his black corns underneath. The crowd came on like flies round jam. At last Danny opened his eyes. Someone brought him a glass of water out of the coffee tavern. He sat up, bowed his shoulders and put his hands over his face as though he was crying. I spotted something then I had never noticed before. There was a big bald hole in his red hair at the top of his head. He looked sickly. But before long he could stand again. I pushed his breast and collar into my pocket and took him back to our lodging house. I looked round but I couldn't see Jordan at all in the crowd. Danny was in bed for a week. He was never the same again. For one thing if he cut himself shaving he didn't bleed. The only thing that came out of the cut was a kind of yellow water.

Before the year was out I had buried Danny. It was wild weather and he caught a cold standing about half-naked in his tights in the fairs and markets. He took to his bed in our lodgings. Soon he was light-headed and then unconscious. Every night I sat by him in our bedroom under the roof with the candle lit listening to his breathing.

One night I dropped off to sleep in the chair and he woke me up screaming. He dreamt Jordan was trying to chop his hands off to make him walk on the stumps. I was terrified at the noise he made. The candle went out and the roar of the wind sawing at the roof of the house was deafening. My heart was thumping like a drum as I tried to relight the candle. I couldn't stop Danny screaming. A few minutes later he died with a yell. Poor Danny. Being a corpse was too much for him. He never struggled out from under the paws of his memories.

The next night the man from the parish came. He asked me if I wasn't ashamed to bury my friend like that. He meant that Danny hadn't had a shave for a week. In the candle-light he had a bright copper beard and he wasn't quite so much like a cow. When the man had gone I started to shave the corpse. It was hard doing it by candle-light. High up on the cheek-bone I must have done something wrong, I must have cut him, because he opened one of his eyes and looked hard at me with it. I was more careful after that. I didn't want to open that vein they say is full of lice.

The morning of the funeral I borrowed a black tie off our landlord. I bummed a wreath on strap. It was very pretty. It was a lot of white flowers on wires made into the shape of a little armchair. In the bars of the back was a card with the word 'Rest' on it done in forget-me-nots. Danny always liked something religious like that.

There was nobody in the funeral except the parson and me and two gravediggers. It was a bad day in autumn and very stormy. The long grass in the graveyard was lying down smooth under the flow of the wind. There were some willow trees around the wall all blown bare except for a few leaves sticking to the thin twigs like hair-nits. The parson in his robes was a thin man but he looked fat in the wind. As he gabbled the service the big dried-up leaves blown along the path scratched at the gravel with webbed fingers, like cut-off hands. I wanted to run away. When Danny was in the earth the gravediggers left. The parson and I sang a funeral hymn. The wind was roaring. As we were singing I heard another voice joining in the distance. It was faint. I had been waiting for it. I didn't need to look round. I knew the sound of the voice and the clicking leg. They came closer and closer. Soon the voice was deafening, the sad hymn roaring like a waterfall beside me. Jordan came right up and stood between me and the parson, touching me. For shaking he was like a giant tree hurling off the storm. His little black book was in his hand. Even in the wind I could smell the strong mouldiness that came off him, clammy as grave-clay. He was bigger than ever. The brim of his black hat was spread out like a roof over my head. As he stood beside me he seemed to be absorbing me. He put his arm with the night-stick in his hand around my shoulders. I felt as though I was gradually disappearing inside his huge body. The ground all around me melted, the path began to flow faster and faster past my feet like a rushing river. I tried to shout out in my terror. I fainted.

When I came round the parson was beside me. We were sitting on the heap of earth beside Danny's open grave. I was as wet as the bed of the river with fright. When I spoke to the parson about Jordan he humoured me. That was a fortnight ago. Yesterday when I cut myself shaving I didn't bleed. All that came out of the cut was a drop or two of yellow water. I won't be long now. I am finished. I wouldn't advise anybody to try crossing Jordan.

DYLAN THOMAS

Patricia, Edith and Arnold

The small boy in his invisible engine, the Cwmdonkin Special, its wheels, polished to dazzle, crunching on the small back garden scattered with breadcrumbs for the birds and white with yesterday's snow, its smoke rising thin and pale as breath in the cold afternoon, hooted under the wash-line, kicked the dog's plate at the washhouse stop, and puffed and pistoned slower and slower while the servant girl lowered the pole, unpegged the swinging vests, showed the brown stains under her arms, and called over the wall: "Edith, Edith, come here, I want you."

Edith climbed on two tubs on the other side of the wall and called back: "I'm here, Patricia." Her head bobbed up above the broken glass.

He backed the Flying Welshman from the washhouse to the open door of the coal-hole and pulled hard on the brake that was a hammer in his pocket: assistants in uniform ran out with the fuel; he spoke to a saluting fireman, and the engine shuffled off, round the barbed walls of China that kept the cats away, by the frozen rivers in the sink, in and out of the coal-hole tunnel. But he was listening carefully all the time, through the squeals and whistles, to Patricia and the next-door servant, who belonged to Mrs Lewis, talking when they should have been working, calling his mother Mrs T., being rude about Mrs L.

He heard Patricia say: "Mrs T. won't be back till six."

And Edith next door replied: "Old Mrs L. has gone to Neath to look for Mr Robert."

"He's on the randy again," Patricia whispered.

"Randy, sandy, bandy!" cried the boy out of the coal-hole.

"You get your face dirty, I'll kill you," Patricia said absent-mindedly.

She did not try to stop him when he climbed up the coal-heap. He stood quietly on the top, King of the Coal Castle, his head touching the roof, and listened to the worried voices of the girls. Patricia was almost in tears, Edith was sobbing and rocking on the unsteady tubs. "I'm standing on top of the coal," he said, and waited for Patricia's anger.

She said: "I don't want to see him, you go alone."

"We must, we must go together," said Edith. "I've got to know."

"I don't want to know."

"I can't stand it, Patricia, you must go with me."

"You go alone, he's waiting for you."

"Please Patricia!"

"I'm lying on my face in the coal," said the boy.

"No, it's your day with him. I don't want to know. I just want to think he loves me."

"Oh, talk sense, Patricia, please! Will you come or no? I've got to hear what he says."

"All right then, in half an hour. I'll shout over the wall."

"You'd better come soon," the boy said, "I'm dirty as Christ knows what."

Patricia ran to the coal-hole. "The language! Come out of there at once!" she said.

The tubs began to slide and Edith vanished.

"Don't you dare use language like that again. Oh! your suit!" Patricia took him indoors.

She made him change his suit in front of her. "Otherwise there's no telling." He took off his trousers and danced around her, crying: "Look at me, Patricia!"

"You be decent," she said, "or I won't take you to the park."

"Am I going to the park, then?"

"Yes, we're all going to the park; you and me and Edith next door."

He dressed himself neatly, not to annoy her, and spat on his hands before parting his hair. She appeared not to notice his silence and neatness. Her large hands were clasped together; she stared down at the white brooch on her chest. She was a tall, thick girl with awkward hands, her fingers were like toes, her shoulders were wide as a man's.

"Am I satisfactory?" he asked.

"There's a long word," she said, and looked at him lovingly. She lifted him up and seated him on the top of the chest of drawers. "Now you're as tall as I am."

"But I'm not so old," he said.

He knew that this was an afternoon on which anything might happen; it might snow enough for sliding on a tray; uncles from America, where he had no uncles, might arrive with revolvers and St. Bernards; Ferguson's shop might catch on fire and all the piece-packets fall on the pavements; and he was not surprised when she put her black, straight-haired heavy head on his shoulder and whispered into his collar: "Arnold, Arnold Matthews."

"There, there," he said, and rubbed her parting with his finger and winked at himself in the mirror behind her and looked down her dress at the back.

"Are you crying?"

"No."

"Yes you are, I can feel the wet."

She dried her eyes on her sleeve. "Don't you let on that I was crying."

"I'll tell everybody, I'll tell Mrs T. and Mrs L., I'll tell the policeman and Edith and my dad and Mr Chapman, Patricia was crying on my shoulder like a nanny goat, she cried for two hours, she cried enough to fill a kettle. I won't really," he said.

As soon as he and Patricia and Edith set off for the park, it began to snow. Big flakes unexpectedly fell on the rocky hill, and the sky grew dark as dusk though it was only three in the afternoon. Another boy, somewhere in the allotments behind the houses, shouted as the first flakes fell. Mrs Ocky Evans opened the top bay-windows of Springmead and thrust her head and hands out, as though to catch the snow. He waited, without revolt, for Patricia to say, "Quick! hurry back, it's snowing!" and to pack him in out of the day before his feet were wet. Patricia can't have seen the snow, he thought at the top of the hill, though it was falling heavily, sweeping against her face, covering her black hat. He dared not speak for fear of waking her, as they turned the corner into the road that led down to the park. He lagged behind to take his cap off and catch the snow in his mouth.

"Put on your cap," said Patricia, turning. "Do you want to catch your death of cold?"

She tucked his muffler inside his coat, and said to Edith: "Will he be there in the snow, do you think? He's bound to be there, isn't he? He was always there on my Wednesdays, wet or fine." The tip of her nose was red, her cheeks glowed like coals, she looked handsomer in the snow than in summer, when her hair would lie limp on her wet forehead and a warm patch spread on her back.

"He'll be there," Edith said. "One Friday it was pelting down and he was there. He hasn't got anywhere else to go, he's always there. Poor Arnold!" She looked white and tidy in a coat with a fur piece, and twice as small as Patricia; she stepped through the thick snow as though she was going shopping.

"Wonders will never cease," he said aloud to himself. This was Patricia letting him walk in the snow, this was striding along in a storm with two big girls. He sat down in the road. "I'm on a sledge," he said, "pull me, Patricia, pull me like an Eskimo."

"Up you get, you moochin, or I'll take you home."

He saw that she did not mean it. "Lovely Patricia, beautiful Patricia," he said, "pull me along on my bottom."

"Any more dirty words, and you know who I'll tell."

"Arnold Matthews," he said.

Patricia and Edith drew closer together.

"He notices everything," Patricia whispered.

Edith said: "I'm glad I haven't got your job."

"Oh," said Patricia, catching him by the hand and pressing it on her arm, "I wouldn't change him for the world!"

He ran down the gravel path on to the upper walk of the park. "I'm spoilt!" he shouted, "I'm spoilt! Patricia spoils me!"

Soon the park would be white all over; already the trees were blurred round the reservoir and fountain, and the training college on the gorse hill was hidden in a cloud. Patricia and Edith took the steep path down to the shelter. Following on the forbidden grass, he slid past them straight into a bare bush, but the bump and the pricks left him shouting and unhurt. The girls gossiped sadly now. They shook their coats in the deserted shelter, scattering snow on the seats, and sat down, close together still, outside the bowling-club window.

PATRICIA, EDITH AND ARNOLD

"We're only just on time," said Edith. "It's hard to be punctual in the snow."

"Can I play by here?"

Patricia nodded. "Play quietly then; don't be rough with the snow."

"Snow! snow! snow!" he said, and scooped it out of the gutter and made a small ball.

"Perhaps he's found a job," Patricia said.

"Not Arnold."

"What if he doesn't come at all?"

"He's bound to come, Patricia; don't say things like that."

"Have you brought your letters?"

"They're in my bag. How many have you got?"

"No, how many have you got, Edith?"

"I haven't counted."

"Show me one of yours," Patricia said.

He was used to their talk by this time; they were old and cuckoo, sitting in the empty shelter sobbing over nothing. Patricia was reading a letter and moving her lips.

"He told me that, too," she said, "that I was his star."

"Did he begin: 'Dear Heart'?"

Edith broke into real loud tears. With a snowball in his hand, he watched her sway on the seat and hide her face in Patricia's snowy coat.

Patricia said, patting and calming Edith, rocking her head: "I'll give him a piece of my mind when he comes!"

When who comes? He threw the snowball high into the silently driving fall. Edith's crying in the deadened park was clear and thin as a whistle, and, disowning the soft girls and standing away from them in case a stranger passed, a man with boots to his thighs, or a sneering, bigger boy from the Uplands, he piled the snow against the wire of the tennis court and thrust his hands into the snow like a baker making bread. As he delved and moulded the snow into loaves, saying under his breath, "This is the way it is done, ladies and gentlemen," Edith raised her head and said: "Patricia, promise me, don't be cross with him. Let's all be quiet and friendly."

"Writing, 'Dear Heart' to us both," said Patricia angrily.

"Did he ever take off your shoes and pull your toes and – "

"No, no, you mustn't, don't go on, you mustn't speak like that!" Edith put her fingers to her cheeks. "Yes, he did," she said.

"Somebody has been pulling Edith's toes," he said to himself, and ran round the other side of the shelter, chuckling. "Edith went to market," he laughed aloud, and stopped at the sight of a young man without an overcoat sitting in the corner seat and cupping his hands and blowing into them. The young man wore a white muffler and a check cap. When he saw the boy, he pulled his cap down over his eyes. His hands were pale blue and the ends of his fingers yellow.

The boy ran back to Patricia. "Patricia, there's a man!" he cried.

"Where's a man?"

"On the other side of the shelter; he hasn't got an overcoat and he's blowing in his hands like this."

Edith jumped up. "It's Arnold!"

"Arnold Matthews, Arnold Matthews, we know you're there!" Patricia called round the shelter, and after a long minute, the young man, raising his cap and smiling, appeared at the corner and leant against a wooden pillar.

The trousers of his sleek blue suit were wide at the bottoms; the shoulders were high and hard, and sharp at the ends; his pointed patent shoes were shining; a red handkerchief stuck from his breast pocket; he had not been out in the snow.

"Fancy you two knowing each other," he said loudly, facing the red-eyed girls and the motionless, open-mouthed boy who stood at Patricia's side with his pockets full of snowballs.

Patricia tossed her head and her hat fell over one eye. As she straightened her hat, "You come and sit down here, Arnold Matthews, you've got some questions to answer!" she said in her washing-day voice.

Edith clutched at her arm: "Oh! Patricia you promised." She picked at the edge of her handkerchief. A tear rolled down her cheek.

Arnold said softly then: "Tell the little boy to run away and play."

The boy ran round the shelter once and returned to hear Edith saying: "There's a hole in your elbow, Arnold," and to see the young man kicking the snow at his feet and staring at the names and hearts cut on the wall behind the girls' heads.

"Who did you walk out with on Wednesdays?" Patricia asked.

Her clumsy hands held Edith's letter close to the sprinkled folds of her chest.

"You, Patricia."

"Who did you walk out with on Fridays?"

"With Edith, Patricia."

He said to the boy: "Here, son, can you roll a snowball as big as a football?"

"Yes, as big as two footballs."

Arnold turned back to Edith, and said "How did you come to know Patricia Davies? You work in Brynmill."

"I just started work in Cwmdonkin," she said. "I haven't seen you since, to tell you. I was going to tell you to-day, but I found out. How could you Arnold? Me on my afternoon off, and Patricia on Wednesdays."

The snowball had turned into a short snow man with a lopsided, dirty head and a face full of twigs, wearing a boy's cap and smoking a pencil.

"I didn't mean any harm," said Arnold. "I love you both."

Edith screamed. The boy jumped forward and the snow man with a broken back collapsed.

"Don't tell your lies, how can you love two of us?" Edith cried, shaking her handbag at Arnold. The bag snapped open, and a bundle of letters fell on the snow.

"Don't you dare pick up those letters," Patricia said.

Arnold had not moved. The boy was searching for his pencil in the snow man's ruins.

"You make your choice, Arnold Matthews, here and now."

"Her or me," said Edith.

Patricia turned her back to him. Edith, with her bag in her hand hanging open, stood still. The sweeping snow turned up the top page of a letter.

"You two," he said, "you go off the handle. Sit down and talk. Don't cry like that, Edith. Hundreds of men love more than one woman, you're always reading about it. Give us a chance, Edith, there's a girl."

Patricia looked at the hearts and arrows and old names. Edith saw the letters curl.

"It's you, Patricia," said Arnold.

Still Patricia turned away from him. Edith opened her mouth to cry, and he put a finger to his lips. He made the shape of a whisper, too soft for Patricia to hear. The boy watched him soothing and promising Edith, but she screamed again and ran out of the shelter and down the path, her handbag beating against her side.

"Patricia," he said, "turn round to me. I had to say it. It's you, Patricia."

The boy bent down over the snow man and found his pencil driven through its head. When he stood up he saw Patricia and Arnold arm in arm.

Snow dripped through his pockets, snow melted in his shoes, snow trickled down his collar into his vest. "Look at you now," said Patricia, rushing to him and holding him by the hands, "you're wringing wet."

"Only a bit of snow," said Arnold, suddenly alone in the shelter.

"A bit of snow indeed, he's as cold as ice and his feet are like sponges. Come on home at once!"

The three of them climbed the path to the upper walk, and Patricia's footprints were large as a horse's in the thickening snow.

"Look, you can see our house, it's got a white roof!"

"We'll be there, ducky, soon."

"I'd rather stay out and make a snow man like Arnold Matthews."

"Hush! hush! your mother'll be waiting. You must come home."

"No she won't. She's gone on a randy with Mr Robert. Randy, sandy, bandy!"

"You know very well she's shopping with Mrs Partridge, you mustn't tell wicked lies."

"Well Arnold Matthews told lies. He said he loved you better than Edith, and he whispered behind your back to her."

"I swear I didn't, Patricia, I don't love Edith at all!"

Patricia stopped walking. "You don't love Edith?"

"No, I've told you, it's you. I don't love her at all," he said. "Oh! my God, what a day! Don't you believe me? It's you Patricia. Edith isn't anything. I just used to meet her; I'm always in the park."

"But you told her you loved her."

The boy stood bewildered between them. Why was Patricia so

angry and serious? Her face was flushed and her eyes shone. Her chest moved up and down. He saw the long black hairs on her leg through a tear in her stockings. Her leg is as big as my middle, he thought. I'm cold; I want tea; I've got snow in my fly.

Arnold backed slowly down the path. "I had to tell her that or she wouldn't have gone away. I had to, Patricia. You saw what she was like. I hate her. Cross my heart!"

"Bang! bang!" cried the boy.

Patricia was smacking Arnold, tugging at his muffler, knocking him with her elbows. She pummelled him down the path, and shouted at the top of her voice: "I'll teach you to lie to Edith! You pig! you black! I'll teach you to break her heart!"

He shielded his face from her blows as he staggered back. "Patricia, Patricia, don't hit me! There's people!"

As Arnold fell, two women with umbrellas up peered through the whirling snow from behind a bush.

Patricia stood over him. "You lied to her and you'd lie to me," she said. "Get up, Arnold Matthews!"

He rose and set his muffler straight and wiped his eyes with the red handkerchief, and raised his cap and walked toward the shelter.

"And as for you," Patricia said, turning to the watching women, "you should be ashamed of yourselves! Two old women playing about in the snow."

They dodged behind the bush.

Patricia and the boy climbed, hand in hand, back to the upper walk.

"I've left my cap by the snow man," he remembered. "It's my cap with the Tottenham colours."

"Run back quickly," she said, "you can't get any wetter than you are."

He found his cap half hidden under snow. In a corner of the shelter, Arnold sat reading the letters that Edith had dropped, turning the wet pages slowly, He did not see the boy, and the boy, behind a pillar, did not interrupt him. Arnold read every letter carefully.

"You've been a long time finding your cap," Patricia said. "Did you see the young man?"

"No," he said, "he was gone."

113

At home, in the warm living-room, Patricia made him change his clothes again. He held his hands in front of the fire, and soon they began to hurt.

"My hands are on fire," he told her, "and my toes, and my face."

After she had comforted him, she said: "There, that's better. The hurting's gone. You won't call the king your uncle in a minute." She was bustling about the room. "Now we've all had a good cry to-day."

SIÂN EVANS

Davis

Fred Davis opened the back door and spat on the manure heap thrown up against the kitchen wall.

"It's no use following me about," he called into the hollow of the passage. "Nagging night and day; it ain't my fault, damn you."

He sighed heavily; his fat, sullen face sagged over a dirty white rag tied round his throat in lieu of a collar, his hands picked at the edges of his pockets; his hair, yellow and plentiful, hung in tags over a flat red brow.

A shrill voice answered like an echo. "That's what you always say; you're lazy, and you know it. Just look at the garden."

Voice and wife approached through the shadows; a woman thrust her face over the man's shoulder, at the same time pointing with a bony arm so that the fingers only appeared round the lintel of the door.

"Call that a garden; look at that hedge. I'd be ashamed to see my wife doing all the work."

Davis shook himself and, turning round, muttered an oath.

"You clear off; leave me alone, can't you?"

His wife now stood on the weedy path, from which vantage-point she poured forth a string of invective and abuse.

"What's happening to us? Bills, no money, no beasts, the place rotting over our heads. Oh, you lazy pig, I wish to God I'd never married you. Too idle to mend the hedge or move the horse manure from off the path. God, the place is worse than a slum, and yet you won't do anything. I can't even find any vegetables to cook, but have to buy what I want. Look at all this garden, wasted, while you lean about all day. It makes me sick. I'm through."

Her voice rose to a shriek, cracked, and was silent.

Davis started to shamble off towards the pigsties, standing at the far end of the path.

"You drive me crazy," he mumbled. "My life's hell."

His wife tore at her hair as though with one frantic gesture to release all her bitterness.

"Hell, that's your destination all right; this ain't a patch on what God'll make you suffer in the world to come."

She turned and disappeared into the house, slamming the door behind her. Davis leaned on the pigsty wall.

He noticed the cracks in the bricks and how the rotten gate swung from one hinge only.

Moss grew like slime on the walls, the roof leaked, stale pig manure and straw-sprouting grass littered the floor.

Again he sighed and the sound seemed ominous, as though by his own breath he stood accused.

God, he was tired. Couldn't she see what an added burden it was to think?

Of course she could, the bitch, that's why she kept goading him. Facing him with his demon till his hands were at his own throat.

He groaned; only with an effort could he bring himself to look at the house.

What had happened? The place was going to ruin.

He remembered how it had looked before his father, old Davis, died. White walls, clean paint, plants in the windows, thick doors fitting without the tremor of a draught, flower-beds under the windows, vegetables in neatly dug patches, pigsties with proper roofs.

The yard, too, looked different; in those days a gate divided the cowsheds, stable, and ricks from the open patch in front of the house; now yard and garden mingled in a puddly mess of straw, rotten stumps of cabbage, and manure.

It had been a prosperous enough place.

Well, something had happened, that was all. A gradual decay.

The garden full of weeds, that large hole in the hedge that made his wife so angry, the patch of horse manure in the middle of the path left when the horse broke in and finished the last of the vegetables, the cracking doors tied together with string.

The yard, unkempt as the garden, standing deserted save for a scraggy horse pulling out tufts of hay from the two remaining ricks, hens scratching in the flower-beds, turning over old tins, cans, and putrid scraps.

Yes, something had happened.

Davis made up his mind to remove the horse manure so that his wife shouldn't see it and scream at him every time she came to the door. He pulled out a cigarette, and while he stood smoking watched the sun disappear beneath the rim of the fields.

Another day gone, too late to do anything now. Tomorrow he'd tidy up the place and mend the hedge.

For a moment his heart seemed to lift in his side, his mind sprang lightly towards the future.

He'd get everything straight, he'd start work seriously.

Again his wife appeared at the door; a lighted candle burned in the passage, throwing a beam that revealed her shape and her thin attenuated arms waving like feelers towards the yard.

"Really!" she screamed, emphasizing each word with a fresh gesture. "Can't you see that horse eating its head off in the yard? Anyone would think we'd got a dozen ricks to waste. Why don't you put it in the stable or shut it in the field? You've been standing out there for nearly an hour. I warn you, I've had about enough."

Davis looked at her, at her small body that, even when still, appeared possessed by a demon of energy, at her hands rapidly unwrapping a scrap of bandage from round her wrist, and her face moving round words that poured from her lips in an endless stream.

"Why can't you do your share? Are you ill, or what? You don't care about anything, no pride ... no nothing."

He bellowed suddenly in a voice choking with anger. "It's your bloody tongue; you take the relish out of anything, work or pleasure. I'm going out, you've driven me out. You do everything yourself, then you can't complain; you always know best, nothing I do's right, you make a man mad." He turned his back on her, setting off towards the road in a great hurry. His blood beat in his temples like pistons, he clutched at his chest uneasily. All this noise and excitement day in, day out; supposing he had a heart attack?

The thought made him feel sickish. When he had turned a corner in the lane he sat down on the roadside and held his head in his hands. No man could stand it.

A great depression fell on him. He kept asking himself questions, although the answers tormented him.

"What shall I do?"

"Work," came the reply like a stone hurled at his head.

"What's the use?"

"Do you want to die, then?"

"No, by God!"

"If everything rots over your head, how will you live?"

"I don't know, something will happen."

"No, it won't."

He began to groan and mumble out loud.

"Things aren't so bad, I'll soon pull them round. I've seen many worse places about."

Then he heard his wife's voice: "You're lazy ... bone lazy."

He jumped to his feet. "That's a lie, a damned lie. Nobody but a bitch would say a thing like that."

He stopped shouting as suddenly as he had commenced.

It was nearly dark, a light mist covered the surrounding fields; standing back, the hills were black against a thickening sky. It looked like rain.

Davis turned and stared at the bank where he had been sitting. A distinct patch where the grass lay flattened revealed the spot.

He looked at it with surprise. "I'm going dotty; anyone would think I'd been drinking...."

He walked about for some time unable to make up his mind, to go down to 'The Angel' for a pint. At last he made for home.

He remembered angrily that he had forgotten to milk the cows.

Never mind, it wouldn't be the first time; they'd have to wait a bit.

When he reached home his wife was washing the milking pails in the back kitchen.

He poked his head round the door, but she kept her head obstinately turned from him. Her tightly compressed lips showed that her silence was the silence of anger and contempt.

He returned to the kitchen and sat warming his feet by the fire.

Presently he slept.

His wife woke him. "Your supper's ready."

It was late, nearly nine o'clock; he sat up with a start.

"All right; you needn't pretend to be surprised it's so late. You needn't say: 'Why didn't you remind me about the cows?' because you knew all along I'd do it, like I always do."

The woman set his plate down as she spoke. There were two red spots burning in her cheeks.

She polished the forks on a cloth and then they started to eat. Neither spoke. While she was making the tea Davis watched his wife sulkily, pulling at his hair with his hands and watching her every movement through half-closed eyes.

As soon as the meal was over she hurried out to the sink and started to wash up.

That night Davis couldn't sleep, but lay on his back staring at the chink of light showing through the bedroom window.

Outside he could hear the rustle of rain mixed with the lifting and falling of branches blowing in the wind.

If only with one sweep of his hand he could put everything right, if only from nothing wealth rose up like a thing solid to the touch, a thing one could snatch without effort and keep locked behind doors while one slept, ate, idled....

His thoughts drifted; he stirred and looked at his wife lying straight and stark beside him; the pallor of her face divided her from the surrounding gloom; her dark hair, braided in two plaits, hung outside the bedclothes.

He felt a dim desire, which, as his thoughts lingered, grew in urgency; he leaned over and touched her with his hands. "Mary, let's be friends, for God's sake."

As though through her sleep she had realised his passion, she at once drew away and answered harshly: "It's useless, quite useless; we can't go on like this."

He seized her arm and ran his fingers up to her bare shoulders; he could feel the blood beating slowly under his touch. There was a clanging in his veins, all his senses seemed gathering for a final revelation; everything was hastening, hastening....

He muttered thickly. "I'm sorry, Mary, don't be hard; I've thought it all out how I'll start tomorrow; I'll mend the hedge, tidy the garden; in a week I'll get the place straight, honest to God I will."

His hands enclosed her breast, dimly he heard her cry. "It's no good, no good."

The lace curtains rustled, swept the fringe of the bed, then lay with a shudder, flat against the window.

Davis swore slowly, half asleep. "I swear it; just you see in the morning."

His wife answered with a kind of wild intensity. "I don't mean to be hard. I try to believe in you, but you make me so bitter."

Her voice broke; Davis fell asleep to the sound of her crying.

He awoke, and at once he was depressed.

Daylight filtered through the window; it fell on the bed, wide, flat, and tousled, on the white counterpane dipping to the floor, on peeling wallpaper and the wash-basin half full of dirty water, standing in the far corner of the room.

He yawned and closed his eyes. Why did the days come on him like a burden?

Downstairs he could hear his wife lighting the fire.

What had he said last night? Something about lighting the fire himself. Well, anyway it was too late now.

With a groan he remembered other promises. He closed his eyes; the warmth in the bed was like the heat from burning logs.

He heard his wife calling out that breakfast was ready. He must have slept again. He turned the clock with its face to the wall and again shut his eyes. His limbs felt like logs.

Drowsily he heard the cows passing under the window on their way to the cowsheds; their feet splashed in the mud, splash, splash, splash.

"Another minute," he started to count slowly. Nearly sixty. What a fool he was to set a limit on time.

Rain ran down the windows and danced in bubbles on the aerial. One, two, three, no man could work in such weather.

Words ran in fragments to the tune of falling rain; they passed through his head and the pulsing of his blood set a rhythm to utterance. "Lazy, bone lazy, one, two, three. What were words?"

He buried his face deeper into the pillows. Once more he slept.

ALUN LEWIS

The Raid

My platoon and I were on training that morning. We've been on training every morning for the last three years, for that matter. On this occasion it was Current Affairs, which always boils down to how long the war is going to last, and when the orderly told me the C.O. wanted me in his office I broke the lads off for a cup of tea from the charwallah and nipped over to the orderly room, tidying myself as I went. I didn't expect anything unusual until I took a cautionary peep through the straw window of his matting shed and saw a strange officer in there. So I did a real dapper salute and braced myself. Self-defence is always the first instinct, self-suspicion the second. But I hadn't been drunk since I came to India and I hadn't written anything except love in my letters. As for politics, as far as they're concerned I don't exist, I'm never in. The other chap was a major and had a red armband.

"Come in, Selden," the colonel said. "This is the D.A.P.M. Head of military police. Got a job for you. Got your map case?"

"No sir. It's in company office."

"Hurry off and fetch it."

When I came back they were hard at it, bending over the inch map. The C.O. looked up. His face got very red when he bent.

"Here's your objective, Selden. This village here, Chaudanullah. Eighteen miles away. Route: track south of Morje, river-bed up to Pimpardi, turn south a mile before Pimpardi and strike across the watershed on a fixed bearing. Work it out with a protractor on the map and set your compass before you march off. Strike the secondary road below this group of huts here, 247568, cross the road and work up the canal to the village. Throw a cordon round the village with

121

two sections of your platoon. Take the third yourself and search the houses methodically. Government has a paid agent in the village who will meet you at this canal bridge here – got it? – at 06.00 hours. The agent reported that your man arrived there last night after dark and is lying up in one of the hovels."

"What man, sir?" I asked.

"Christ, didn't I tell you? Why the devil didn't you stop me? This fellow, what's-his-name – it's all on that paper there – he's wanted. Remember the bomb in the cinema last Tuesday, killed three British other ranks? He's wanted for that. Read the description before you go. Any questions so far? Right. Well, you'll avoid all houses, make a detour round villages, keep off the road all the way. Understand? News travels faster than infantry in India. He'll be away before you're within ten miles if you show yourself. Let's see. Twenty miles by night. Give you ten hours. Leave here at 19.30 hours. Arrive an hour before first light. Go in at dawn, keep your eyes skinned. M.T. will R.V. outside the village at dawn. Drive the prisoner straight to jail, D.A.P.M. will be there."

"Very good, sir. Dress, sir?" I said.

"Dress? P.T. shoes, cloth caps, overalls, basic pouches, rifles, 50 rounds of .303 per man, and grenades. 69 grenades if he won't come out, 36 grenades if he makes a fight of it. Anything else?"

"No, sir."

"Good. Remember to avoid the villages. Stalk him good and proper. Keep up-wind of him. I'm picking you and your platoon because I think you're the best I've got. I want results, Selden."

"I'll give you a good show, sir."

"Bloody good shot with a point 22, Selden is," the C.O. said to the D.A.P.M. by way of light conversation. "Shot six mallard with me last Sunday."

"Of course we want the man alive, sir, if it's at all possible," the D.A.P.M. said, fiddling with his nervous pink moustache. "He's not proved guilty yet, you see, sir, and with public opinion in India what it is."

"Quite," said the colonel. "Quite. Make a note of that, Selden. Tell your men to shoot low."

"Very good, sir."

"Got the route marked on your talc?"

"Yes, sir." I'd marked the route in chinograph pencil and the Chaudanullah place in red as we do for enemy objectives. It was all thick.

"Rub it all off, then. Security. Read his description. Have you read it? What is it?"

"Dark eyes, sir. Scar on left knee. Prominent cheekbones. Left corner of mouth droops. Front incisor discoloured. Last seen wearing European suit, may be dressed in native dhoti, Mahratta style."

"And his ring?" said the C.O. He's as keen as mustard the old man is.

"Oh yes, sir. Plain gold wedding ring."

"Correct. Don't forget these details. Invaluable sometimes. Off with you."

I saluted and marched out.

"Damn good fellow, Selden," I heard the C.O. say. "Your man is in the bag."

I felt pretty pleased with that. Comes of shooting those six mallard.

The platoon was reassembling after their tea and I felt pretty important, going back with all that dope. After all, it was the first bit of action we'd seen in two and a half years. It would be good for morale. I knew they'd moan like hell, having to do a twenty-mile route march by night, but I could sell them that all right. So I fell them in threes and called them to attention for disciplinary reasons and told them they'd been picked for a special job and this was it....

They were very impressed by the time I'd finished.

"Any questions?" I said.

"Yes, sir," said Chalky White. He was an L.P.T.B. conductor and you won't find him forgetting a halfpenny. "Do we take haversack rations and will we be in time for breakfast?" He thinks the same way as Napoleon,

"Yes," I said. "Anything else?"

"What's this fellow done, sir?" Bottomley asked, then. Bottomley always was a bit Bolshie, and he's had his knife into me for two and a half years because I was a bank clerk in Civvy Street and played golf on Sundays.

"Killed three troops, I think," I said. "Is that good enough?"
I felt I'd scored pretty heavy over his Red stuff this time.

"Right," I said. "Break off till 19.00 hours. Keep your mouths shut. White will draw rations at the cookhouse. No cigarettes or matches will be taken."

I did this for disciplinary purposes. They didn't say a word. Pretty good.

We crossed the start line dead on 19.30 hours and everybody looked at us with some interest. I felt mighty 'hush-hush'. My security was first class. Hadn't told a soul, except Ken More and Ted Paynter.

"Bring 'em back alive," a soldier jeered outside the cookhouse.

Somebody's let the cat out of the bag. Damn them all. Can't trust a soul in the ranks with the skin of a sausage.

Anyway, we got going bang away. I knew the first stretch past Morje and Pimpardi and we did about three miles an hour there. The night was breathless and stuffy; we put hankies round our foreheads to keep the sweat out of our eyes. And the perpetual buzzing of the crickets got on my nerves like a motor horn when the points jam and all the pedestrians laugh. I suppose I was a bit worked up. Every time a mosquito or midge touched me I let out a blow fit to knacker a bull. But I settled down after a while and began to enjoy the sense of freedom and deep still peace that informs the night out in the tropics. You've read all about tropical stars; well, it's quite true. They're marvellous; and we use some of them for direction-finding at night too. The Plough, for instance, and one called Cassiopeia that you bisect for the Pole Star.

Then there was the tricky bit over the mountain by compass. I just hoped for the best on that leg. Luckily the moon came up and put the lads in a good mood. I allowed them to talk in whispers for one hour and they had to keep silent for the next hour for disciplinary reasons. We halted for half an hour on the crest of the watershed and ate our bully beef sandwiches with relish, though bully tastes like a hot poultice out here. It was a damn fine view from that crest. A broad valley a thousand feet below with clusters of fires in the villages and round a hill temple on the other side. Either a festival or a funeral, obviously. I could hear the drums beating there, too; it was very clear and echoing, made my flesh creep. You feel so out of it in India somehow. You just slink around in the wilds and you feel very white and different. I don't know.... You know, I'd have said that valley hated us that night, on those rocky crests. Queer.

I didn't know which group of huts was which, but I could see the canal glittering in the moonlight so I was near enough right, praise be. The jackals were howling too, and some creature came right up to us, it gave me a scare. I knew that bully had a pretty bad stench. Anyway we got on the move again, Chalky White saying next stop Hammersmiff Bridge, and we slithered down as quietly as we could, hanging on to each other's rifles on the steep bits. We made our way between the villages and the drums beat themselves into a frenzy that had something personal about it. Then we went up the canal for about four miles, keeping about a hundred yards off the path and pretty rough going it was. Then we came to what I felt must be our objective, a cluster of crumbled huts on the foothills, pretty poor show even for these parts, and the boys were blistered and beat so I scattered them under the bushes and told them to lie low. It was only 5.30 a.m. and the agent fellow wasn't due until six. I had a nap myself, matter of fact, though it's a shootable offence. I woke up with a start and it was five past six, and I peered round my tree and there wasn't a sound. No drums, no jackals, no pie dogs. It was singing in my ears, the silence, and I wished to God we'd got this job over. It could go wrong so easily. He might fight, or his pals might help him, or he might have got wind of us, or I might have come to the wrong place. I was like an old woman. I loaded my Colt and felt better. Then I went down the canal to look for the chowkey fellow. I took a pretty poor view of a traitor, but I took a poorer view of him not turning up. He wasn't there and I walked up the path and just when I was getting really scared he appeared out of nowhere and I damn near shot him on the spot.

"Officer sahib huzzoor," he said. "Mai Sarkar ko dost hai," or something. And he said the name of the man I was after, which was the password.

"Achiba," I said, meaning good show. "Tairo a minute while I bolo my phaltan and then we'll jao jillo." He got the idea.

I nipped back and roused the lads quietly from under the trees and we moved up like ghosts on that village. I never want to see that village again. It was so still and fragile in the reluctant grey light. Even the pie dogs were asleep, and the bullocks lying on their sides. Once I travelled overnight from Dieppe to Paris and the countryside looked just as ghostly that morning. But this time it was dangerous. I had a feeling that somebody was going to die and there'd be a hell of a shemozzle. And at the same time the houses looked so poor and harmless, almost timid somehow. And the chowkey bloke was like a ghost. It was seeing him so scared that put me steady again. He was afraid of being seen with us as far as I could make out, and said he'd show us where this fellow was lying up and then he'd disappear please. I said never mind about the peace, let's get the war over first, and I told Bottomley to watch the bloke in case he had anything up his sleeve.

We got to the ring of trees outside the village without a sound, and the two section leaders led their men round each side of the village in a pincer movement. All the boys were white and dirty and their eyes were like stones. I remember suddenly feeling very proud of them just then.

I gave them ten minutes to get into position and close the road at the rear of the village. And then a damned pie dog set up a yelp over on the right flanks and another replied with a long shivering howl. I knew things would start going wrong if I didn't act quickly. We didn't want the village to find out until we'd gone if possible. For political reasons. And for reasons of health, I thought. So I gave the Follow-me sign and closed in on the huddled houses. There were a couple of outlying houses with a little shrine, and then the village proper with a crooked street running down it. The chowkey seemed to know where to go. I pointed to the single buildings and he said, "Nan, sahib," and pointed to the street. So I posted a man to picket the shrine and led the rest through the bush behind our scruffy guide. He moved like a beaten dog, crouching and limping, bare-foot. There was a dead ox in the bush and a pair of kites sleeping and gorged beside it. It stank like a bad death. Turned me. We hurried on. The bushes were in flower, sort of wisteria, the blossoms closed and dropping. We crept along under a tumbledown wall and paused, kneeling, at the street corner. I posted two men there, one on each side with fixed bayonets, to fire down the street if he bolted. The other two sections would be covering it from the other end. Then I nudged the chowkey man and signalled to my grenade man and rifleman to cover me in. I slipped round the corner and went gingerly down the street. Suddenly I feel quite cool and excited at the same time. The chowkey went about fifteen yards down the street and then slunk against the wall on his knees, pointing inwards to the house he was kneeling against. It was made of branches woven with straw and reed, a beggared place. He looked up at me and my revolver and he was sweating with fear. He had the pox all over his face, too. I took a breath to steady myself, took the first pressure on my trigger, kicked the door lattice aside and jumped in. Stand in the light in the doorway and you're a dead man.

I crouched in the dark corner. It was very dark in there still. There was a pile of straw on the floor and straw heaped in the corner. And some huge thing moved ponderously. I nearly yelped. Then I saw what it was. It was a cow. Honestly. A sleepy fawn cow with a soft mild face like somebody's dream woman.

"She never frew no bomb," Chalky said. He was my rifleman. Cool as ice. His voice must have broken the fellow's nerve. There was a huge rustle in the straw in the corner behind the cow and a man stood up, a man in a white dhoti, young, thin, sort of smiling. Discoloured teeth. Chalky lunged his bayonet. The chap still had plenty of nerve left. He just swayed a little.

"Please," he said. "Have you got a smoke upon you?"

"Watch him, White," I said. I searched him.

"Please," he said. "I have nothing." He was breathing quickly and smiling.

"Come on," I said. "Quietly."

"You know you are taking me to my death?" he said. "No doubt?"

"I'm taking you to Poona," I said. "You killed three of our men."

The smile sort of congealed on his face. Like a trick. His head nodded like an old doll. "Did I?" he said. "Three men died? Did I?"

"Come on," I said. "It's daylight."

"It's dreadful," he said. He looked sick. I felt sorry for him, nodding his head and sick, sallow. Looked like a student, I should say.

"Keep your hands up," Chalky said, prodding him in the back.

We went quietly down the street, no incident at all, and I signalled the two enveloping sections together and we got down the road out of sight. I was in a cold sweat and I wanted to laugh.

The truckers weren't there. God, I cursed them, waiting there. They might bitch the whole show. The villagers were going to the well quite close.

"What did you do it for, mate?" I heard Bottomley ask.

After a long silence the chap said very quietly. "For my country."

Chalky said, "Everybody says that. Beats me." Then we heard the trucks, and Chalky said, "We ought to be there in time for breakfast, boys."

RICHARD HUGHES

The Swans

Two ugly women in summer dresses stood under a tree: a fountain of a tree, with heavy scent streaming from its pink-and-white burden of blossoms. There was dapple sunshine shifting on the lawn: a nightingale singing before its time. Daisies and dropt flowers from the trees played at damask on the grass. The tall woman pulled down a bough towards her: hid her face a moment in the flowers: let it fly back:

"What is its name?"

"I don't know."

They forgot about it: not noticing the blossoms sticking to their hair. They swung their hands a little, walking away behind a dark shrubbery, not to appear again. The nightingale tuned his voice to new excellencies: and next across the lawn a tiny boy, all round, and as ill-balanced on his legs as cuckoo-spit on a grass-blade. He ran slowly and seriously, but as if to stop running were to fall. Like a grey woolly ball on pink stalks, he too wavered round the shrubbery, leaving the lawn as if empty.

It was set with seats, some shadowed, some in the sun, where a few people were sitting: for the garden was almost public. In one seat was a knitting woman. Two children in ugly skimped frocks were playing far away under the sunshine. The elder ecstatically threw an armful of mown grass into the air: it fell upon the other, so that she capered about: but it was too far off to smell the steam of the grass. Then they ran both together to the knitting woman, surprising her from behind. One of them wore a dress of tight white cotton, dog-toothed at the edge, and was quite straight: she was about twelve, and had not much black hair, but she tossed it up against the breeze, and the holes in her stockings did not show much. The other may have been ten, and although she was not so thin, was no better shaped, but wore her pink frock stiffly, as though it was padded. They surprised the knitting woman from behind, and took away from her the baby that was with her: it could toddle slowly. They lured it away with enticing, provocative sounds, telling it to catch them. They would show themselves from behind the shrubbery for a moment: the baby chuckled and began to wobble towards them: then they would flee back like the wind, screaming in quite real terror. The baby would fall over; and when it got up, start back again towards its mother. They showed themselves once more, and it all happened over again. Sometimes they would stay hidden for a long time, giggling in a high tone as if concocting some wicked plot.

Beyond the shrubbery, away to the right, was a small lake: the trees grew down so low over it that you could only see the reflections of the people on the far side; and there were two swans that broke up the reflections by leaping across the water, three-quarters out of it, from side to side, clapping their wings with a noise like a carpenter driving nails. One of them clambered out on to the further bank: it was darting its head angrily and pecking upwards as if someone unseen was teasing it. It grew very angry, ready to murder anyone small that should pass.

Meanwhile the hopeless game of catch by the shrubbery still went on: and I was waiting to see the little one cry. Presently it would grow tired, and feel the unfairness of it all, and fall down weeping. Each time it toddled slower and slower. Then two delicate-pretty little girls came into the garden, dressed one in soft white, the other in flame: they walked the flowered grass as if it was nothing earthly, treading with a lark's quick lightness. The baby ran towards them in mistake, and sat down suddenly once more.

But the two delicate children went towards the lake; following the path that led round it to the other side, where the swan was still flashing furiously up and down in the sunlight.

The baby got up no more, but lay there still and quiet. It did not cry; and the sisters came and danced round it, making goading noises, running up to it and away again, but it lay still. So they took runs, and jumped over it and over it, lower and more wildly each time. It rolled a little sometimes; and when they nearly trod on it, they shrieked. But they grew tired of this, and stopped. As if her ingenuity had dried up, and she could think of nothing better to do, the pink sister began to roll about violently. The straight white one stood irresolute. Then she began to dance; not gracefully, but with great skill, turning and pirouetting and doing most ingenious steps – in front, behind, in front: first clutching the bottom of her frock in mockery of a skirt-dance, then waving her arms in the manner of a ballet. She danced listlessly; it was a memory test, the recapitulation of a lesson once learnt. Presently the sun shone behind her, showing a quite ludicrous outline – the thick stuff petticoat under her cotton frock. Then the pink one stood up and whirled round and about furiously, arms and ugly frills flying out grotesquely, till she grew giddy and fell dispread on the grass.

But the two little girls who had started round the lake had paused under some dark trees; between, sunlit midges were dancing against the black background. Presently they went on: they seemed suddenly to turn black as they passed under a low stone arch, then bright again for a moment in the framed sunlight beyond it, before they disappeared. The baby began to crawl back towards the knitting woman: the elder two to quarrel on the grass with the anger and heat of giddiness. The swans were flashing ferociously up and down in the sun: while the two little girls had passed out of sight towards them.

RHYS DAVIES

The Chosen One

A letter, inscribed 'By Hand', lay inside the door when he arrived home just before seven o'clock. The thick, expensive-looking envelope was black-edged and smelled of stale face powder. Hoarding old-fashioned mourning envelopes would be typical of Mrs Vines, and the premonition of disaster Rufus felt now had nothing to do with death. But he stared for some moments at the penny-sized blob of purple wax sealing the flap. Other communications he had received from Mrs Vines over the last two years had not been sent in such a ceremonious envelope. The sheet of ruled paper inside, torn from a pad of the cheapest kind, was more familiar. He read it with strained concentration, his brows drawn into a pucker. The finely traced handwriting, in green ink, gave him no special difficulty, and his pausings over words such as 'oral', 'category' and 'sentimental', while his full-fleshed lips shaped the syllables, came from uncertainty of their meaning.

> Sir
>
> In reply to your oral request to me yesterday, concerning the property, Brychan Cottage, I have decided not to grant you a renewal of the lease, due to expire on June 30th next. This is final.
>
> The cottage is unfit for human habitation, whether you consider yourself as coming under that category or not. It is an eyesore to me, and I intend razing it to the ground later this year. That you wish to get married and continue to live in the cottage with some factory hussy from the town is no affair of mine, and that my father, for sentimental reasons, granted your grandfather a seventy-five-year lease for the paltry sum of a hundred pounds

is no affair of mine either. Your wretched family has always been a nuisance to me on my estate and I will not tolerate one of them to infest it any longer than is legal, or any screeching, jazz-dancing slut in trousers and bare feet to trespass and contaminate my land. Although you got rid of the pestiferous poultry after your mother died, the noise of the motor cycle you then bought has annoyed me even more than the cockerel crowing. Get out.

Yours truly, Audrey P Vines

He saw her brown-speckled, jewel-ringed hand moving from word to word with a certainty of expression beyond any means of retaliation from him. The abuse in the letter did not enrage him immediately; it belonged too familiarly to Mrs Vines' character and reputation, though when he was a boy he had known different behaviour from her. But awareness that she had this devilish right to throw him, neck and crop, from the home he had inherited began to register somewhere in his mind at last. He had never believed she would do it.

Shock temporarily suspended full realisation of the catastrophe. He went into the kitchen to brew the tea he always made as soon as he arrived home on his motor bike from his factory job in the county town. While he waited for the kettle to boil on the oil stove, his eye kept straying warily to the table. That a black-edged envelope lay on it was like something in a warning dream. He stared vaguely at the familiar objects around him. A peculiar silence seemed to have come to this kitchen that he had known all his life. There was a feeling of withdrawal from him in the room, as though already he were an intruder in it.

He winced when he picked up the letter and put it in a pocket of his leather jacket. Then, as was his habit on fine evenings, he took a mug of tea out to a seat under a pear tree shading the ill-fitting front door of the cottage, a sixteenth-century building in which he had been born. Golden light of May flooded the well-stocked garden. He began to re-read the letter, stopped to fetch a tattered little dictionary from the living room, and sat consulting one or two words which still perplexed him. Then, his thick jaw thrust out in his effort at sustained concentration, he read the letter through again.

The sentence "This is final" pounded in his head. Three words had smashed his plans for the future. In his bewilderment, it did not occur to him that his inbred procrastination was of importance. Until the day before, he had kept postponing going to see the evil-tempered mistress of Plas Idwal about the lease business, though his mother, who couldn't bear the sight of her, had reminded him of it several times in her last illness. He had just refused to believe that Mrs Vines would turn him out when a date in a yellowed old document came round. His mother's forebears had occupied Brychan Cottage for hundreds of years, long before Mrs Vines' family bought Plas Idwal.

Slowly turning his head, as though in compulsion, he gazed to the left of where he sat. He could see, beyond the garden and the alders fringing a ditch, an extensive slope of rough turf on which, centrally in his vision, a great cypress spread branches to the ground. Higher, crowning the slope, a rectangular mansion of russet stone caught the full light of the sunset. At this hour, he had sometimes seen Mrs Vines walking down the slope with her bulldog. She always carried a bag, throwing bread from it to birds and to wild duck on the river below. The tapestry bag had been familiar to him since he was a boy, but it was not until last Sunday that he learned she kept binoculars in it.

She could not be seen anywhere this evening. He sat thinking of last Sunday's events, unable to understand that such a small mistake as his girl had made could have caused the nastiness in the letter. Gloria had only trespassed a few yards on Plas Idwal land. And what was wrong with a girl wearing trousers or walking bare-foot on clean grass? What harm was there if a girl he was courting screeched when he chased her on to the river bank and if they tumbled to the ground? Nobody's clothes had come off.

He had thought Sunday was the champion day of his life. He had fetched Gloria from the town on his motor bike in the afternoon. It was her first visit to the cottage that he had boasted about so often in the factory, especially to her. Brought up in a poky terrace house without a garden, she had been pleased and excited with his pretty home on the Plas Idwal estate, and in half an hour, while they sat under this pear tree, he had asked her to marry him, and she said she would. She had laughed and squealed a lot in the garden and by the river, kicking her shoes off, dancing on the grassy river bank; she was only eighteen. Then, when he went indoors to put the kettle on for tea, she had jumped the narrow dividing ditch on to Mrs Vines' land – and soon after came dashing into the cottage. Shaking with fright, she said that a terrible woman in a torn fur coat had come shouting from under a big tree on the slope, binoculars in her hand and threatening her with a bulldog. It took quite a while to calm Gloria down. He told her of Mrs Vines' funny ways and the tales he had heard from his mother. But neither on Sunday nor since did he mention anything about the lease of Brychan Cottage, though remembrance of it had crossed his mind when Gloria said she'd marry him.

On Sunday, too, he had kept telling himself that he ought to ride up to the mansion to explain about the stranger who ignorantly crossed the ditch. But three days went by before he made the visit. He had bought a high-priced suede windcheater in the town, and got his hair trimmed during his dinner hour. He had even picked a bunch of polyanthus for Mrs Vines when he arrived home from the factory – and then, bothered by wanting to postpone the visit still longer, forgot them when he forced himself at last to jump on the bike. It was her tongue he was frightened of, he had told himself. He could never cope with women's tantrums.

But she had not seemed to be in one of her famous tempers when he appeared at the kitchen door of Plas Idwal, just after seven. "Well, young man, what do you require?" she asked, pointing to a carpenter's bench alongside the dresser, on which he had often sat as a boy. First, he had tried to tell her that the girl who strayed on her land was going to marry him. But Mrs Vines talked to the five cats that, one after the other, bounded into the kitchen from upstairs a minute after he arrived. She said to them, "We won't have these loud-voiced factory girls trespassing on any part of my property, will we, my darlings?" Taking her time, she fed the cats with liver she lifted with her fingers from a pan on one of her three small oil stoves. Presently he forced himself to say, "I've come about the lease of Brychan Cottage. My mother told me about it. I've got a paper with a date on it." But Mrs Vines said to one of the cats, "Queenie, you'll have to swallow a pill tomorrow!" After another wait, he tried again, saying, "My young lady is liking Brychan Cottage very much." Mrs

Vines had stared at him not saying a word for about a minute, then said, "You can go now. I will write you tomorrow about the lease."

He had left the kitchen feeling a tightness beginning to throttle him, and he knew then that it had never been fear he felt towards her. But, as he tore at full speed down the drive, the thought came that it might have been a bad mistake to have stopped going to Plas Idwal to ask if he could collect whinberries for her up on the slopes of Mynydd Baer, or find mushrooms in the Caer Tegid fields, as he used to do before he took a job in a factory in the town. Was that why, soon after his mother died, she had sent him a rude letter about the smell of poultry and the rooster crowing? He had found that letter comic and shown it to the chaps in the factory. But something had told him to get rid of the poultry.

He got up from the seat under the pear tree. The strange quiet he had noticed in the kitchen was in the garden too. Not a leaf or bird stirred. He could hear his heart thumping. He began to walk up and down the paths. He knew now the full meaning of her remark to those cats that no trespassers would be allowed on 'my property'. In about six weeks he himself would be a trespasser. He stopped to tear a branch of pear blossom from the tree and looked at it abstractedly. The pear tree was his! His mother had told him it was planted on the day he was born. Some summers it used to fruit so well that they had sold the whole load to Harries in the town, and the money was always for him.

Pacing, he slapped the branch against his leg, scattering the blossom. The tumult in his heart did not diminish. Like the kitchen, the garden seemed already to be withdrawn from his keeping. She had walked there that day, tainting it. He hurled the branch in the direction of the Plas Idwal slope. He did not want to go indoors, he went through a thicket of willows and lay on the river bank, staring into the clear, placidly flowing water. Her face flickered in the greenish depths. He flung a stone at it. Stress coiled tighter in him. He lay flat on his back, sweating, a hand clenched over his genitals.

The arc of serene evening sky and the whisper of gently lapping water calmed him for a while. A shred of common sense told him that the loss of Brychan Cottage was not a matter of life and death. But he could not forget Mrs Vines. He tried to think how he could appease her with some act of service. He remembered that until he was about seventeen she would ask him to do odd jobs for her, such as clearing fallen branches, setting fire to wasp holes, and – she made him wear a bonnet and veil for this – collecting the combs from her beehives. But what could he do now? She had shut herself away from everybody for years.

He could not shake off thought of her. Half-forgotten memories of the past came back. When he was about twelve, how surprised his mother had been when he told her that he had been taken upstairs in Plas Idwal and shown six kittens born that day! Soon after that, Mrs Vines had come down to this bank, where he had sat fishing, and said she wanted him to drown three of the kittens. She had a tub of water ready outside her kitchen door, and she stood watching while he held a wriggling canvas sack under the water with a broom. The three were males, she said. He had to dig a hole close to the greenhouses for the sack.

She never gave him money for any job, only presents from the house – an old magic lantern, coloured slides, dominoes, a box of crayons, even a dolls' house. Her big brown eyes would look at him without any sign of temper at all. Once, when she asked him, "Are you a dunce in school?" and he said, "Yes, bottom of the class," he heard her laugh aloud for the first time, and she looked very pleased with him. All that, he remembered, was when visitors had stopped going to Plas Idwal, and there was not a servant left; his mother said they wouldn't put up with Mrs Vines' bad ways any more. But people in the town who had worked for her said she was a very clever woman, with letters after her name, and it was likely she would always come out on top in disputes concerning her estate.

Other scraps of her history returned to his memory – things heard from old people who had known her before she shut herself away. Evan Matthews, who used to be her estate keeper and had been a friend of his father's, said that for a time she had lived among African savages, studying their ways with her first husband. Nobody knew she had got rid of that husband, or the whole truth about her second one. She used to disappear from Plas Idwal for months, but when her father died she never went away from her old home again. But it was when her second husband was no longer seen in Plas Idwal that she shut herself up there, except that once a month she hired a Daimler from the county town and went to buy, so it was said, cases of wine at Drapple's, and stuff for her face at the chemist's. Then even those trips had stopped, and everything was delivered to Plas Idwal by tradesmen's vans or post.

No clue came of a way to appease her. He rose from the river bank. The sunset light was beginning to fade, but he could still see clearly the mansion facade, its twelve bare windows, and the crumbling entrance portico, which was never used now. In sudden compulsion, he strode down to the narrow, weed-filled ditch marking the boundary of Brychan Cottage land. But he drew up at its edge. If he went to see her, he thought, he must prepare what he had to say with a cooler head than he had now.

Besides, to approach the mansion that way was forbidden. She might be watching him through binoculars from one of those windows.

An ambling sound roused him from this torment of indecision. Fifty yards beyond the river's opposite bank, the 7.40 slow train to the county town was approaching. Its passage over the rough stretches of meadowland brought back a reminder of his mother's bitter grudge against the family at Plas Idwal. The trickery that had been done before the railroad was laid had never meant much to him, though he had heard about it often enough from his mother. Late in the nineteenth century, her father, who couldn't read or write, had been persuaded by Mrs Vines' father to sell to him, at a low price, not only decaying Brychan Cottage but, across the river, a great many acres of useless meadowland included in the cottage demesne. As a bait, a seventy-five-year retaining lease of the cottage and a piece of land to the river bank were granted for a hundred pounds. So there had been some money to stave off further dilapidation of the cottage and to put by for hard times. But in less than two years after the transaction, a railroad loop to a developing port in the west had been laid over that long stretch of useless land across the river. Mrs Vines' father had known of the project and, according to the never-forgotten grudge, cleared a big profit from rail rights. His explanation (alleged by Rufus' mother to be humbug) was that he wanted to preserve the view from possible ruination by buildings such a gasworks; a few trains every day, including important expresses and freight traffic, did not matter.

Watching, with a belligerent scowl, the 7.40 vanishing into the sunset fume, Rufus remembered that his father used to say that it wasn't Mrs Vines herself who had done the dirty trick. But was the daughter proving herself to be of the same robbing nature now? He could not believe that she intended razing Brychan Cottage to the ground. Did she want to trim it up and sell or rent at a price she knew he could never afford? But she had plenty of money already – everybody knew that. Was it only that she wanted him out of sight, the last member of his family, and the last man on the estate?

He strode back to the cottage with the quick step of a man reaching a decision. Yet when he entered the dusky, low-ceilinged living room the paralysis of will threatened him again. He stood gazing round at the age-darkened furniture, the steel and copper accoutrements of the cavernous fireplace, the ornaments, the dim engravings of mountains, castles, and waterfalls as though he viewed them for the first time. He could not light the oil lamp, could not prepare a meal, begin his evening routine. A superstitious dread assailed him. Another presence was in possession here.

He shook the spell off. In the crimson glow remaining at the deep window, he read the letter once more, searching for some hint of a loophole. There seemed none. But awareness of a challenge penetrated his mind. For the first time since the death of his parents an important event was his to deal with alone. He lit the lamp, found a seldom-used stationery compendium, and sat down. He did not get beyond, "Dear Madam, Surprised to receive your letter...." Instinct told him he must wheedle Mrs Vines. But in what way? After half an hour of defeat, he dashed upstairs, ran down naked to the kitchen to wash at the sink, and returned upstairs to rub scented oil into his tough black hair and dress in the new cotton trousers and elegant windcheater of green suede that had cost him more than a week's wages.

Audrey Vines put her binoculars into her tapestry bag when Rufus entered Brychan Cottage and, her uninterested old bulldog at her heels, stepped out to the slope from between a brace of low-sweeping cypress branches. After concealing herself under the massive tree minutes before the noise of Rufus' motor cycle had come, as usual, a few minutes before seven, she had studied his face and followed his prowlings about the garden and river bank for nearly an hour. The clear views of him this evening had been particularly unsatisfactory. She knew it was a dictionary he had consulted under the pear tree, where he often sat drinking from a large Victorian mug. The furious hurling of a branch in the direction of the cypress had pleased her; his stress when he paced the garden had been as rewarding as his stupefied reading of the deliberately perplexing phraseology of her letter.

"Come along, Mia. *Good* little darling! We are going in now."

Paused on the slope in musing, the corpulent bitch grunted, blinked, and followed with a faint trace of former briskness in her bandily aged waddle. Audrey Vines climbed without any breathlessness herself, her pertinacious gaze examining the distances to right and left. She came out every evening not only to feed the birds but to scrutinize her estate before settling down for the night. There was also the passage of the 7.40 train to see; since her two watches and every clock in the house needed repairs, it gave verification of the exact time, though this, like the bird feeding, was not really of account to her.

It was her glimpses of Rufus that provided her long day with most interest. For some years she had regularly watched him through the powerful Zeiss binoculars from various concealed spots. He renewed an interest in studies begun during long-ago travels in countries far from Wales, and she often jotted her findings into a household-accounts book kept locked in an old portable escritoire. To her eye, the prognathous jaw, broad nose, and gypsy-black hair of this heavy-bodied but personable young man bore distinct atavistic elements. He possessed too, a primitive bloom, which often lingered for years beyond adolescence with persons of tardy mental development. But this throwback descendant of an ancient race was also, up to a point, a triumph over decadence. Arriving miraculously late in his mother's life, after three others born much earlier to the illiterate woman had died in infancy, this last-moment child had flourished physically, if not in other respects.

Except for the occasion when, as a boy and youth, he used to come to Plas Idwal to do odd jobs and run errands, her deductions had been formed entirely through the limited and intensifying medium of her binoculars. She had come to know all his outdoor habits and activities around the cottage. These were rewarding only occasionally. The days when she failed to see him seemed bleakly deficient of incident. While daylight lasted, he never bathed in the river without her knowledge, though sometimes, among the willows and reeds, he was as elusive as an otter. And winter, of course, kept him indoors a great deal.

"Come, darling. There'll be a visitor for us tonight."

Mia, her little question-mark tail unexpectedly quivering, glanced up with the vaguely deprecating look of her breed. Audrey Vines had reached the balustraded front terrace. She paused by a broken sundial for a final look round at the spread of tranquil uplands and dim woods afar, the silent river and deserted meadows below, and, lingeringly, at the ancient trees shading her estate. Mild and windless though the evening was, she wore a long draggled coat of brown-dyed ermine and, pinned securely on skeins of vigorous hair unskilfully home-dyed to auburn tints, a winged hat of tobacco-gold velvet. These, with her thick bistre face powder and assertive eye pencilling, gave her the look of an uncompromisingly womanly woman in an old-style sepia photograph, a woman halted for ever in the dead past. But there was no evidence of waning powers in either her demeanour or step as she continued to the side terrace. A woman of leisure ignoring time's urgencies, she only suggested an unruffled unity with the day's slow descent into twilight.

The outward calm was deceptive. A watchful gleam in her eyes was always there, and the binoculars were carried for a reason additional to her study of Rufus. She was ever on the lookout for trespassers and poachers or tramps on the estate, rare though such were. When perhaps three or four times a year, she discovered a stray culprit, the mature repose would disappear in a flash, her steps accelerate, her throaty voice lash out. Tradesmen arriving legitimately at her kitchen door avoided looking her straight in the eye, and C.W. Powell, her solicitor, knew exactly how far he could go in sociabilities during his quarterly conferences with her in the kitchen of Plas Idwal. Deep within those dissociated eyes lay an adamantine refusal to acknowledge the existence of any friendly approach. Only her animals could soften that repudiation.

"Poor Mia! We won't stay out so long tomorrow, I promise! Come along." They had reached the unbalustraded side terrace. "A flower for us tonight, sweetheart, then we'll go in," she murmured.

She crossed the cobbled yard behind the mansion. Close to disused greenhouses, inside which overturned flowerpots and abandoned garden tools lay under tangles of grossly overgrown plants sprouting to the broken roofing, there was a single border of wallflowers, primulas, and several well-pruned rosebushes in generous bud. It was the only evidence in all the Plas Idwal domain of her almost defunct passion for flower cultivation. One pure white rose, an early herald of summer plenty, had begun to unfold that mild day; she had noticed it when she came out. Raindrops from a morning shower sprinkled on to her wrist as she plucked this sprightly first bloom, and she smiled as she inhaled the secret odour within. Holding the flower aloft like a trophy, she proceeded to the kitchen entrance with the same composed gait. There was all the time in the world.

Dusk had come into the spacious kitchen. But there was sufficient light for her activities from the curtainless bay window overlooking the yard and the flower borders in which, long ago, Mia's much loved predecessor had been buried. Candles were not lit until it was strictly necessary. She fumbled among a jumble of oddments in one of the gloomy little pantries lying off the kitchen, and came out with a cone-shaped silver vase.

Light pattering sounds came from beyond an open inner door, where an uncarpeted back staircase lay, and five cats came bounding down from the first-floor drawing room. Each a ginger tabby of almost identical aspect, they whisked, mewing, around their mistress, tails up.

"Yes, yes, my darlings," she said. "Your saucers in a moment." She crossed to a sink of blackened stone, humming to herself.

A monster Edwardian cooking range stood derelict in a chimneyed alcove, with three portable oil stoves before it holding a covered frying pan, an iron stewpan, and a tin kettle. Stately dinner crockery and a variety of canisters and tinned foodstuff packed the shelves of a huge dresser built into the back wall. A long table stretching down the centre of the kitchen was even more crowded. It held half a dozen bulging paper satchels, biscuit tins, piles of unwashed plates and saucers, two stacks of *The Geographical Magazine*, the skull of a sheep, heaped vegetable peelings, an old wooden coffee grinder, a leatherette hatbox, a Tunisian birdcage used for storing meat, several ribboned chocolate boxes crammed with letters, and a traveller's escritoire of rosewood. On the end near the oil stoves, under a three-branched candelabra of heavy Sheffield plate encrusted with carved vine leaves and grapes, a reasonably fresh cloth of fine lace was laid with silver cutlery, a condiment set of polished silver, a crystal wine goblet, and a neatly folded linen napkin. A boudoir chair of gilded wood stood before this end of the table.

When the cold-water tap was turned on at the sink, a rattle sounded afar in the house and ended in a groaning cough – a companionable sound, which Mrs Vines much liked. She continued to hum as she placed the rose in the vase, set it below the handsome candelabra, and stepped back to admire the effect. Pulling out a pair of long, jet-headed pins, she took off her opulent velvet hat.

"He's a stupid lout, isn't he, Queenie?" The eldest cat, her favourite, had leaped on the table. "Thinking he was going to bed that chit down here and breed like rabbits!"

She gave the cats their separate saucers of liver, chopped from cold slices taken from the frying pan. Queenie was served first. The bulldog waited for her dish of beef chunks from the stewpan, and, given them, stood morosely for a minute, as if counting the pieces. Finally, Audrey Vines took for herself a remaining portion of liver and a slice of bread from a loaf on the dresser, and fetched a half bottle of champagne from a capacious oak chest placed between the two pantries. She removed her fur coat before she settled on the frail boudoir chair and shook out her napkin.

Several of these meagre snacks were taken every day, the last just after the 11.15 night express rocked away to the port in the west. Now, her excellent teeth masticating with barely perceptible movements, she ate with fastidious care. The bluish light filtering through the grimy bay window soon thickened, but still she did not light the three candles. Her snack finished, and the last drop of champagne taken with a sweet biscuit, she continued to sit at the table, her oil-stained tea gown of beige chiffon ethereal in the dimness.

She became an unmoving shadow. A disciplined meditation or a religious exercise might have been engaging her. Mia, also an immobile smudge, lay fast asleep on a strip of coconut matting beside the gilt chair. The five cats, tails down, had returned upstairs immediately after their meal, going one after the other as though in strict etiquette, or like a file of replete orphans. Each had a mahogany cradle in the drawing room, constructed to their mistress' specifications by an aged craftsman who had once been employed at Plas Idwal.

She stirred for a minute from the reverie, but her murmuring scarcely disturbed the silence. Turning her head in mechanical habit to where Mia lay, she asked, "Was it last January the river froze for a fortnight?.... No, not last winter. But there were gales, weren't there? Floods of rain.... Which winter did I burn the chairs to keep us warm? That idiotic oilman didn't come. Then the candles and matches gave out, and I used the electricity. One of Queenie's daughters died that winter. It was the year he went to work in a factory."

Time had long ago ceased to have calendar meaning in her life; a dozen years were as one. But lately she had begun to be obsessed by dread of another severe winter. Winters seemed to have become colder and longer. She dreaded the deeper hibernation they enforced. Springs were intolerably long in coming, postponing the time when her child of nature became visible again, busy under his flowering trees and splashing in the river. His reliable appearances brought back flickers of interest in the world; in comparison, intruders on the estate, the arrival of tradesmen, or the visits of her solicitor were becoming of little consequence.

She lapsed back into silence. The kitchen was almost invisible, when, swiftly alert, she turned her head towards the indigo blue of the bay window. A throbbing sound had come from far away. It mounted to a series of kicking spurts, roared, and became a loudly tearing rhythm. She rose from her chair and fumbled for a box of matches on the table. But the rhythmic sound began to dwindle, and her hand remained over the box. The sound floated away.

She sank back on the chair. "Not now, darling!" she told the drowsily shifting dog. "Later, later."

The headlamp beam flashed past the high entrance gates to Plas Idwal, but Rufus did not even glance at them. They were wide open and, he knew, would remain open all night. He had long ceased to wonder about this. Some people said Mrs Vines wanted to trap strangers inside, so that she could enjoy frightening them when they were nabbed, but other townsfolk thought that the gates had been kept open for years because she was always expecting her second husband to come back.

At top speed, his bike could reach the town in less than ten minutes. The fir-darkened road was deserted. No cottage or house bordered it for five miles. A roadside farmstead had become derelict, but in a long vale quietly ascending towards the mountain range some families still continued with reduced sheep farming. Rufus knew them all. His father had worked at one of the farms before the decline in agricultural prosperity set in. From the outskirts of the hilly town he could see an illuminated clock in the Assembly Hall tower. It was half-past nine. He did not slow down. Avoiding the town centre, he tore past the pens of a disused cattle market, a recently built confectionery factory, a nineteenth-century Nonconformist chapel, which had become a furniture depository, then past a row of cottages remaining from days when the town profited from rich milk and tough flannel woven at riverside mills. Farther round the town's lower folds, he turned into an area of diminutive back-to-back dwellings, their fronts ranging direct along narrow pavements.

Nobody was visible in these gaslit streets. He stopped at one of the terraces, walked to a door, and, without knocking, turned its brass knob. The door opened into a living room, though a sort of entrance lobby was formed by a chenille curtain and an upturned painted drainpipe used for umbrellas. Voices came from beyond the curtain. But only Gloria's twelve-year-old brother sat in the darkened room, watching television from a plump easy chair. His spectacles flashed up at the interrupting visitor.

"Gone to the pictures with Mum." The boy's attention returned impatiently to the dramatic serial. "Won't be back till long after ten."

Rufus sat down behind the boy and gazed unseeingly at the

screen. A feeling of relief came to him. He knew now that he didn't want to show the letter to Gloria tonight, or tell her anything about the lease of Brychan Cottage. Besides, she mustn't read those nasty insults about her in the letter. He asked himself why he had come there, so hastily. Why hadn't he gone to Plas Idwal? Mrs Vines might give way. Then he needn't mention anything at all to Gloria. If he told her about the letter tonight, it would make him look a shifty cheat. She would ask why he hadn't told her about the lease before.

He began to sweat. The close-packed little room was warm and airless. Gloria's two married sisters lived in poky terrace houses just like this one, and he became certain that it was sight of Brychan Cottage and its garden last Sunday that convinced her to marry him. Before Sunday, she had always been a bit offhand, pouting if he said too much about the future. Although she could giggle and squeal a lot, she could wrinkle up her nose, too, and flounce away if any chap tried any fancy stuff on her in the factory recreation room. He saw her little feet skipping and running fast as a deer's.

The torment was coming back. This room, instead of bringing Gloria closer to him, made her seem farther off. He kept seeing her on the run. She was screeching as she ran. That loud screech of hers! He had never really liked it. It made his blood go cold, though a chap in the factory said that screeches like that were only a sign that a girl was a virgin and that they disappeared afterwards. Why was he hearing them now? Then he remembered that one of Mrs Vines' insults was about the screeching.

His fingers trembled when he lit a cigarette. He sat a little while longer telling himself he ought to have gone begging to Plas Idwal and promised to do anything if he could keep the cottage. He would work on the estate evenings and weekends for no money; a lot of jobs needed doing there. He'd offer to pay a good rent for the cottage, too. But what he ought to get before going there, he thought further, was advice from someone who had known Mrs Vines well. He peered at his watch and got up.

"Tell Gloria I thought she'd like to go for a ride on the bike. I won't come back tonight."

"You'll be seeing her in the factory tomorrow," the boy pointed out.

It was only a minute up to the town centre. After parking the bike behind the Assembly Hall, Rufus crossed the quiet market square to a timbered old inn at the corner of Einon's Dip. He had remembered that Evan Matthews often went in there on his way to his night job at the reservoir. Sometimes they'd had a quick drink together.

Thursdays were quiet nights in pubs; so far, there were only five customers in the cozily rambling main bar. Instead of his usual beer, he ordered a double whisky, and asked Gwyneth, the elderly barmaid, if Evan Matthews had been in. She said that if he came in at all it would be about that time. Rufus took his glass over to a table beside the fireless inglenook. He didn't know the two fellows playing darts. An English-looking commercial traveller in a bowler sat at a table scribbling in a notebook. Councillor Llew Pryce stood talking in Welsh to Gwyneth at the counter, and sitting at a table across the bar from himself, the woman called Joanie was reading the local newspaper.

Staring at his unwatered whisky, he tried to decide whether to go to Evan's home in Mostyn Street. No, he'd wait a while here. He wanted more time to think. How could Evan help, after all? A couple of drinks – that's what he needed now. Empty glass in hand, he looked up. Joanie was laying her newspaper down. A blue flower decorated her white felt hat, and there was a bright cherry in her small wineglass.

He watched, in a fascination like relief, as she bit the cherry from its stick and chewed with easy enjoyment. She'd be about thirty-five, he judged. She was a Saturday-night regular, but he had seen her in The Drovers on other nights, and she didn't lack company as a rule. He knew of her only from tales and jokes by chaps in the factory. Someone had said she'd come from Bristol, with a man supposed to be her husband, who had disappeared when they'd both worked in the slab-cake factory for a few months.

Joanie looked at him, and picked up her paper. He wondered if she was waiting for someone. If Evan didn't come in, could he talk to her about his trouble, ask her the best way to handle a bad-tempered old money-bags? She looked experienced and good-hearted, a woman with no lumps in her nature. He could show her the letter; being a newcomer to the town, she wouldn't know who Mrs Vines was.

He rose to get another double whisky but couldn't make up his mind to stop at Joanie's table or venture a passing nod. He stayed at the counter finishing his second double, and he was still there when Evan came in. He bought Evan a pint of bitter, a single whisky for himself, and Joanie forgotten, led Evan to the inglenook table.

"Had a knockout when I got home this evening." He took the black-edged envelope from a pocket of his windcheater.

Evan Matthews read the letter. A sinewy well-preserved man, he looked about fifty and was approaching sixty; when Mrs Vines had hired him as estate keeper and herdsman, he had been under forty. He grinned as he handed the letter back, saying, "She's got you properly skewered, boyo! I warned your dad she'd do it when the lease was up."

"What's the reason for it? Brychan Cottage isn't unfit for living in, like she says – there's only a bit of dry rot in the floor boards. I've never done her any harm."

"No harm, except that you're a man now."

Uncomprehending, Rufus scowled. "She used to like me. Gave me presents. Is it more money she's after?"

"She isn't after money. Audrey P. Vines was open-fisted with cash – I'll say that for her. No, she just hates the lot of us."

"Men, you mean?"

"The whole bunch of us get her dander up." Recollection lit Evan's eyes. "She gave me cracks across the head with a riding crop that she always carried in those days. I'd been working hard at Plas Idwal for five years when I got my lot from her."

"Cracks across the head?" Rufus said, sidetracked.

"She drew blood. I told your dad about it. He said I ought to prosecute her for assault. But when she did it I felt sorry for her, and she knew it. It made her blood boil the more."

"What you'd done?"

"We were in the cowshed. She used to keep a fine herd of Jerseys, and she blamed the death of a calving one on me – began raging that I was clumsy pulling the calf out, which I'd been obliged to do." Evan shook his head. "It wasn't that got her flaring. But she took advantage of it and gave me three or four lashes with the crop. I just stood looking at her. I could see she wanted me to hit back and have a proper set-to. Of course, I was much younger then, and so was she! But I only said, 'You and I must part, Mrs Vines.' She lifted that top lip of hers, like a vixen done out of a fowl – I can see her now – and went from the shed without a word. I packed up that day. Same as her second husband had walked out on her a couple of years before – the one that played a violin."

"You mean…" Rufus blurted, after a pause of astonishment. "You mean, you'd *been* with her?"

Evan chuckled. "Now, I didn't say that!"

"What's the *matter* with the woman?" Rufus exclaimed. The mystery of Mrs Vines' attack on himself was no clearer.

"There's women that turn themselves into royalty," Evan said. "They get it into their heads they rule the world. People who knew little Audrey's father used to say he spoiled her up to the hilt because her mother died young. He only had one child. They travelled a lot together when she was a girl, going into savage parts, and afterwards she always had a taste for places where there's no baptized Christians. I heard that her first husband committed suicide in Nigeria, but nobody knows for certain what happened." He took up Rufus' empty whisky glass, and pushed back his chair. "If he did something without her permission, he'd be for the crocodiles."

"I've had two doubles and a single and I haven't had supper yet," Rufus protested. But Evan fetched him a single whisky. When it was placed before him, Rufus stubbornly asked, "What's the best thing for me to do?"

"Go and see her." Evan's face had the tenderly amused relish of one who knows that the young male must get a portion of trouble at the hands of women. "That's what she wants. I know our Audrey." He glanced again at this slow-thinking son of an old friend. "Go tonight," he urged.

"It's late to go tonight," Rufus mumbled. Sunk in rumination, he added. "She stays up late. I've seen a light in her kitchen window when I drive back over the rise after I've been out with Gloria." He swallowed the whisky at a gulp.

"If you want to keep Brychan Cottage, boyo, *act*. Night's better than daytime for seeing her. She'll have had a glass or two. Bottles still go there regularly from Jack Drapple's."

149

"You mean, soft-soap her?" Rufus asked with a grimace,

"No, not soft-soap. But give her what she wants." Evan thought for a moment, and added, a little more clearly, "When she starts laying into you – and she will, judging by that letter – you have a go at *her*. I wouldn't be surprised she'll respect you for it. Her and me in the cowshed was a different matter – I wasn't after anything from her. Get some clouts in on her, if you can."

Rufus shook his head slowly. "She said in the letter it was final," he said.

"Nothing is final with women, boyo. Especially what they put down in writing. They send letters like that to get a man springing up off his tail. They can't bear us to sit down quietly for long." Evan finished his beer. It was time to leave for his watchman's job at the new reservoir up at Mynydd Baer, the towering mountain from which showers thrashed down.

"Brychan Cottage belongs to me! Not to that damned old witch!" Rufus had banged the table with his fist. The dart players turned to look; Joanie lowered her paper; the commercial traveller glanced up from his notebook, took off his bowler, and laid it on the table. Gwyneth coughed and thumped a large Toby jug down warningly on the bar counter.

Evan said, "Try shouting at *her* like that – she won't mind language – but pipe down here. And don't take any more whisky."

"I'll tell her I won't budge from Brychan Cottage!" Rufus announced. "Her father cheated my grandfather over the railway – made a lot of money. She won't try to force me out. She'd be disgraced in the town."

"Audrey Vines won't care a farthing about disgrace or gossip." Evan buttoned up his black mackintosh. "I heard she used to give her second husband shocking dressings-down in front of servants and the visitors that used to go to Plas Idwal in those days. Mr Oswald, he was called. A touch of African tarbrush in him, and had tried playing the violin for a living." A tone of sly pleasure was in his voice. "Younger than Audrey Vines. One afternoon in Plas Idwal, she caught him with a skivvy in the girl's bedroom top of the house, and she locked him in there for twenty-four hours. She turned the electricity off at the main, and there the two stayed without food or water all that time." Evan took from his pocket a tasselled monkey cap of white wool, kept for his journey by motor bike into the mountains. "If you go to see her tonight, give her my love. Come to Mostyn Street tomorrow to tell me how you got on."

"What happened when the two were let out of the bedroom?"

"The skivvy was sent flying at once, of course. Mari, the housekeeper, told me that in a day or two Mrs Vines was playing her piano to Mr Oswald's fiddle as usual. Long duets they used to play most evenings, and visitors had to sit and listen. But it wasn't many weeks before Mr Oswald bunked off, in the dead of night. The tale some tell that he is still shut away somewhere in Plas Idwal is bull." He winked at Rufus.

"I've heard she keeps the gates open all the time to welcome him back," Rufus persisted, delaying Evan still longer. It was as though he dreaded to be left alone.

"After all these years? Some people like to believe women get love on the brain. But it's true they can go sour when a man they're set on does a skedaddle from them. And when they get like that, they can go round the bend without much pushing." He rose from the table. "But I'll say this for our Audrey. After Mr Oswald skedaddled, she shut herself up in Plas Idwal and wasn't too much of a nuisance to people outside. Far as I know, I was the only man who had his claret tapped with that riding crop!" He drained a last swallow from his glass. "Mind, I wouldn't deny she'd like Mr Oswald to come back, even after all these years! She'd have ways and means of finishing him off." He patted Rufus' shoulder. "In the long run it might be best if you lost Brychan Cottage."

Rufus' jaw set in sudden obstinate sullenness. "I've told Gloria we're going to live there for ever. I'm going to Plas Idwal tonight."

When he got up, a minute after Evan had left, it was with a clumsy spring; the table and glasses lurched. But his progress to the bar counter was undeviating. He drank another single whisky, bought a half bottle, which he put inside his elastic-waisted windcheater, and strode from the bar with a newly found hauteur.

She came out of her bedroom above the kitchen rather later than her usual time for going down to prepare her last meal of the day,

Carrying a candleholder of Venetian glass shaped like a water lily, she did not descend by the adjacent back staircase tonight but went along a corridor and turned into another, off which lay the front drawing room. Each of the doors she passed, like every other inside the house, was wide open; a bronze statuette of a mounted hussar kept her bedroom door secure against slamming on windy nights.

She had dressed and renewed her make-up by the light of the candle, which was now a dripping stub concealed in the pretty holder. Her wide-skirted evening gown of mauve taffeta had not entirely lost a crisp rustle, and on the mottled flesh of her bosom a ruby pendant shone vivaciously. Rouge, lip salve, and mascara had been applied with a prodigal hand, like the expensive scent that left whiffs in her wake. She arrayed herself in this way now and again – sometimes if she planned to sit far into the night composing letters and always for her solicitor's arrival on the evening of the quarter day, when she would give him soup and tinned crab in the kitchen.

She never failed to look into the first-floor drawing room at about eleven o'clock, to bid a good night to the cats. The bulldog, aware of the custom, had preceded her mistress on this occasion and stood looking in turn at the occupants of five short-legged cradles ranged in a half circle before a gaunt and empty fireplace of grey stone. Pampered Queenie lay fast asleep on her eiderdown cushion; the other tabbies had heard their mistress approaching and sat up, stretching and giving themselves a contented lick. Blue starlight came from four tall windows, whose satin curtains were drawn back tightly into dirt-stiff folds, rigid as marble. In that quiet illumination of candle and starlight, the richly dressed woman moving from cradle to cradle, stroking and cooing a word or two, had a look of feudally assured serenity. Mia watched in pedigreed detachment; even her squashed face achieved a debonair comeliness.

"Queenie, Queenie, won't you say good night to me? Bowen's are sending fish tomorrow! Friday fish! Soles, darling! *Fish fish!*"

Queenie refused to stir from her fat sleep. Presently, her ceremony performed, Audrey Vines descended by the front staircase, candle in hand, Mia stepping with equal care behind her. At the rear of the panelled hall, she passed through an archway, above which hung a Bantu initiatory mask, its orange and purple stripes dimmed under grime. A baize door in the passage beyond was kept open with an earthenware jar full of potatoes and onions. In the kitchen, she lit the three-branched candelabra from her pink-and-white holder, and blew out the stub. This was always the hour she liked best. The last snack would be prepared with even more leisure than the earlier four or five. Tonight, she opened a tin of sardines, sliced a tomato and a hard-boiled egg, and brought from one of the dank little pantries a jar of olives, a bottle of mayonnaise, and a foil-wrapped triangle of processed cheese. While she buttered slices of bread, the distant rocking of the last train could be heard, its fading rhythm leaving behind all the unruffled calm of a windless night. She arranged half a dozen sponge fingers clockwise on a Chelsea plate, then took a half bottle of champagne from the chest, hesitated, and exchanged it for a full-sized one.

Mia had occupied herself with a prolonged examination and sniffing and scratching of her varicoloured strip of matting; she might have been viewing it for the first time. Noticing that her mistress was seated, she reclined her obdurate bulk on the strip. Presently, she would be given her usual two sponge fingers dipped in champagne. She took no notice when a throbbing sound came from outside or when it grew louder.

"Our visitor, sweetheart. I told you he'd come."

Audrey Vines, postponing the treat of her favourite brand of sardines until later, dapped mayonnaise on a slice of egg, ate, and wiped her lips. "Don't bark!" she commanded. "There's noise enough as it is." Becoming languidly alert to the accumulating roar, Mia had got on to her bandy legs. A light flashed across the bay window. The roar ceased abruptly. Audrey Vines took a slice of bread as footsteps approached outside, and Mia, her shred of a tail faintly active, trundled to the door. A bell hanging inside had tinkled.

"Open, open!" Mrs Vines' shout from the table was throaty, but strong and even. "Open and come in!"

Rufus paused stiffly on the threshold, his face in profile, his eyes glancing obliquely at the candlelit woman sitting at the table's far end. "I saw your lighted window," he said. The dog returned to the matting after a sniff of his shoes and a brief upward look of approval.

"Thank God I shall not be hearing the noise of that cursed motor cycle on my land much longer. Shut the door, young man, and sit over there."

He shut the door and crossed to the seat Mrs Vines had indicated, the same rough bench placed against a wall between the dresser and the inner door on which he used to sit during happier visits long ago. He sat down and forced himself to gaze slowly down the big kitchen, his eyes ranging over the long, crowded table to the woman in her evening gown, to the single, red jewel on her bare chest, and, at last, to her painted face.

Audrey Vines went on with her meal. The silence continued. A visitor might not have been present. Rufus watched her leisurely selection of a slice of tomato and an olive, the careful unwrapping of foil from cheese. Her two diamond rings sparkled in the candlelight. He had never seen her eating, and this evidence of a normal habit both mesmerized and eased him.

"I've come about the letter."

The words were out, he sat up, taut in justification of complaint. But Mrs Vines seemed not to have heard. She sprinkled pepper and salt on the cheese, cut it into small pieces, and looked consideringly at the untouched sardines in their tin, while the disregarded visitor relapsed into silent watching. Three or four minutes passed before she spoke.

"Are you aware that I could institute a police charge against you for bathing completely naked in the river on my estate?"

It stirred him anew to a bolt-upright posture. "There's nobody to see."

She turned a speculative, heavy-lidded eye in his direction. "Then how do I know about it? Do you consider me nobody?" Yet there was no trace of malevolence as she continued. "You are almost as hairy as an ape. Perhaps you consider that is sufficient covering?" Sedate as a judge in court, she added, "But your organs are exceptionally pronounced."

"Other people don't go about with spying glasses." Anger gave his words a stinging ring.

Turning to the dog, she remarked, "An impudent defence from the hairy bather!" Mia, waiting patiently for the sponge fingers, blinked, and Audrey Vines, reaching for the tin of sardines, said,

154

"People in the trains can see."

"I know the times of the trains."

"You have bathed like that all the summer. You walk to the river from Brychan Cottage unclothed. You did not do this when your parents were alive."

"You never sent me a letter about it."

"I delivered a letter at Brychan Cottage today. *That* covers everything."

There was another silence. Needing time to reassemble his thoughts, he watched as she carefully manipulated a sardine out of the tin with her pointed fingernails. The fish did not break. She held it aloft by its tail end to let oil drip into the tin, and regally tilted her head back and slowly lowered it whole into her mouth. The coral-red lips softly clamped about the disappearing body, drawing it in with appreciation. She chewed with fastidiously dawdling movements. Lifting another fish, she repeated the performance, her face wholly absorbed in her pleasure.

She was selecting a third sardine before Rufus spoke. "I want to go on living in Brychan Cottage," he said, slurring the words. The sardine had disappeared when he continued. "My family always lived in Brychan Cottage. It belonged to us hundreds of years before your family came to Plas Idwal."

"You've been drinking," Audrey Vines said, looking ruminatively over the half-empty plates before her. She did not sound disapproving, but almost amiable. Rufus made no reply. After she had eaten a whole slice of bread, ridding her mouth of sardine taste, she reached for the bottle of champagne. A long time was spent untwisting wire from cork. Her manipulating hands were gentle in the soft yellow candlelight, and in the quiet of deep country night filling the room she seemed just then an ordinary woman sitting in peace over an ordinary meal, a flower from her garden on the table, a faithful dog lying near her chair.

Making a further effort, he repeated, "My family always lived in Brychan Cottage."

"Your disagreeable mother," Audrey Vines responded, "allowed a man to take a photograph of Brychan Cottage. I had sent the creature packing when he called here. The photograph appeared in a ridiculous guidebook. Your mother knew I would not approve of attracting such flashy attention to my estate. My solicitor showed me the book."

Unable to deal with this accusation, he fell into headlong pleading. "I've taken care of the cottage. It's not dirty. I could put new floor boards in downstairs and change the front door. I can cook and do cleaning. The garden is tidy. I'm planning to border the paths with more fruit trees, and – "

"Why did your parents name you Rufus?" she interrupted. "You are dark as night, though your complexion is pale ... and pitted like the moon's surface." The wire was off the cork. "I wonder were you born hairy-bodied?"

He subsided, baffled. As she eased the cork out, there was the same disregard of him. He jerked when the cork shot in his direction. She seemed to smile as the foam spurted and settled delicately in her crystal glass. She took a sip, and another, and spoke to the saliva-dropping dog.

"Your bikkies in a second. Aren't you a nice quiet little Mia! A pity *he* isn't as quiet, darling."

"Got a bottle of whisky with me. Can I take a swig?" The request came in a sudden desperate burst.

"You may."

She watched in turn while he brought the flat, half-sized bottle from inside his windcheater, unscrewed its stopper, and tilted the neck into his mouth. She took further sips of her wine. Absorbed in his own need, Rufus paused for only a moment before returning the neck to his mouth. About half the whisky had been taken when, holding the bottle at the ready between his knees, his eyes met hers across the room's length. She looked away, her lids stiffening. But confidence increased in Rufus.

He repeated, "I want to live in Brychan Cottage all my life."

"You wish to live in Brychan Cottage. I wish to raze it to the ground." A second glass of wine was poured. "So there we are, young man!" She wetted a sponge finger in her wine and handed it to Mia.

"My mother said the cottage and land belonged to us for ever at one time. Your father cheated us out of...." He stopped, realizing his foolishness, and scowled.

"Mia, darling, how you love your drop of champagne!" She dipped another sponge finger; in her obliviousness, she might have been courteously overlooking his slip. "Not good for your rheumatism, though! Oh, you dribbler!"

He took another swig of whisky – a smaller one. He was sitting in Plas Idwal and must not forget himself so far as to get drunk. Settling back against the wall, he stared in wonder at objects on the long table and ventured to ask, "What ... what have you got that skull for? It's a sheep's, isn't it?"

"That? I keep it because it shows pure breeding in its lines and therefore is beautiful. Such sheep are not degenerate, as are so many of their so-called masters. No compulsory education, state welfare services, and social coddling for a sheep!" Rufus' face displayed the blank respect of a modest person hearing academic information beyond his comprehension, and she appended, "The ewe that lived inside that skull was eaten alive by blowfly maggots. I found her under a hedge below Mynydd Baer." She finished her second glass, and poured a third.

As though in sociable alliance, he allowed himself another mouthful of whisky. Awareness of his gaffe about her cheating father kept him from returning to the subject of the cottage at once. He was prepared to remain on the bench for hours; she seemed not to mind his visit. His eyes did not stray from her any more; every trivial move she made held his attention now. She reached for a fancy biscuit tin and closely studied the white roses painted on its shiny blue side. He waited. The silence became acceptable. It belonged to the late hour and this house and the mystery of Mrs Vines' ways.

Audrey Vines laid the biscuit tin down unopened, and slowly ran a finger along the lace tablecloth, like a woman preoccupied with arriving at a resolve. "If you are dissatisfied with the leasehold deeds of Brychan Cottage," she began, "I advise you to consult a solicitor. Daniel Lewis welcomes such small business, I believe. You will find his office behind the Assembly Hall. You have been remarkably lackadaisical in this matter.... No, *not* remarkably, since he is as he is! He should live in a tree." She had turned to Mia.

"I don't want to go to a solicitor." After a pause, he mumbled, half sulkily, "Can't ... can't we settle it between us?"

She looked up. Their eyes met again. The bright ruby on her chest flashed as she purposelessly moved a dish on the table. But the roused expectancy in Rufus' glistening eyes did not fade. After a moment, he tilted the bottle high into his mouth, and withdrew it with a look of extreme surprise. It was empty.

Audrey Vines drank more wine. Then, rapping the words out, she demanded, "How much rent are you prepared to pay me for the cottage?"

Rufus gaped in wonder. Had Evan Matthews been right, then, in saying that nothing was final with women? He put the whisky bottle down on the bench and offered the first sum in his mind. "A pound a week?"

Audrey Vines laughed. It was a hoarse sound, cramped and discordant in her throat. She straightened a leaning candle and spoke with the incisiveness of a nimble businesswoman addressing a foolish client. "Evidently you know nothing of property values, young man. My estate is one of the most attractive in this part of Wales. A Londoner needing weekend seclusion would pay ten pounds a week for my cottage, with fishing rights."

It had become 'my cottage'. Rufus pushed a hand into his sweat-damp black hair, and mumbled, "Best to have a man you know near by you on the estate."

"For a pound! I fail to see the advantage I reap."

"Thirty shillings, then? I'm only drawing a clear nine pounds in Nelson's factory." Without guile, he sped on, "Haven't got enough training yet to be put on the machines, you see! They've kept me in the packing room with the learners."

"That I can well believe. Nevertheless, you can afford to buy a motor cycle and flasks of whisky." She clattered a plate on to another. "My cottage would be rent-free to the right man. Would you like a couple of sardines with your whisky?"

The abrupt invitation quenched him once more. He lowered his head, scowling, his thighs wide apart. His hands gripped his knees. There was a silence. When he looked up, she was straining her pencilled eyes towards him, as though their sight had become blurred. But now he could not look at her in return. His gaze focused on the three candle flames to the left of her head.

"Well, sardines or not?"

"No," he answered, almost inaudibly.

"Grind me some coffee, then," she rapped, pointing to the handle-topped wooden box on the table. "There are beans in it. Put a little water in the kettle on one of those oil stoves. Matches are here. Coffeepot on the dresser." She dabbed her lips with her napkin, looking at the stain they left, and refilled her glass.

He could no longer respond in any way to these changes of mood. He neither moved nor spoke. Reality had faded, the kitchen itself became less factual, objects on the table insubstantially remote. Only the woman's face drew and held his eyes. But Audrey Vines seemed not to notice this semi-paralysis; she was allowing a slow-thinking man time to obey her command. She spoke a few words to Mia. She leaned forward to reach for a lacquered box, and took from it a pink cigarette. As she rose to light the gold-tipped cigarette at a candle, he said, "Brychan Cottage always belonged to my family."

"He keeps saying that!" she said to Mia, sighing and sitting back. Reflective while she smoked, she had an air of waiting for coffee to be served, a woman retreated into the securities of the distant past, when everybody ran to her bidding.

"What do you want, then?" His voice came from deep in his chest, the words flat and earnest in his need to know.

The mistress of Plas Idwal did not reply for a minute. Her gaze was fixed on the closely woven flower in its silver vase. And a strange transformation came to her lulled face. The lineaments of a girl eased its contours, bringing a smooth texture to the skin, clothing the stark bones with a pastel-like delicacy of fine young flesh. An apparition, perhaps an inhabitant of her reverie, was fugitively in possession.

"I want peace and quiet," she whispered.

His head had come forward. He saw the extraordinary transformation. Like the dissolving reality of the room, it had the nature of an hallucination. His brows puckering in his efforts to concentrate, to find exactness, he slowly sat back, and asked, "You want me to stay single? Then I can keep Brychan Cottage?"

In a sudden, total extinction of control, her face became contorted into an angry shape of wrinkled flesh. Her eyes blazed almost sightlessly. She threw the cigarette on the floor and screamed, "Did you think I was going to allow that slut to live there? Braying and squealing on my estate like a prostitute!" Her loud breathing was that of someone about to vomit.

With the same flat simplicity, he said, "Gloria is not a prostitute." "Gloria! Good God, *Gloria!* How far in idiocy can they go? Why not Cleopatra? I don't care a hair of your stupid head what happens to you and that wretched creature. You are not going to get the cottage. I'll burn it to the ground rather than have you and that born prostitute in it!" Her hands began to grasp at plates and cutlery on the table, in a blind semblance of the act of clearing them. "Stupid lout, coming here! By the autumn there won't be a stone of that cottage left. Not a stone, you hear!"

Her demented goading held such pure hatred that it seemed devoid of connection with him. She had arrived at the fringe of sane consciousness; her gaze fixed on nothing, she was aware only of a dim figure hovering down the room, beyond the throw of candlelight. "The thirtieth of June, you hear? Or the police will be called to turn you out!"

He had paused for a second at the far end of the table, near the door. His head was averted. Four or five paces away from him lay release into the night. But he proceeded in her direction, advancing as though in deferential shyness, his head still half turned away, a hand sliding along the table. He paused again, took up the coffee grinder, looked at it vaguely, and lowered it to the table. It crashed on the stone floor.

She became aware of the accosting figure. The screaming did not diminish. "Pick that thing up! You've broken it, clumsy fool, Pick it up!"

He looked round uncertainly, not at her but at the uncurtained bay window giving on to the spaces of night. He did not stoop for the grinder.

"*Pick it up!*" The mounting howl swept away the last hesitation in him. He went towards her unwaveringly.

She sat without a movement until he was close to her. He stopped, and looked down at her. Something like a compelled obedience was in the crouch of his shoulders. Her right hand moved, grasping the tablecloth fringe into a tight fistful. She made no attempt to speak, but an articulation came into the exposed face that was lifted to him. From the glaze of her eyes, from deep in unfathomable misery, came entreaty. He was the chosen one. He alone held the power of deliverance. He saw it, and in that instant of mutual recognition his hand grasped the heavy candelabra and lifted it high. Its three flames blew out in the swiftness of the plunge. There was a din of objects crashing to the floor from the tugged tablecloth. When he rose from beside the fallen chair and put the candelabra down, the whimpering dog followed him in the darkness to the door, as though pleading with this welcome visitor not to go.

He left the motor bike outside the back garden gate of Brychan Cottage, walked along a wicker fence and, near the river, jumped across the ditch on to Plas Idwal land. Presently, he reached a spot where, long before he was born, the river had been widened and deepened to form an ornamental pool. A rotting summer-house, impenetrable under wild creeper, overlooked it, and a pair of stone urns marked a short flight of weed-hidden steps. The soft water, which in daytime was as blue as the distant mountain range where lay its source, flowed through in lingering eddies. He had sometimes bathed in this prohibited pool late at night; below Brychan Cottage the river was much less comfortable for swimming.

He undressed without haste, and jumped into the pool with a quick and acrobatically high leap. He swam underwater, rose, and went under again, in complete ablution. When he stood up beside the opposite bank, where the glimmering water reached to his chest, he relaxed his arms along the grassy verge and remained for moments looking at the enormous expanse of starry sky, away from the mansion dimly outlined above the pool.

He was part of the anonymous liberty of the night. This bathe was the completion of an act of mastery. The river was his; returning to its depths, he was assimilated into it. He flowed downstream a little way and, where the water became shallow, sat up. His left hand spread on pebbles below, he leaned negligently there, like a deity of pools and streams risen in search of possibilities in the night. He sat unmoving for several minutes. The supple water running over his loins began to feel much colder. It seemed to clear his mind of tumult.

Slowly, he turned his head towards the mansion.

He saw her face in the last flare of the candles, and now he knew why she had tormented him. She had been waiting long for his arrival. The knowledge lodged, certain and tenacious, in his mind. Beyond his wonder at her choice, it brought, too, some easing of the terror threatening him. Further his mind would not go; he retreated from thinking of the woman lying alone in the darkness of that mansion up there. He knew she was dead. Suddenly, he rose, waded to the bank, and strode to where his clothes lay.

His movements took on the neatness and dispatch of a man acting entirely on a residue of memory. He went to Brychan Cottage only to dry and dress himself in the kitchen. When he got to the town, all lamps had been extinguished in the deserted streets. The bike tore into the private hush of an ancient orderliness. He did not turn into the route he had taken earlier that night but drove on at top speed through the market place. Behind the medieval Assembly Hall, down a street of municipal offices and timbered old houses in which legal business was done, a blue lamp shone alight. It jutted clearly from the porch of a stone building, and the solid door below yielded to his push.

Inside, a bald-headed officer sitting at a desk glanced up in mild surprise at this visitor out of the peaceful night, and, since the young man kept silent, asked, "Well, what can we do for you?"

BRENDA CHAMBERLAIN

The Return

It isn't as if the Captain took reasonable care of himself," said the postmaster.

"No," she answered. She was on guard against anything he might say.

"A man needs to be careful with a lung like that," said the postmaster.

"Yes," she said. She waited for sentences to be laid like baited traps. They watched one another for the next move. The man lifted a two-ounce weight from the counter and dropped it with fastidious fingers into the brass scale. As the tray fell, the woman sighed. A chink in her armour. He breathed importantly and spread his hands on the counter. From pressure on the palms, dark veins stood up under the skin on the backs of his hands. He leaned his face to the level of her eyes. Watching him, her mouth fell slightly open.

"The Captain's lady is very nice indeed; Mrs Morrison is a charming lady. Have you met his wife, Mrs Ritsin?"

"No," she answered; "she has not been to the Island since I came." She could not prevent a smile flashing across her eyes at her own stupidity. Why must she have said just that, a ready-made sentence that could be handed on without distortion. She has not been to the Island since I came. Should she add: no doubt she will be over soon; then I shall have the pleasure of meeting her? The words would not come. The postmaster lodged the sentence carefully in his brain to be retailed to the village.

They watched one another. She, packed with secrets behind that innocent face, damn her, why couldn't he worm down the secret passages of her mind? Why had she come here in the first place, this

Mrs Ritsin? Like a doll, so small and delicate, she made you want to hit or pet her, according to your nature. She walked with small strides, as if she owned the place, as if she was on equal terms with man and the sea. Her eyes disturbed something in his nature that could not bear the light. They were large, they looked farther than any other eyes he had seen. They shone with a happiness that he thought indecent in the circumstances.

Everyone knew, the whole village gloated and hummed over the fact that Ceridwen had refused to live on the Island and that she herself was a close friend of Alec Morrison. But why, she asked herself, why did she let herself fall into their cheap traps? The sentence would be repeated almost without a word being altered, but the emphasis, O my God, the stressing of the *I*, to imply a malicious woman's triumph. But all this doesn't really matter, she told herself, at least it won't once I am back there. The Island. She saw it float in front of the postmaster's face. The rocks were clear and the hovering, wind-swung birds; she saw them clearly in front of the wrinkles and clefts on his brow and chin. He coughed discreetly and shrugged with small deprecatory movements of the shoulders. He wished she would not stare at him as if he was a wall or invisible. If she was trying to get at his secrets she could try till crack of doom. All the same. As a precautionary measure he slid aside and faced the window.

"Seems as though it will be too risky for you to go back this evening," he said; "there's a bit of fog about. You'll be stopping the night in Porthbychan?"

"– and he wouldn't let her go on holiday in the winter: said, if she did, he'd get a concubine to keep him warm, and he meant –"

A woman was talking to her friend outside the door.

"You cannot possibly cross the Race alone in this weather, Mrs Ritsin," persisted the postmaster.

"I must get back tonight, Mr Davies."

He sketched the bay with a twitching arm, as if to say: I have bound the restless wave. He became confidential, turning to stretch across the counter.

"My dear Mrs Ritsin, no woman has ever before navigated these waters. Why, even on a calm day the Porthbychan fishers will not enter the Race. Be warned, dear lady. Imagine my feelings if you were to be washed up on the beach, here."

Bridget Ritsin said, "I am afraid it is most important that I should get back tonight, Mr Davies."

Ann Pritchard from the corner house slid from the glittering evening into the shadows of the post office. She spoke out of the dusk behind the door. "It isn't right for a woman to ape a man, doing a man's work."

"Captain Morrison is ill. He couldn't possibly come across today. That is why I'm in charge of the boat," Bridget answered.

Two other women had slipped in against the wall of the shop. Now, four pairs of eyes bored into her face. With sly insolence the women threw ambiguous sentences to the postmaster, who smiled as he studied the grain in the wood of his counter. Bridget picked up a bundle of letters and turned to go. "The tide will be about right now," she said. "Good evening, Mr Davies."

"Be very, very careful, Mrs Ritsin, and remember me to the Captain."

Laughter followed her into the street. It was like dying in agony, while crowds danced and mocked. O, my darling, my darling over the cold waves. She knew that while she was away he would try to do too much about the house. He would go to the well for water, looking over the fields he lacked strength to drain. He would be in the yard, chopping sticks. He would cough and spit blood. "It isn't as if the Captain took reasonable care of himself." When he ran too hard, when he moved anything heavy and lost his breath, he only struck his chest and cursed: "Blast my lung." "Alec dear, you should not run so fast up the mountain." He never heeded her. He had begun to spit blood.

By the bridge over the river, her friend Griff Owen was leaning against the side of a motor-car, talking to a man and woman in the front seats. He said to them, "Ask her", as she came past.

"Excuse me, Miss, could you take us over to see the Island?"

"I'm sorry," she said, "there's a storm coming up. It wouldn't be possible to make the double journey."

They eyed her, curious about her way of life.

Griff Owen, and the grocer's boy carrying two boxes of provisions, came down to the beach with her.

"I wouldn't be you; going to be a dirty night," said the man.

The waves were chopped and the headland was vague with hanging cloud. The two small islets in the bay were behind curtains of vapour. The sea was blurred and welcomeless. To the Island, to the Island. Here in the village, you opened a door: laughter and filthy jokes buzzed in your face. They stung and blinded. O my love, be patient, I am coming back to you, quickly, quickly, over the waves.

The grocer's boy put down the provisions on the sand near the tide edge. Immediately a shallow pool formed round the bottoms of the boxes.

"Wind seems to be dropping," said Griff.

"Yes, but I think there will be fog later on," she answered, "sea fog." She turned to him. "Oh, Griff, you are always so kind to me. What would we do without you?"

He laid a hand on her shoulder. "Tell me, how is the Captain feeling in himself? I don't like the thought of him being so far from the doctor."

"The doctor can't do very much for him. Living in the clean air from the sea is good. These days he isn't well, soon he may be better. Don't worry, he is hanging on to life and the Island." They began to push the boat down over rollers towards the water. Last week Alec had said quite abruptly as he was stirring the boiled potatoes for the ducks: "At least, you will have this land if I die."

At least, I have the Island.

"Well, well," said the man, making an effort to joke; "tell the Captain from me that I'll come over to see him if he comes for me himself. Tell him I wouldn't trust my life to a lady, even though the boat has got a good engine and knows her way home."

He shook her arm: "You are a stout girl."

"Mr Davies coming down," said the boy, looking over his shoulder as he heaved on the side of the boat. The postmaster came on to the beach through the narrow passage between the hotel and the churchyard. His overcoat flapped round him in the wind. He had something white in his hand. The boat floated; Bridget waded out and stowed away her provisions and parcels. By the time she had made a second journey Mr Davies was at the water's edge.

"Another letter for you, Mrs Ritsin," he said. "Very sorry, it had got behind the old-age-pension books." He peered at her, longing to know what was in the letter, dying to find out what her feelings would be when she saw the handwriting. He had already devoured the envelope with his eyes, back and front, reading the postmark and the two sentences written in pencil at the back. He knew it was a letter from Ceridwen to her husband.

"A letter for the Captain," said the postmaster, and watched her closely.

"Thank you." She took it, resisting the temptation to read the words that caught her eye on the back of the envelope. She put it away in the large pocket of her oilskin along with the rest.

The postmaster sucked in his cheeks and mumbled something. "So Mrs Morrison will be back here soon," he suddenly shot at her. Only the grocer's boy, whistling as he kicked the shingle, did not respond to what he said. Griff looked from her to the postmaster, she studied the postmaster's hypocritical smile. Her head went up, she was able to smile: "Oh, yes, of course, Mrs Morrison is sure to come over when the weather is better." What did he know, why should he want to know?

It was like a death; every hour that she had to spend on the mainland gave her fresh wounds.

"Thank you, Mr Davies. Good-bye Griff, see you next week if the weather isn't too bad." She climbed into the motor-boat and weighed anchor. She bent over the engine and it began to live. The grocer's boy was drifting away, still kicking the beach as if he bore it a grudge. Mr Davies called in a thin voice "… great care … wish you would … the Race and …"

Griff waved and roared like a horn: "Tell him I'll take the next calf if it is a good one."

It was his way of wishing her God-speed. Linking the moment's hazard to the safety of future days.

She waved her hand. The men grew small, they and the gravestones of blue and green slate clustered round the medieval church at the top of the sand. The village drew into itself, fell into perspective against the distant mountains.

It was lonely in the bay. She took comfort from the steady throbbing of the engine. She drew Ceridwen's letter from her pocket,

She read: "If it is *very* fine, Auntie Grace and I will come over next week-end. Arriving Saturday tea-time Porthbychan. Please meet."

Now she understood what Mr Davies had been getting at. Ceridwen and the aunt. She shivered suddenly and felt the flesh creeping on her face and arms. The sea was bleak and washed of colour under the shadow of a long roll of mist that stretched from the level of the water almost to the sun. It was nine o'clock in the evening. She could not reach the anchorage before ten and, though it was summertime, darkness would have fallen before she reached home. She hoped Alec's dog would be looking out for her on the headland.

The wind blew fresh, but the wall of mist did not seem to move at all. She wondered if Penmaen du and the mountain would be visible when she rounded the cliffs into the Race. Soon now she should be able to see the Island mountain. She knew every Islandman would sooner face a storm than fog.

So Ceridwen wanted to come over, did she? For the week-end, and with the aunt's support. Perhaps she had heard at last that another woman was looking after her sick husband that she did not want but over whom she was jealous as a tigress. The weekend was going to be merry hell. Bridget realized that she was very tired.

The mainland, the islets, the cliff-top farms of the peninsula fell away. Porpoise rolling offshore towards the Race made her heart lift for their companionship.

She took a compass-bearing before she entered the white silence of the barren wall of fog. Immediately she was both trapped and free. Trapped because it was still daylight and yet she was denied sight, as if blindness had fallen, not blindness where everything is dark, but blindness where eyes are filled with vague light and they strain helplessly. Is it that I cannot see, is this blindness? The horror was comparable to waking on a black winter night and being unable to distinguish anything, until in panic she thought, has my sight gone? And free because the mind could build images on walls of mist, her spirit could lose itself in tunnels of vapour.

The sound of the motor-boat's engine was monstrously exaggerated by the fog. Like a giant heart it pulsed: thump, thump. There was a faint echo, as if another boat, a ghost ship, moved near by. Her mind had too much freedom in these gulfs.

The motor-boat began to pitch like a bucking horse. She felt depth upon depth of water underneath the boards on which her feet were braced. It was the Race. The tide poured across her course. The brightness of cloud reared upward from the water's face. Not that it was anywhere uniform in density; high up there would suddenly be a thinning, a tearing apart of vapour with a wan high blue showing through, and once the jaundiced, weeping sun was partly visible, low in the sky, which told her that she was still on the right bearing. There were grey-blue caverns of shadow that seemed like patches of land, but they were effaced in new swirls of cloud, or came about her in imprisoning walls, tunnels along which the boat moved only to find nothingness at the end. Unconsciously, she had gritted her teeth when she ran into the fog-bank. Her tension remained. Two ghosts were beside her in the boat, Ceridwen, in a white fur coat, was sitting amidships and facing her, huddled together, cold and unhappy in the middle of the boat, her knees pressed against the casing of the engine. Alec's ghost sat in the bows. As a figurehead he leaned away from her, his face half lost in opaque cloud.

"I will get back safely, I will get home," she said aloud, looking ahead to make the image of Ceridwen fade. But the phantom persisted; it answered her spoken thought.

"No, you'll drown, you won't ever reach the anchorage. The dogfish will have you."

"I tell you I can do it. He's waiting for me, he needs me."

Alec turned round, his face serious. "When you get across the Race, if you can hear the foghorn," he said quietly, "you are on the wrong tack. If you can't hear it, you're all right; it means you are cruising safely along the foot of the cliffs.... When you get home, will you come to me, be my little wife?"

"Oh, my dear," she answered, "I could weep or laugh that you ask me now, here. Yes, if I get home."

"Soon you'll be on the cold floor of the sea," said Ceridwen.

Spouts of angry water threatened the boat that tossed sideways. Salt sprays flew over her.

"Careful, careful," warned Alec. "We are nearly on Pen Cader, the rocks are near now, we are almost out of the Race."

A seabird flapped close to her face, then with a cry swerved away, its claws pressed backwards.

Above the noise of the engine there was now a different sound, that of water striking land. For an instant she saw the foot of a black cliff. Wet fangs snapped at her. Vicious fangs, how near they were. Shaken by the sight, by the rock death that waited, she turned the boat away from the Island. She gasped as she saw white spouting foam against the black and slimy cliff. She was once more alone. Alec and Ceridwen, leaving her to the sea, had been sucked into the awful cloud, this vapour without substance or end. She listened for the foghorn. No sound from the lighthouse. A break in the cloud above her head drew her eyes. A few yards of the mountaintop of the Island was visible, seeming impossibly high, impossibly green and homely. Before the eddying mists rejoined, she saw a thin shape trotting across the steep grass slope, far, far up near the crest of the hill. Leaning forward, she said aloud: "O look, the dog." It was Alec's dog keeping watch for her. The hole in the mist closed up, the shroud fell thicker than ever. It was terrible, this loneliness, this groping that seemed as if it might go on for ever.

Then she heard the low-throated blaring into the fog. It came from somewhere on her right hand. So in avoiding the rocks she had put out too far to sea and had overshot the anchorage. She must be somewhere off the southern headland near the pirate's rock. She passed a line of lobster floats.

She decided to stop the engine and anchor where she was, hoping that the fog would clear at nightfall. Then she would be able to return on to her proper course. There was an unnatural silence after she had cut off the engine. Water knocked against the boat.

Cold seeped into her bones from the planks. With stiff wet hands she opened the bag of provisions, taking off the crust of a loaf and spreading butter on it with her gutting knife. As she ate, she found that for the first time in weeks she had leisure in which to review her life. For when she was on the farm it was eat, work, sleep, eat, work, sleep, in rotation.

I have sinned or happiness is not for me, she thought. It was her heart's great weakness that she could not rid herself of superstitious beliefs.

Head in hands, she asked: But how have I sinned? I didn't steal another woman's husband. They had already fallen apart when I first met Alec. Is too great happiness itself a sin? Surely it's only because I am frightened of the fog that I ask, have I sinned, is this my punishment? When the sun shines I take happiness with both hands. Perhaps it's wrong to be happy when half the people of the world are chainbound and hungry, cut off from the sun. If you scratch below the surface of most men's minds you find that they are bleeding inwardly. Men want to destroy themselves. It is their only hope. Each one secretly nurses the death-wish, to be god and mortal in one; not to die at nature's order, but to cease on his own chosen day. Man has destroyed so much that only the destruction of all life will satisfy him.

How can it be important whether I am happy or unhappy? And yet it's difficult for me to say, I am only one, what does my fate matter? For I want to be fulfilled like other women. What have I done to be lost in winding sheets of fog?

And he will be standing in the door wondering that I do not come.

For how long had she sat in the gently rocking boat? It was almost dark and her eyes smarted from constant gazing. Mist weighed against her eyeballs. She closed her eyes for relief.

Something was staring at her. Through drawn lids she felt the steady glance of a sea-creature. She looked at the darkening waves. Over an area of a few yards she could see; beyond, the wave was cloud, the cloud was water. A dark, wet-gleaming thing on the right. It disappeared before she could make out what it was. And then, those brown beseeching eyes of the seal cow. She had risen near by, her mottled head scarcely causing a ripple. Lying on her back in the grey-green gloom of the sea she waves her flippers now outwards to the woman, now inwards to her white breast, saying, come to me, come to me, to the caverns where shark bones lie like tree stumps, bleached, growth-ringed like trees.

Mother seal, seal cow. The woman stretched out her arms. The attraction of those eyes was almost strong enough to draw her to salt death. The head disappeared. The dappled back turned over in the opaque water, and dived. Bridget gripped the side of the boat, praying that this gentle visitant should not desert her.

Hola, hola, hola, seal mother from the eastern cave.

Come to me, come to me, come to me. The stone-grey head reappeared on the other side, on her left. Water ran off the whiskered face, she showed her profile; straight nose, and above, heavy lids drooping over melancholy eyes. When she plunged, showing off her prowess, a sheen of pearly colours ran over the sleek body.

They watched one another until the light failed to penetrate the fog. After the uneasy summer twilight had fallen, the woman was still aware of the presence of the seal. She dozed off into a shivering sleep through which she heard faintly the snorting of the sea creature. A cold, desolate sound. Behind that again was the bull-throated horn bellowing into the night.

She dreamed: Alec was taking her up the mountain at night under a sky dripping with blood. Heaven was on fire. Alec was gasping for breath. The other islanders came behind, their long shadows stretching down the slope. The mountain top remained far off. She never reached it.

Out of dream, she swam to consciousness, painfully leaving the dark figures of fantasy. A sensation of swimming upwards through fathoms of water. The sea of her dreams was dark and at certain levels between sleeping and waking a band of light ran across the waves. Exhaustion made her long to fall back to the sea-floor of oblivion, but the pricking brain floated her at last on to the surface of morning.

She awoke with a great wrenching gasp that flung her against the gunwhale. Wind walked the sea. The fog had gone, leaving the world raw and disenchanted in the false dawn. Already, gulls were crying for a new day. Wet and numb with cold, the woman looked about her. At first it was impossible to tell off what shore the boat was lying. For a few minutes it was enough to know that she was after all at anchor so close to land.

Passing down the whole eastern coastline, she had rounded the south end and was a little way past Mallt's bay on the west. The farmhouse, home, seemed near across the foreshortened fields. Faint light showed in the kitchen window, a warm glow in the grey landscape. It was too early for the other places, Goppa, Pen Isaf, to show signs of life. Field, farm, mountain, sea and sky. What a simple world. And below the undercurrents.

Mechanically she started up the engine and raced round to the anchorage through mounting sea spray and needles of rain.

She made the boat secure against rising wind, then trudged through seaweed and shingle, carrying the supplies up into the boat-house. She loitered inside after putting down the bags of food. Being at last out of the wind, no longer pitched and tumbled on the sea, made her feel that she was in a vacuum. Wind howled and thumped at the walls. Tears of salt water raced down the body of a horse scratched long ago on the window by Alec. Sails stacked under the roof shivered in the draught forced under the slates. She felt that she was spinning wildly in some mad dance. The floor rose and fell as the waves had done. The earth seemed to slide away and come up again under her feet. She leant on the windowsill, her forehead pressed to the pane. Through a crack in the glass wind poured in a cold stream across her cheek. Nausea rose in her against returning to the shore for the last packages. After that there would be almost the length of the Island to walk. At the thought she straightened herself, rubbing the patch of skin on her forehead where pressure on the window had numbed it. She fought her way down to the anchorage. Spume blew across the rocks, covering her sea boots. A piece of wrack was blown into the wet tangle of her hair. Picking up the bag of provisions, she began the return journey. Presently she stopped, put down the bag, and went again to the waves. She had been so long with them that now the thought of going inland was unnerving. Wading out until water swirled round her knees she stood relaxed, bending like a young tree under the wind's weight. Salt was crusted on her lips and hair. Her feet were sucked by outdrawn shingle. She no longer wished to struggle but to let a wave carry her beyond the world.

"I want sleep," she said to the sea. "O God, I am so tired, so tired." The sea sobbed, sleep, the wind mourned, sleep.

Oystercatchers flying in formation, a pattern of black and white and scarlet, screamed: we are St Bride's birds, we saved Christ, we rescued the Saviour.

A fox-coloured animal was coming over the weedy rocks of the point. It was the dog, shivering and mist-soaked as if he had been out all night. He must have been lying in a cranny and so missed greeting her when she had landed. He fawned about her feet, barking unhappily.

They went home together, passing Pen Isaf that slept; Goppa too. It was about four o'clock of a summer daybreak. She picked two mushrooms glowing in their own radiance. Memories came of her first morning's walk on the Island. There had been a green and lashing sea and gullies of damp rock, and parsley fern among loose stones. Innocent beginning, uncomplicated, shadowless. As if looking on the dead from the pinnacle of experience, she saw herself as she had been.

She opened the house door: a chair scraped inside. Alec stood in the kitchen, white with strain and illness.

"So you did come," he said dully.

"Yes," she said with equal flatness, putting down the bags.

How sick, how deathly he looked.

"Really, you shouldn't have sat up all night for me." He stirred the pale ashes; a fine white dust arose.

"Look, there's still fire, and the kettle's hot." He coughed. They drank the tea in silence, standing far apart. Her eyes never left his face. And the sea lurched giddily under her braced feet. Alec went and sat before the hearth. Bridget came up behind his chair and pressed her cheek to his head. She let her arms fall slackly round his neck. Her hands hung over his chest. Tears grew in her eyes, brimming the lower lids so that she could not see. They splashed on to his clenched fists. He shuddered a little. Without turning his head, he said: "Your hair's wet. You must be tired."

"Yes," she said, "so tired. Almost worn out."

"Come, let us go to bed for an hour or two."

"You go up," she answered, moving away into the back kitchen; "I must take off my wet clothes first."

"Don't be long. Promise me you won't be long." He got up out of the wicker chair, feeling stiff and old, to be near her where she leant against the slate table. One of her hands was on the slate, the other was peeling off her oilskin trousers.

He said: "Don't cry. I can't bear it if you cry."

"I'm not, I'm not. Go to bed, please."

"I thought you would never get back."

She took the bundle of letters out of the inner pocket of her coat and put them on the table. She said: "There's one for you from Ceridwen."

"Never mind about the letters. Come quickly to me." She stood naked in the light that spread unwillingly from sea and sky. Little channels of moisture ran down her flanks, water dripped from her hair over the points of her breasts. As she reached for a towel he watched the skin stretch over the fragile ribs. He touched her thigh with his fingers, almost a despairing gesture. She looked at him shyly, and, swiftly bending, began to dry her feet. Shaking as if from ague, she thought her heart's beating would be audible to him.

He walked abruptly away from her, went upstairs. The boards creaked in his bedroom.

Standing in the middle of the floor surrounded by wet clothes, she saw through the window how colour was slowly draining back into the world. It came from the sea, into the wild irises near the well, into the withy beds in the corner of the field. Turning, she went upstairs in the brightness of her body.

He must have fallen asleep as soon as he lay down. His face was bleached, the bones too clearly visible under the flesh. Dark folds of skin lay loosely under his eyes. Now that the eyes were hidden, his face was like a death-mask. She crept quietly into bed beside him.

Through the open window came the lowing of cattle. The cows belonging to Goppa were being driven up for milking. Turning towards the sleeping man, she put her left hand on his hip. He did not stir.

She cried then as if she would never be able to stop, the tears gushing down from her eyes until the pillow was wet and stained from her weeping.

What will become of us, what will become of us?

RON BERRY

Rosebud Prosser

It was stiffening cold. A driving north-east wind carried stinging dust from derelict Hafod colliery. The rusted winding gear, screens and railway siding squatted inside a triangle of slag tips. Fine location for council houses, ideal environment, all sweetness and light. Off at a dog-leg from the siding, Sebon Lakes are full of caked slurry. Two small kidney-shaped lakes, once the tranquil roach pools of boyhood generations, NCB filter beds for twenty years, abandoned when they closed Hafod. Here in South Wales, we have been civilised by utility pollution and sincere blight.

Three hundred council houses, forty-eight-year-old Ivor Prosser, the foreman carpenter, green slouch hat slanted above his peacock eyes, thin wide mouth below a dago moustache, and the swagger of vanity. Vanity slippery as terrazzo.

"Dai Sam, how's progress up there?" he shouted.

We were fixing ceiling joists and noggins in a block of four houses. From the wall plate I saw him down below, his gloved hands fisted in the pockets of a company donkey coat. Slag dust tamping off the brickwork, hissed all day like seeds.

"We're on target unless you interfere," I said.

"Dai, I need your labourer!"

Still in his teens, a drop-out from Newport Art College, our labourer had the attitude of a self-trained loner. "Ivor," I said, "you can't take Musketeer away now, not after he's done all the hard graft on this block. He's been humping four by twos since we came on the job this morning."

"Emergency!" yelled Ivor. He crab-walked, straddling himself across a narrow conduit trench in the frozen mud. "Wocky's

176

unloading cement! For God's sake listen to me! Essential we unload that stuff before knocking off time!"

I said, "Find another bloke."

"Point blank refusal to co-operate! No damn principle! Me and you, we travel in the cab with Wocky!" He spun away from the wind, threatening, "Al'right, Dai Sam, no more favours!"

The following week we were roofing. Four chippies sharing bonus. Casual Musketeer, he dropped my hammer down a wall cavity. We lost money while I blindly fiddled and failed to hook the hammer with a length of wire. I had to leave it there, a fine clawed, nicely balanced hammer. From Musketeer came, "Sorry, Dai. Hey um, how much do I owe you?"

"Too much," I said.

But thank God the north-east wind eased. Human nature is caricatured by extreme climates.

"Snow forecast," Wocky said, gearing down for the climb up Heol Gwyn mountain. On crystal mornings you can see the Bristol Channel from the top of Heol Gwyn, glimmering flat in the distance, twenty odd miles away. Originally a shank's pony track, Heol Gwyn rises two thousand feet above sea level, with horseshoe and hairpin bends each side of the barren summit.

"Ha, snow, good for the soil," Ivor said. He blabbed exaggerations and lies about horticulture. The Prosser family were indoctrinated by a grandfather who worked for settlement Quakers during the Depression.

Behind us in the lorry, twelve blokes were huddled under a plastic canopy. Every day two lorries grinding up and over Heol Gwyn. Red lorries, yellow canopies.

"Slam your foot down, it's quarter to eight," urged Ivor, delirious, the way big fish madden themselves in small ponds.

Wocky dry-spat disgust. "Shurrup. My wagon, this. I'm responsible. You, you couldn't drive a pram." Blunt Wocky (Cynlais) Eynon, a born and bred industrialised Celt.

Ivor grinned indulgence. "Where were you drinking last night, Cynlais?"

"Same place."

"Where though, man, where?"

. Wocky elbowed him. "Don't keep on. Shift over a bit. I can't get at the stick."

Ivor crowded me against the cab door. Wocky pushed into high as we cleared the brow, slid into a cutting between low drystone walls holding back peat bogs, then began the long twisting run down hill.

At five to eight we piled out of the lorries. By ten o'clock the first flurries of snow sprinkled Hafod slag tips. Next day the same, sudsy flakes wandering from a gun-metal grey sky. Sleet froze on Heol Gwyn. Council workmen sprayed rock salt.

Thursday morning, Wocky promised, "We'll get it today."

Ivor laughed, gay as a bandit.

Anyhow, the world turned white by lunch-time.

"There it is," Wocky said, dummying a half-nelson on Ivor to make him look up at Heol Gwyn. "Means we'll have to go round-about. Across Sebon Common and up the other valley. Forty miles. Hour and a quarter each way."

"We'll make it over the mountain," insisted Ivor. He grabbed my arm. "I'll pay this Dai Sam to gallop behind us with a whip."

Wocky sneered, "Your mouth's in the wrong fuckin' place, mate."

"Hush't, don't panic. I'll sort things out with the general foreman." Ivor's promise guaranteed nothing. They were still arguing an hour later, the G.F., the firm's agent, two card stewards and Ivor Prosser. Of course the G.F. and the agent didn't have to cross Heol Gwyn before putting their feet under the table.

All in all a shabby housing contract. Brickies, chippies and labourers came and went like shy, troubled birds. Sure sign of a cut-throat firm.

So, at ten past three our lorries pulled away from outside the site office, through a few inches of snow, winter's soft blanket fall, which tilted, came slashing horizontally as we climbed Heol Gwyn.

"Them wipers pack in and I'm beat," said Wocky, leaning forward, twitchy-eyed, snowflakes ragged as wet cotton sedge smudging across the windscreen.

"Mush! Mush!" cried Ivor.

Sullen Wocky, he said, "Clever waster you are."

Lighting his slim-line pipe, Ivor sucked and whoofed tobacco smoke. "Men, listen, we ought to arrange a Saturday night on the beer. Just the three of us."

I recommended the Footbridge Arms.

"Right! Bring some birds in. Through and through in the snug," boasted Ivor.

Wocky huffed, muttering to himself, "By the Jesus Christ, hark at him."

We were crawling now, up into blizzard weather, Wocky on his feet, reaching out his arm, clearing the windscreen with his cap, Ivor shrinking from the draught, pipe jiggling in his teeth, his collar drawn up to the slouch hat.

Vicious umbrage from Wocky. "Where's the bloody road? I can't see the marker stones." Pause: "Come on, Charlie, c'mon-c'mon." Charlie drove the second lorry, tailing us, blurred as a war machine in the white welter.

"Footbridge Arms next Saturday night," confirmed Ivor. "Let me tell you from personal experience, there's no price to leisure time. Regardless of expense, every man should have his fair whack."

"Whattew smokin', old socks?" asked Wocky.

Ivor sang, "*Everybody loves Saturday night, everybody loves Saturday night, Everybody everybody everybody everybody, everybody loves Saturday night.*" He had a ringing high register baritone, his slim-line pipe ratt-tatting West Indian rhythm, doing lieu for a bongo pebble rattler.

"Not bad, mate," begrudged Wocky. The wipers jerked to and fro. Wocky stayed in bottom gear, steering around the first horseshoe bend. "I gave you proper warning, Ivor. We're the only dull bastards travelling this road."

Ivor snuggled between us. "Cynlais-boy, never let it be said your father reared a jibber."

We rounded the horseshoe, bedlam howlings coming from inside the canopy, our fellow workers caught in a chute of blizzard, then we climbed below high buttresses, sheep tucked like hibernators at the foot of the rocks. Another slow turn fed us head-on into the blizzard. We were two hundred yards from the cutting on top of Heol Gwyn when a small herd of mountain ponies fanned out, ghost shapes trekking down to lower ground.

Wocky tished sympathy. "Poor buggers."

Ivor braced his forearm against my neck, peering out and yipping like a cowboy. More yelps came from under the canopy. The shaggy ponies trudged heedlessly.

"Wouldn't mind me a ramping big stallion," Ivor hooping himself, jockeying, stroking the insides of his thighs. "Ride to hounds like the spunk faced aristocracy. That's the life for Ivor Prosser."

"You'd fall off a feed bag," said Wocky.

"I'll be riding some lush bird next Saturday night!"

Wocky said, "Your missis, she'd dose you with Paraquat."

I felt goose pimples – this crazy banter from the building trade as we nosed into a snowdrift. Wocky reversed, inched forward, stuck, reversed, rammed at the drift, snarling, "Right, gerrout and walk."

Ivor's charisma went absent. Lips stretched off his choppers, eyes bulging fear under the brim of his green slouch, he looked like a peon doomed to bullets in the stomach.

I opened the cab door. It was arctic all right. Men were dropping off at the back of the lorry, staying bunched, hop-hopping in the lee. Charlie came, followed by his passengers. Six foot three Charlie bent double, crouched in the swarming headlights of his lorry.

Wocky shouted, "This is it! I knew! Nobody'd listen to me!"

"Two bloody coffins on wheels," said Charlie.

Ivor scuttled into the gang, donkey coat clutched to his throat. He choked on panic. "Every man for himself!" Barging through the crowd, he rested his forehead on the tailboard. "I'm bronchial, Dai. Can't breathe. It catches me in the tubes," but he raised his arms like a preacher, "every man for himself!"

Ivor's inane bravado.

The snowdrift inclined sharply, filling the cutting between the drystone retaining walls. There weren't any heroes. We lost direction. Musketeer rambled, wailing for help, chest deep in bog and snow. Hands grabbed him, hauled him back to the main ruck. We were blinded, every man-jack floundering legless, the blizzard sucking air from our lungs. Bear right, I kept saying to myself, remembering the left-ward oblivion circling of lost souls. Genuine cannibal, the human heart.

Ivor Prosser suffered. He moaned. He chittered. All the time stumbling, falling, moaning. One grizzled old pipelayer stopped, turned his back on the blizzard. I caught his arm, pivoted him around – he was mumbling, maybe praying, in Welsh, the hearth language of his childhood. "Diolch," he said, his cold lips at my ear.

We linked hands, tall Charlie in front, then Wocky, Ivor, the rest of us strung behind, the awkwardest crocodile since homo sapiens rose up off all-fours, down through the Eskimo weather, downhill two miles from the seething crown of Heol Gwyn. Strange as dreaming the blizzard thinned away to gusts. Soon we were boot deep in Christmas card snow. Again the soft, threatless blanket fall. We chatted, shared cigarettes, enjoyed each other like citizens converted to peace for evermore. Except Wocky Eynon. He swore the lorries would remain trapped for days.

They were, too.

Saturday night with Wocky in the Footbridge Arms, for the fourth successive weekend we befriended Olive and Megan with vodkas. Bland Olive and brash Megan. We didn't expect to see Ivor. Cars were chaining cautiously up and down the slushed valley. Half way up to Heol Gwyn, the council abandoned a snowplough until daylight. Dumps of rock salt were empty. In the crowded lounge bar, love buds were ripening favourably by ten o'clock, when Ivor shouted from the lobby, "Dai Sam! Where's Dai Samuels?"

He was wearing a fawn duffle coat with mock bone toggles, green and brown checkered suit, primrose yellow pullover, blue pinstripe shirt, pale silvery tie and oil-shining hair accurately parted along the side of his head. "Found this boy in the Royal Hotel," he said, parading Musketeer into the lounge. Musketeer wore elephant corduroys, zipped boots, khaki ganzi with suede elbow patches, a Spanish guitar draped down his back, and the benign, lorn face of a folksy troubadour. In his triple ringed left hand, a glass of rosé wine. Musketeer nodded without smiling.

Squeezing himself between Olive and Megan, our foreman carpenter mimed strumming. "Righto, kid, let's hear from you."

"Oh yes, please," Megan said, coaxing.

Ivor flashed his gay bandit's grin. "Listen, gel, you with Dai or Cynlais? No matter, what are you drinking?"

Megan frosted him, Olive doubling the snub, leaning across the front of his natty pullover, whispering to Megan, "Here's a scraper from God knows where."

"I think he's wearing a toupée," said Megan.

Musketeer sang slow, dirgy verses about fields, hedges and dewponds disappearing under motorways. Musketeer's tired, mournful style, effective yet somehow unreal, like artificial insemination. I forgave him for dropping my hammer down a wall cavity. Half starved in his soul, that young Musketeer. I saw his name once, on a pay docket: Billy Rowlands.

Afterwards the lounge bar crowd made some decent harmony, mixing pop and ballads until stop tap. Buffing up his charm, Ivor failed to impress Olive and Megan. While he sang 'Persian Rosebud', Musketeer stroking chords, searching for the tune, the girls went to the Ladies' place. Unique baritone, Ivor Prosser, the sad, foppish bastard.

We filed out into the cold night, Megan and Olive pulling each other away from Ivor. Schoolgirlish romping. He fawned like a poacher's long-dog, Olive slapping at his hands, Megan chogging a wristy smack on his head, a beautifully timed accident as she tugged into her overcoat. Wocky had phone-called a taxi, Ivor reduced to pleading by now, all teeth, moustache and gleaming hair. "Room for one more?"

"Not on, can't take five," said the taxi driver.

Wocky slammed the door. "Tarra, Rosebud, see you Monday morning. Mind your feet!" the nearside tyres squirting slush at Ivor as we left the kerb.

Megan whaowed. "That fella Prosser reminded me of a vampire."

"I wouldn't trust him at all," agreed Olive.

"Me neither! Never!"

"Slyness in his eyes," said Olive.

Megan heaved a throaty squawk, Wocky nudging her, "Cut the bloody inquest, ah? If you don't mind?"

I said, "What happened to Musketeer? He disappeared after Ivor's 'Persian Rosebud'."

"Lovely boy," sang the girls, twin toning like Zulu descant.

Megan stressed to Olive, "Ever such a clever boy, quiet, really lovely."

"Mm," said Olive, coolish, the Mm for politeness.

They had a flat above Pegler's Stores. Steady bachelor girls on television assembly, unworried about settling down with meal ticket husbands. They heated pre-packed chicken curries for supper. Wocky helped Megan wheel her single bed into the living room. As usual, for the fourth time, sometime during the night he left Megan. Wocky went home. Late Sabbath morning toast and tea for three, relaxed chit-chat, the flat gently washed over by nonstop scrape-scrape tinkle-tinkle radio music from next door.

On Monday Wocky drove a hired van, grumpy behind the wheel, sogged from all-day Sunday boozing. We travelled the round-about route across Sebon Common. Snow-bound Cymru. No sign of thaw. A dozen men were crammed on the floor of the van like convicts, the same in Charlie's van.

"How did she perform?" asked Ivor.

"You're the arteest," I said. " 'Persian Rosebud', terr-rrific."

"By damn, I'm the man should have taken her home." Ivor pumped phallic uppercuts, howling, "Oompah oompah!"

Wocky's eyelids were swollen. "Rosebud," he said, "anything the matter with your missis? Doesn't make sense to me, old tiger like you chasing around like a whoormaster."

He cracked short laughs, loosely clasped his hands to his stomach, shoulders hoisted like a trouper soloist, tidily arranged himself and broke out on 'Persian Rosebud'.

Communal singing then, all the way to Hafod colliery. Unnatural on a bitter January morning.

Outside the canteen shed, Wocky unlocked the rear door to let the men out, at the same time cursing the white hulk of Heol Gwyn mountain.

"Dai," explained Ivor, anxiously knotted to confession, "between you and me now, confidential, right? My wife's retired from cooking school dinners. Yes, she, her and myself, we got married late in life, consequence being as regards certain matters, y'know Dai, it's a question of respect. No alternative. It's separate beds. See what I mean?"

I said, "You should have had voice training thirty years ago."

He aimed his pipe like a pistol. "It isn't for me to brag, others have mentioned exactly the same thing."

"Water under the bridge, Ivor," I said.

Perversely manful, jigging up on his toes, his alibi sounded like destiny. "Circumstances! Widowed mother! Trouble was, Dai Sam, I waited until my mother passed away before getting married. Good to me, my old lady, a saint in her own right."

"Some mothers are way out, fantastic," I said. "Can you spare us a man this morning? We'll have to clear snow off the scaffold and the wall plates before we drive a nail in."

Ivor cupped his hands around his mouth. "Wocky!"

Wocky grinned. "What's the trouble, Rosebud?"

"Look, Cynlais, borrow a shovel from the concrete ganger. Help Dai Sam and his mates for half an hour."

"No problem, Rosebud," Wocky said. "Anything else, Rosebud, apart from those two lorries stuck up on the mountain?"

It was inevitable, Wocky tabbed him for the rest of his life: Rosebud Prosser, foreman carpenter.

DANNIE ABSE

My Father's Red Indian

Look at a good map of South Wales and you'll see Ogmore-by-Sea plainly marked. It is halfway between Swansea and Cardiff, on the coast, of course, facing the small hills of Somerset that I can now observe hazily, fifteen miles away, across the grey, twitching, Saturday evening sea of the Bristol Channel. Not quite a village, not quite a resort, it is a place where sheep outnumber seagulls, where seagulls outnumber dogs, where dogs outnumber its human denizens.

My father loved Ogmore. He regularly drove the car down the A48 so that he could fish where the river, trying to rid itself of all the Welsh rain from the inland mountains, pours itself ceaselessly into the sea. "I'll catch a salmon bass today," my father would say optimistically in those far, long-ago days before the war when I was a small boy flying low over that Ogmore beach with my arms outstretched, or kicking a pebble into the rocks and shouting "Goal!" or just playing with my yo-yo and whispering, "Knock, knock, who's there?" while the sea wind replied threateningly, "Me, the bogeyman, me, Adolf Hitler, and I'll make you and little Audrey cry and cry and cry."

I love Ogmore as much as my father did. That's why, since I've been in South Wales a week now, staying with my mother, I drove out here on my own today. I like the open acres of sheep-cropped turf that spread upwards from the rocks to the bluish ribbon road where the post office is and the petrol pump and the small Sea View Hotel. I like the green ferns, the gorse in yolk-yellow flower that smells of Barmouth biscuits, and the old grey stone walls flecked with mustard lichen. I like the tons and tons of sweet air, and the extra air between the fleeing clouds and the blue. I like the dramatic, slow, chemically coloured sunsets – unpaintable, unbeatable – and those lights of Porthcawl across the bay that in an hour or so will suddenly appear, so many shivering distant dots as darkness deepens. I like even those scattered bungalows over there that seer the slopes of Ogmore-by-Sea, hideous as they are with their tidy lawns and hydrangea bushes and their neat, little surrounding red-brick walls. Bungalows called Sea Breeze or Cap Dai or Balmoral or Cartref.

Just after tea I overheard a lady, a stranger to me, who lived in one of the bungalows, say in the post office, "Jack Evans, 'e ought to be put away, I'm tellin' you, stark ravin', stark ravin', duw."

Jack Evans, I thought, I wonder if it's the same Jack Evans? He would be an old man now.

A common enough name in Wales. I did not like to question this lady who wore a green scarf tied about her head and who said nothing more about Jack Evans, "Ta-ta," she called as she closed the door that made a bell briefly, sadly, tinkle.

"*South Wales Echo*, please," I said, and carrying the newspaper I walked down towards the sea, towards a dog barking.

After the war, when I was a student, my father continued regularly to visit Ogmore-by-Sea. But the river had become polluted, the Bristol Channel more of a sewer, and he caught no more salmon bass, no more of those little flat dabs either, that my mother liked so much. Even the skate, with their horrible human lips, had vanished. Nothing lived in that sea except an occasional conger eel and the urine-coloured seaweed. Still my father stood there with his rod, all day uselessly until sunset when his silent silhouette listened to the crashing, deranged rhythms of the sea.

"Stark ravin', stark ravin'," the woman had said in the post office. And didn't my mother think Dad stark ravin' as he stood in his footprints throwing a line of hooks and raw pink ragworms into the barren waves?

"Might as well fish in the dirty bathwater upstairs," my mother grumbled.

"But I'm not the only one," father growled one day defensively. "Since two weeks now another fella comes to fish near me. We'll catch something one of these days."

"Who's this other crazy fisherman?" my mother asked.

"Name of Jack Evans," my father replied. Then he hesitated and with his left thumb and index finger pulled at his lower lip. He was obviously going to announce something important. But he mumbled something. I didn't hear what he said that made my mother laugh. She laughed, stopped, laughed again, and choking cheerfully gasped, "That's a good one, ha ha."

My father, uneasy because of her response, ignored me when I asked, "What did you say, Dad?"

My mother, chuckling, tried to wipe tears from her eyes. "Your father says, ha ha ha, that this Jack Evans is ha ha ha ha ha ha, oh dear, oh dear."

"What?" I asked, irritated.

"Ha ha ha," my mother continued, "a *Red Indian*, ha ha ha."

"He is too," shouted my father, angry now. "For heaven's sake, stop laughing. His mother was an American Indian, his father Welsh. What's funny about that?"

My father picked up a newspaper but didn't put on his glasses. He just stared at the paper and said, "He's a Welsh Red Indian. When his mother died Jack was sixteen so his father brought him back to Bridgend which is where the Evans family come from."

"We're Welsh Jews," I said to my mother. "So why should we laugh at Welsh Indians?"

"You and your old fishing stories," my mother said dismissively and disappeared into the kitchen.

My father put down the newspapers. "He's a very interesting man is Jack Evans," my father said, pensively, quietly.

Next time my father went fishing by the river mouth at Ogmore maybe I would go with him and meet Jack Evans, interesting Welsh Red Indian. My father drove the twenty-odd miles to Ogmore most weekends but somehow I never found time to go with him. There was a film to see, a party to go to, or I just wasted time playing poker in the students' union. So I did not meet Jack Evans. My father, though, became more and more expert in the culture and history of the American Indian.

"Oh aye," said my father. "We do 'ave some very hinteresting conversations, me and Jack."

"No fish, though," I said.

My father was not a religious man, not a philosophical man either, but standing there, by the side of the sea with Jack Evans, both men silent for the most part I should think, they must have thought thoughts, dreamed dreams that all men do who confront the man-absent seascape for hours and hours. My father never spoke a word of praise about the altering light in the water and the changing skies but he did occasionally stammer out some of his new-found Jack Evans knowledge, and when he did so my mother gazed at him with unaccustomed, suspicious eyes as if he were unwell, or as if he had brought home, uncharacteristically, a bunch of flowers.

"D'ye know," he told us, "the American Indians are a bit like Jews? They 'ave no priest between man and his Creator, see."

"No mediator, no intercessor?" I asked.

"Exactly," my father continued. "And like Jews, would you believe it, they don't kneel to pray. They stand up erect, aye."

"So what?" my mother said, disturbed.

"They don't try and convert people either – like Jews, see. An' they have a sort of bar mitzvah, a sort of confirmation, when they're thirteen."

"I don't like Jack Evans," my mother suddenly declared as if she had decided he was a savage. "What does he want?"

But I was curious to learn more about the Red Indian confirmation ceremony and so I asked my father to tell us more about it. It seemed, according to Jack Evans anyway, that after a purifying vapour bath the thirteen-year-old Red Indian would climb the highest point in the vicinity. Wishing to stand before God in all humility the youth would strip and stand naked and motionless and silent on top of hill, or top of mountain, exposed to the wind and the sun. For two days and one night, for two sunrises and two sunsets, the naked boys would stand erect watching all the stars coming out and all the stars disappearing.

"Good night," said my mother. "What an ordeal for a young boy."

We sat in the room, none of us speaking for a while. Then my mother said, "I bet that Jack Evans could do with a vapour bath. Bet he smells and could do with some Lifebuoy soap under his armpits."

My father looked up, pained. "I'd like to meet Jack Evans," I said quietly. "I'll come to Ogmore with you next weekend, Dad."

"All right," my father said. "I've told 'im you write poetry. He was very interested to hear that. Soft in the head I told him you were. But I 'spec' he'll be glad to meet you."

"Fishing by there in Ogmore, both of them," my mother said. "Blockheads."

The next weekend I sat in the back of my father's Morris Minor next to his fishing tackle, next to the worm bait in an old tobacco tin. My mother, at the last moment, decided to come too. "Just for the ride," she explained. Like me, though, I'm sure she was curious to meet my father's own Red Indian. On the other hand, my mother always did, still does, delight in travelling in a car. Always she sat next to the driver's seat, the window on her side open a little, however chill a wind screeched in to freeze the other back-seat, protesting passengers.

"Just an inch," she would plead. And content to be driven, to rest from her house chores, ten miles outside the town she'd sit there regal, giving my father directions or humming happily the gone music-hall songs that have faded into nostalgia.

As we came down Crack Hill to leave the A48 for Ogmore her hum became louder and soon words, wrong words, replaced the hum. "I know she loves me, because she says so, because she says so, she is the Lily of Caerphilly, she is the Lily – Watch the sheep," she suddenly shouted. The hedges and green fields raced backwards and there, ahead of us in the bending road, forty yellow eyes stared at us. Afterwards, when father accelerated again, my mother asked in a voice too loud, "He doesn't wear feathers an' things, does he?"

"For heaven's sake," my father said. "Don't be tactless. Don't ask him damn soft things like that."

"Good night," my mother replied. "I won't speak to the man at all."

She pulled out some Mintos from her handbag, gave me one and unwrapped another to push into my father's mouth as he stared steadily ahead at the road. Through the window now the landscape had changed. Down there in the valley, beyond turf and farms, the river snaked its way this side of the high sand dunes and then, abruptly, as we climbed an incline the open sea fanned out, the dazzle on the sea, the creamy edge of it all visible below us as it curved elliptically on the beach from the promontory of Porthcawl all the way round Happy Valley towards Ogmore and the mouth of the river.

Such a deception that sea. So beautiful to look upon but so empty of fish. Even the seagulls of Ogmore looked thin, famished, not like those who feasted on these shores before the war.

"Can't see anyone fishing down there," I said to my father.

"Tide's coming in," he replied. "Jack'll be by presently."

Jack Evans seemed in no hurry. My father fished alone and my mother and I waited until we became tired of waiting. We went for a turfy walk and when we returned we found my father on his own still, casting his line into the incoming sea. We decided to go for tea in the Sea View Hotel and we left my father the flask and sandwiches. When we came back again, still Jack Evans was absent. There was just the derelict wind and out there a distant coal tramp steamer edging its way on the silver dazzle towards Cardiff.

"Brr," my mother said. "It's an arctic wind. We'll wait in the car. Don't be long."

We did not meet Jack Evans that day and the next weekend it was raining monotonously. Besides I wanted to see Henry Fonda in a film called *Strange Incident*.

"Duw, you want to see a cowboy film," my father mocked me, "when you could come with me an' meet a real live Red Indian."

"It's raining, Dad," I said.

"He'll be down there this week, sure as eggs," my father said. So father drove that Saturday to Ogmore alone and that night when he returned he gave me a note. "'Ere," he said. "Jack Evans 'as written this out for you. He said sorry to 'ave missed you last week. But you might like this Red Indian poem of his. Read it out loud to your mother. It's short, go on."

I opened up the piece of paper. I have never seen such big handwriting – bigger than a child's. *You up there*, I read to myself and then I read it out loud for my mother sat there inquisitively. "It's about a falling star," I said.

> You up there
> you who sewed to the black garment
> of endless night
> all those shining button-stars
> how your big fingers
> must have been cold.

For the buttons do not hold
some are loose
some fall off.
Look how one drops now
down and in towards us
and out of sight.

My mother nodded. "Very nice," she said, My father seemed triumphant. "Even I understand that, son – it's about a shooting star – now why can't you write clear stuff like that instead of those *modern* poems you produce?"

"That's how Red Indians think," my mother interrupted him. "They don't understand about shooting stars. I mean they don't know the scientific explanation. They think God's fingers were just numb with cold. Fancy. Good night."

I stared down at the handwriting. Nobody genuinely wrote like that, I thought. And then it occurred to me: Jack Evans didn't exist. My father had made him up. Why not? Some people wrote novels, others plays, or worked at poems like me. So why shouldn't my father have invented a character? And yet? How would my father have got hold of that poem or all those facts about Red Indian religion? My father was no scholar. Somebody with erudition had talked to him ... so why not Jack Evans? All the same I looked at my father suspiciously.

"I'll come with you to Ogmore again one of these days," I said.

I did too. About once a month I accompanied my father on his fishing trips. But I never met Jack Evans.

"Funny," said my father, "how he never makes it when you or your mother come."

"He's got Red Indian second sight," I muttered.

I remembered it was 21 June, the longest day of the year, when I ambled into Cardiff Central Library and saw in the spacious reference room my own father studiously reading a book – something he never did at home. At once I guessed the book was about American Indian culture. Now I was certain he had invented Jack Evans, that his recently acquired knowledge about American Indian history and religion and poetry had been culled from books – not from any real, gossiping individual. My father sat, the other side of the room, at a long black table, bent over a book, unaware that his son was watching him. And I felt guilty standing there, finding out his secret. I felt furtive and quickly left the reference room lest he should look up. My own father ... crazy! Fooling us like that. As I ran down the steps of the library, disturbed, I do not know why I wanted to cry. My own father whom I loved, who was a bit eccentric, yes – but I'd thought not this crazy – living in a fantasy world, having a fantasy companion fishing with him in the sea that contained no fish. Hell, I thought, good grief! I decided not to say anything to my mother.

That night after a silent supper my father brought a piece of paper out of his pocket. "I went to the library today," he announced. "I wanted to find a Red Indian poem for Jack. They were very 'elpful. The girl in the library let me 'ave a look at a book called *Literature of the American Indian*. Very hinteresting. I found this in it. It's an Eskimo poem, really. I'm not sure whether it's the same thing as a Red Indian one."

He handed me the piece of paper and I felt relieved. I wanted to laugh. So my father hadn't made up Jack Evans. Now I felt ashamed that I had ever thought he had. I stared at my father's handwriting that was simple but small, mercifully small.

"Read it out, son," said my mother.

"It's called 'The Song of the Bad Boy'," I said.

My father stared at me bright-eyed, his mouth a little open. My mother smoothed back her hair. They were waiting so I read it out loud, 'The Song of the Bad Boy'.

> I am going to run away from home, *hayah*
> In a great big boat, *hayah*
> To hunt for a sweet little girl, *hayah*
> I shall get her some beads, *hayah*
> The kind that look like boiled ones, *hayah*
> Then after a while, *hayah*
> I shall come back home, *hayah*
> I shall call all my relations together, *hayah*
> And I shall give them all a thrashing, *hayah*
> I shall marry two girls at once, *hayah*
> One of the sweet little darlings, *hayah*
> I shall dress in spotted seal-skins, *hayah*

And the other dear little pet, *hayah*
Shall wear skins of the hooded seal only, *hayah*.

My mother laughed when I finished and said, "The little demon,"
And my father said, "What does *hayah* mean?" I didn't know. Did it
mean anything? Did it mean Hooray?
"You can ask Jack Evans!" said my mother.
He never did though. Jack Evans never turned up in Ogmore
again. Regularly my father went fishing, regularly he stood near the
river's mouth on his own. First he assumed that Jack Evans was ill.
He did not know exactly where he lived. In Bridgend, probably. In
some ways, my father admitted, Jack Evans was a mystery man. "An'
I can't look him up in any damned phone book," Dad said. "There
are so many Evanses about."
Gradually, catching nothing except seaweed week after week, and
having no companions, my father became discouraged. Only in the
best blue weather would he drive the car to Ogmore and even then
he would rarely go fishing. His chest already had begun to play him
up. He would sit in the car and cough and cough, gasping for breath,
while my mother muttered anxiously, "Good night, I do wish you'd
give up smoking."
The next year he did give up smoking. He gave up everything.
The one Sunday we did go to Ogmore he did not even take his fishing
tackle with him. He sat for hours silently, then almost shouted, "They
spoilt it, they ruined it. Oh the fools, the fools!" And he stared
morosely at the polluted sea.
The years have not made me forget the timbre of his voice, nor
the righteousness of his anger. I strolled over the turfy hillocks above
the rocks and stared at the wronged sea. I remembered my mother,
now an old lady in her Cardiff flat, still saying, "Good night," and I
continued walking towards the sea and the sunset. I wondered if there
would be any fishermen this Saturday evening down by the mouth
of the river. Because of the woman with the green scarf in the post
office I half expected Jack Evans to be fishing there – an ancient
grey-haired man not quite right in the head, standing where my father
stood, wearing Wellingtons like my father did, as the smallest waves
collapsed near his feet. "Stark ravin', stark ravin'."

I quickened my pace as the strong sea wind moistened my eyes. There was not going to be much of a sunset. A few seagulls floated like paper towards the flat rocks on my left. Soon I would be beyond the small sand dunes on my right and the grey wall and the last bungalows. Then the river mouth would be visible. Indeed, three minutes later I saw the river below me and, in the distance, one solitary man holding a bending rod. I wanted to run. I scrambled over the rocks, shuffled over pebbles until my feet became silent on sand. As I approached the fisherman, I saw that he was, alas, quite young and I felt stupid as I walked towards him, still carrying my *South Wales Echo*.

He had seen me and I veered away a little but the stranger called, "Got the football results?"

I glanced momentarily at the newspaper in my hand. "No," I said. "I got this paper earlier. Too early."

The fisherman nodded and I asked, hesitating, "Any fish in these seas?"

Perhaps the wind carried my words the wrong way for he replied. "Costs 'ell of a lot these days, mun. The price of bait, duw, shocking."

"Do you ever catch fish here?" I asked again louder.

"They caught a cod down by there near the flat rocks last week," he replied. "I'm 'oping for a salmon bass meself."

He probably lived in Ogmore-by-Sea. Perhaps he would know about the Jack Evans "who ought to be put away".

"Jack Evans?" he replied. "No."

I nodded and was about to turn back when he surprised me with, "You don't mean Mac Evans by any chance?"

I wanted to laugh. I was looking for a Welsh Red Indian not a Welsh Scotsman!

"No, no," said my new-found fisherman friend. "Max Evans, mun. We just call him Mac for short."

"Is Mac ... Max Evans a bit ... er ... crazy?"

His hands tightened on his rod so that his knuckles whitened and he laughed. Suddenly he stopped laughing. "By Christ," he said. And solemn, he paused again as if to tell me of some disaster. "You should see Mac on a motorbike," he continued.

I grinned, half turned and raised my hand. He smiled back. I walked away up the crunching pebbles, over the rocks, onto the turf. Way at the top, on the road, the lamp posts jerked on and Ogmore-by-Sea immediately became darker. Lights came on too in the post office and the Sea View Hotel, and as I walked up the slope the moon in the sky became more and more bright.

EMYR HUMPHREYS

The Arrest

i

A short stocky man stood in the middle of a room lined with books. He was in his shirt sleeves. His clenched fists inside his trouser pockets pressed down hard so that the tough elastic in his braces was fully stretched. He shut his eyes and breathed deeply. When his tight lips expanded with the conscious effort of subduing his excitement, he looked pleased with himself. He opened his eyes. They were a piercing innocent blue. A beam of the morning sunlight caught the framed photograph of his college football team hanging above the door. He saw himself picked out plainly in the back row, his arms folded high across his chest a tight smile on his face, his head crowned with golden hair cut short at the back and sides and brushed back in close even waves. It was a head of hair to be proud of. A blackbird in one of the cherry trees at the bottom of the garden burst into a prolonged cadenza. His hand opened and passed softly over the trim white waves that remained to him, still cut close in the old style.

His wife appeared in the study doorway. Her grey head was held to one side. She dry-washed her long white hands and smiled at him winningly.

"I don't think they are coming today, Gwilym."

Her voice was quiet, a little tremulous with anxiety and respect.

"Cat and mouse."

His thumbs planed up and down inside his braces.

"It's obvious what they are up to. Cat and mouse. Trying to break my will. Trying to make me give in."

His wife lowered her head. Her concern seemed tinged with guilt. "Let him stew a bit longer. You can hear them say it."

The room reverberated with his resonant nasal baritone. He was a minister who enjoyed the art of preaching. His wife's attitude of troubled and reverential concern urged him on.

"The magistrates were very polite. Very gracious. The narrow iron hand in the thick velvet glove. A month to pay. That month expired, Olwen, ten days ago. And still they have not been to get me.... That's the way things are done in this little country of ours. It's all persuasion, moderation, compromise. As I said yesterday, an entire population is guided, herded like a vast flock by the sheepdogs of the communication media into the neat rectangular pens of public obedience. And we still don't realise that those pens are process machines and that we have all become units of mass government analogous to units of mass production: uniformed wrapped and packaged products of the state machine."

She closed her eyes before taking a step into the room. Her hands spread out in a gesture of pleading.

"Gwilym," she said. "You've made your stand. The congregation understands and admires you. That's something a minister can be proud of. Why not pay now and have done with it!"

He lifted a warning finger.

"I have forbidden any member of my congregation to pay my fine! I have made a legal statement to the effect that all our property, such as it is, including our little Morris Minor, is in your name, 'Mrs Olwen Dora Ellis'. They can come when they like to arrest me."

She moved to the window and looked forlornly at their narrow strip of garden and the circular rockery they had built together. The aubretia was already in flower. The north wall of the chapel was faced with slates that looked less austere in the vibrant sunlight. The minister ran his finger lightly along a row of volumes on a shelf.

"The role of the church in the modern world et cetera et cetera," he said. "How readily we take the word for the deed. It's deep in our psyche. What we need is more preachers in prison."

"Yes, but why you, Gwilym?"

The question was intended as a humble appeal: but she could not prevent it sounding sulky. He waved it aside.

"Yes but where are the young ones? You are a man of fifty-six, Gwilym. You have certain physical ailments sometimes...."

"Piles," he said.

He spoke as one at all times determined to be frank.

"Otherwise I'm extremely fit."

"It worries me. I can't bear to think of you going to prison for a month."

"Twenty eight days."

"It really worries me. I don't think I can stand it."

They both stood still as though they were listening to the uninterrupted song of the blackbird in the cherry tree. He wanted to comfort her but her distress embarrassed him too much.

"We've been over this before," he said. "Somebody has to take a lead. Our language is being driven out of the homes of our people and our religion is being swept away with it. We *must* have an all-Welsh television channel. That's all there is to it. That's what our campaign is all about. When words fail, actions must follow. Stand firm, Olwen."

At last he moved closer to her and put his arm over her shoulders.

"Now what about a cup of coffee?"

ii

It was while they sat in the kitchen drinking it, the police arrived. Mrs Ellis glimpsed a blue helmet moving above the lace curtain.

"They've come," she said. "Oh my God ... they're here."

She stared so wildly at her husband, she could have been urging him to run away and hide. He sat at the table, pale and trembling a little. He spoke in spite of himself.

"Didn't think they would come today," he said.

The peremptory knock on the back door agitated Mrs Ellis so much she pressed both her hands on her grey hair and then against her cheeks.

"I've got fifteen pounds in the lustre jug," she said. "Do you think they'll take them, Gwilym, if I offer them?"

The colour began to return to his cheeks.

"They don't really want you to go. The prisons are too full

anyway. I read that in the paper only a week ago. They're too full you see. I meant to cut it out to show you. They won't have room for you, when it comes to it...."

The minister breathed very deeply and rose to his feet.

"It's not a place for you anyway. Not a man like you Gwilym. This is your proper place where you're looked after properly, so that you can do the work you have been called to do. A son of the Manse living in the Manse. There isn't a man in the Presbytery who works half as hard as you do...."

"Olwen! Pull yourself together! Be worthy."

A second series of knocks sent him rushing to the back door. He threw it open and greeted the two policemen with exaggerated geniality.

"Gentlemen! Please come in! I've been expecting you and yet I must confess I'm not absolutely ready to travel, as you can see. Won't you come in?"

He led them into the parlour. The room was conspicuously clear but crowded with heavy old-fashioned furniture. It smelt faintly of camphor. In a glass-fronted cabinet there were ceramic objects Mrs Ellis had collected. Two matching Rembrandt reproductions hung on either side of the black marble mantle-piece. The minister invited the policemen to sit down. The senior policeman removed his helmet. A dull groove encircled his thick black hair. Sitting in a low armchair he nursed both the charge-sheet attached to a clip-board and his helmet on his knees. His companion stood at ease in the doorway until he realised that Mrs Ellis was behind him. She recoiled nervously when he turned and pressed himself against the door so that she could pass into the room. He was a young policeman with plump cheeks and wet suckling lips. When she saw how young he was she looked a little reassured. The older policeman twisted in his chair to speak to her. His voice was loud with undue effort to be normal and polite.

"I don't expect you remember me?"

She moved forward to inspect his face more closely. His false teeth flashed under his black moustache and drew attention to his pock-marked cheeks and small, restless eyes. The minister's wife shook her head a little hopelessly.

"I am Gwennie's husband. Gwennie Penycefn. You remember Gwennie."

"Gwennie...."

Mrs Ellis repeated the name with affectionate recognition. She looked at her husband hopefully. He was still frowning with the effort of identification.

"You taught her to recite when she was small."

Mrs Ellis nodded eagerly.

"And Mr Ellis here confirmed her. I don't mind telling you she burst into tears after breakfast. When I told her where I was going and the job I had to do. 'Not Mr Ellis,' she said. 'He baptised me and he confirmed me'. Poor Gwennie. She was very upset."

The minister nodded solemnly. He stood in front of the empty fireplace, squaring his shoulders, his hands clasped tightly together behind his back. The armchair creaked as the policeman lowered his voice and leaned forward.

"What about paying, Mr Ellis? You've made your stand. And we respect you for it. It's our language too isn't it, after all. I don't want to see a man of your calibre going to prison. Honestly I don't."

"Oh dear...."

In spite of her effort at self-control, Mrs Ellis had begun to sigh and tremble. The policeman turned his attention to her, gruff but confident in his own benevolence.

"Persuade him, Mrs Ellis bach. You should see the other one I've got waiting in the station. And goodness knows what else the van will have to collect. The refuse of society, Mrs Ellis. Isn't that so, Pierce?"

He invited a confirming nod from his young colleague.

"Scum," Pierce said in his light tenor voice. "That one tried to kill himself last night, if you please."

"Oh no."

Mrs Ellis put her hands over her mouth.

"Younger than me too. Now he needs a stretch. Do him good."

"Officer."

The minister was making an effort to sound still and formal.

"This man you say tried to kill himself. What was his trouble?"

"Drugs."

The older policeman answered the question.

"Stealing. Breaking and entering. Driving without a licence. Drugs."

The policeman spoke the last word as if its very sound had polluted his lips, His colleague had managed to tighten his wet lips to demonstrate total abomination. He made a strange sound in his throat like the growl of an angry watchdog.

"Will you give me a moment to ... dress ... and so on?"

The policeman sighed.

"You don't need anything, my dear Mr Ellis. You go in wet and naked like the day you were born."

Mrs Ellis moved into the crowded room. Even in her distress she navigated her way between the furniture without ever touching their edges. Her arms floated upwards like a weak swimmer giving in to the tide.

"I'll pack a few things," she said. "In your little week-end case."

Her eyes were filling with tears and it was clear that she had not taken in the policeman's last words.

"Wear your round collar, Gwilym," she said.

She spoke in a pleading whisper and made a discreet gesture towards her own throat.

"There's still respect for the cloth, isn't there?"

"I go like any other man who has broken the English law," he said. "Get me my coat, Olwen. That's all I shall need."

The younger policeman looked suddenly annoyed.

"Look," he said. "Why cause all this fuss for nothing? It's only a bit of a telly licence. Why don't you pay the fine here and now like any sensible chap and have done with it?"

The minister looked at him.

"You have your duty," he said. "I have mine."

iii

The rear door of the van opened suddenly. The minister had a brief glimpse of men out in a yard smoking and enjoying the May sunshine: they were plain-clothes men and policeman in uniform. They paid little attention to the van, even when a bulky youth in frayed jeans was lifted bodily and pushed into it. He collapsed on the cold metal floor near the minister's feet. His large head was a mass of uncombed curls. When his face appeared his lips were stretched in a mooncalf smile. He was handcuffed and there were no laces in his dirty white pumps. His wrists were heavily bandaged in blood-stained crepe. His nose was running and he lifted both hands to try and wipe it. A plainclothes detective bent over him, still breathing hard.

"Now look, Smyrna," he said. "You promise to behave yourself and I'll take these off. Otherwise you'll be chained to the pole see? With a ring through your nose like a bull."

Smyrna was nodding and smiling foolishly.

"You've got a real minister to look after you now. So you behave yourself and I'll bring you a fag before we leave."

His boots stamped noisily on the metal. The slamming of the rear doors reverberated in the dim interior of the police van. Smyrna, still sitting on the floor raised his arms to stare at his wrists. The minister nodded at him and moved to make room for him on the narrow bench. Smyrna's tongue hung out as he searched the pockets of his jeans for a cigarette. He found a flattened stump, rolled it between his dirty fingers and stuck it between his lips.

"Got a match?"

The minister felt about in his pockets before he shook his head. He looked apologetic. The young man sucked the wet stump. He lifted his bandaged wrists so that the minister could observe them.

"You know what he said?"

"Who?"

"That sergeant. That detective sergeant. 'Didn't make a good job of it, did you?'"

The minister leaned forward to scrutinise the lateral scratches ascending both the young man's strong arms.

"That's sympathy for you. I was upset. It's a terrible thing to happen to anybody. Eighteen months in prison. And that was all the sympathy I got."

The minister gathered up the ends of his clerical grey macintosh and leaned forward as far as he could to show intense sympathy.

"How did you do it?"

Smyrna's lips stretched in a proud smile, the cigarette stump still in the corner of his mouth.

"Smashed my arms through the glass. Thick it was. Frosted. Too thick really."

He mimed the act of scratching his arms with pieces of broken glass. Then he pulled a face to indicate his pain. The minister was distressed.

"Is it hurting now?" he said.

"Aye. A bit."

Smyrna's head sank on to his chest. The van lurched abruptly out of the yard. Through the small window the minister caught a glimpse of familiar landmarks warmed by the brilliant sunshine: boarding houses, a deserted slate quay, a wooded corner of the island across the sandy straits. Smyrna was on his knees communicating with the two policemen who rode in front. A plainclothes man the minister had not seen before, lit a cigarette in his own mouth and then passed it between the bars to the young prisoner. Smyrna settled as last on the bench, enjoying the luxury of the smoke, staring most of the time at the bandages on his wrists, lifting first one and then the other for a closer inspection.

The minister asked him questions. He wanted details of his background. As the van travelled faster the interior grew colder and more draughty. Smyrna's eyes shifted about as he tried to work out the ulterior motive behind Mr Ellis's probing solicitude. He pulled his tattered combat jacket closer about his body and sniffed continuously to stop his nose running. His answers became monosyllabic and he began to mutter and complain about the cold and the noise. His eyes closed. He sagged in his seat and his large body shook passively with the vibrations of the uncomfortable vehicle.

The van turned into the rear of a large police headquarters. It reversed noisily up a narrow concrete passage to get as close as possible to a basement block of cells. Smyrna jerked himself up nervously and called out.

"Where are we then?"

The minister tried to give a reassuring smile.

"I've no idea," he said.

The van stood still, the engine running. There were shouts outside and the jovial sounds of policemen greeting one another. Smyrna's mouth opened and his eyeballs oscillated nervously in their sockets as he listened.

When the doors at last opened a smartly dressed young man jumped in. He wore large tinted spectacles and his straight hair was streaked and tinted. He wore his bright handcuffs as if they were a decoration. He sat opposite the other two, giving them a brief nod and a smile of regal condescension. There was no question of removing his handcuffs. His escort examined the interior and then decided to ride in front with his colleagues. As soon as the doors were locked the van moved off at speed. Smyrna unsteadily attempted to wipe his nose first with the back of one hand and then the other. He stared at the newcomer's handcuffs with a curiosity that made him miss his own nose. His mouth hung open. A fastidious expression appeared on the new prisoner's face.

"You're a dirty bugger aren't you?"

A modish disc-jockey drawl had been superimposed on his local accent. The effect would have been comic but for the menacing stillness of his narrow head. It was held in some invisible vice of his own making. His eyes, pale and yet glinting dangerously, were also still beyond the grey tint of the thin convex lenses.

"I don't like dirty buggers near me. I can tell you that now. What do they call you?"

Smyrna's jaw stretched out as he considered the quiet words addressed to him. Was this a new threat forming itself? Had his environment become totally hostile? The well-dressed prisoner was handcuffed after all. He was a man of slight build. He looked down unhappily at his own powerful arms and began once again to examine the bandages on his wrists.

"Smyrna," he said. "Smyrna. That's what they call me."

"What's that for Christ's sake. Some bloody Welsh chapel, or something?"

He bared the bottom of his immaculate teeth in an unfriendly smile.

"Now look here...."

The minister felt obliged to intervene.

"You must understand that our young friend here isn't at all well. You can see for yourself."

The cold eyes shifted to examine the minister for the first time.

"Who the hell are you? His old dad or something?"

He directed the same question to Smyrna with the slightest nod towards the minister. He was amused by his own remarks.

"Your old dad, is he? Come for the ride?"

The minister made an appeal for sociability.

"Now look here," he said. "We are all in the same boat. In the same van anyway. Let us make an effort to get on together, and help each other."

The handcuffed man studied the minister with the absorbed but objective interest of an ornithologist examining a known if unfamiliar species in the wholly inappropriate habitat.

"How long you in for, Moses?"

"A month. Twenty eight days that is."

The minister was prepared to be relaxed and jovial.

"Oh dearie me. That's a very long time isn't it? What about you snotty Smyrna?"

"Eighteen months."

Smyrna's large head sank on his chest. His jaw began to work. In the depth of his misery he seemed unaware of a trickle of mucus that ran from his nostril over the edge of his upper lip.

"Wipe your snot, you dirty bugger."

The handcuffed prisoner's voice rose sharply to assert itself above the noise of the engine taking a hill in low gear.

"I bet you're one of those miserable sods who grind their bloody teeth in their sleep. Aren't you?"

Smyrna smiled rather foolishly. He had no defence except to try and be friendly.

"How long you in for then?"

He put the question with amiable innocence and waited patiently for an answer. A pulse began to beat visibly in the handcuffed man's tightened jaws.

"Nine."

He spoke at last, but so quietly Smyrna leaned forward as though he were about to complain he hadn't heard. One of the police escort shifted in his cramped seat to peer back at them through the steel bars. The scream of the engine subsided a little.

"Nine months did you say?"

Smyrna was smiling inanely.

"Nine fucking years you snotty piece of crap. If they can hold me."

He lifted his handcuffed hands to the breast pocket of his smart suit and let them fall again.

"Here...."

He was ordering Smyrna to extract a packet of cigarettes from the pocket. Smyrna glanced apprehensively at the broad backs of the policeman in front.

"Never mind them, snotty. When you're inside you do as I tell you. You may as well start now."

Smyrna was permitted a cigarette himself. He was instructed to sit alongside his new master to enjoy it.

"You sit there mate, and then I won't have to bloody look at you."

Smyrna settled down, inhaling deeply and giggling. He blew on the end of the cigarette and pointed it at Mr Ellis.

"He's a minister," he said.

"Is he now? Well, well. He should be sorry for us."

He held out his handcuffed wrists and nudged Smyrna to do the same. When he understood the order, Smyrna shook so much with silent giggles that he had difficulty in keeping his bandaged wrists level and close to the handcuffs.

"We make a pair. A pair of Jacks. Isn't that so, Snotty? A pair of Jacks."

Smyrna laughed delightedly. He let his arms drop but a glance from his new companion made him raise them again.

"What is it then. What is it you're in for?"

The minister cleared his throat. He straightened his back.

"For refusing to buy my television licence," he said. "On principle."

"Oh my God. One of them language fanatics. I tell you what I'd do, Moses, if I was in charge. I'd stick the bloody lot of you up against a wall –"

"You don't understand," the minister said. "I'm not blaming you. You've never had a chance to understand."

"Do you hear that?"

The man in handcuffs elbowed Smyrna again to show him he could lower his arms if he wanted to since he had decided the joke was over.

"He's a fucking Welsh hero. That's what he is. In for twenty days and then out for a fucking laurel crown made of leeks. That's him. I tell you what we'll do, snotty. We'll be in the same cell tonight. And I won't be wearing my bracelets. How about knitting him a nice little crown of thorns?"

Smyrna inhaled cigarette smoke to the bottom of his lungs and nodded gleefully.

GLENDA BEAGAN

Scream, Scream

It is quiet on the ward. There are only three bed patients. Nurse Sandra looks at her watch. It is so still. There is the faint hum of a mechanical mower on lawns far away, that is all. No birds are singing. Mrs Jessop is snoring quietly. She's had a bad night. It is on the report.

Linda is about to make her move. Nurse Sandra senses it. She smooths her apron, flicks through a magazine with studied carelessness watching sideways through her hair as Linda shifts her slow carcase off the bed. Even now as those bare arms emerge Nurse Sandra has to steel herself. She looks up, clenched. Sioned, the anorexic girl in the top bed is semaphoring wildly. Linda begins.

"Is my heart still beating?"

"Yes, Linda." Nurse Sandra sighs, tries to smile. How well she knows this never ending litany.

"Are you sure?"

"Yes."

"Can you hear it?"

"Not from here I can't, no."

"Come and listen."

"Again, Linda?"

"Yes. I think it's stopped."

"No luv, silly. Course it hasn't stopped. You wouldn't be sitting up talking to me if it had stopped, would you?"

"No."

"There you are then."

Now the familiar pause.

"Is my baby dead?"

This was the bit she dreaded. Day after day, hour after hour, the same question. And still she dreaded it.

"It's a long time ago now, Linda."

"How long?"

"Two years."

"I killed my baby didn't I?"

"No, you didn't kill your baby. You know you didn't."

"Heroin killed my baby."

"Yes."

"Not me."

"No."

"But I did really. I know I did."

Nurse Sandra gulps. Linda never wants platitudes. Sometimes she'll accept them. Mostly she won't.

Nurse Sandra still finds she winces inside at the sight of those arms: the half healed scars she'd cleaned of pus months before are still lurid among the tattoos, the roses, crowns and mermaids, the names JIMMY and MOTHER, the waste, the pointlessness. Linda is dying, her liver, which is all of twenty three years old, is ready to pack up on her. She has respiratory problems. Her legs are hideously ulcerated. She has come here to die because there is nowhere else for her to go.

"Have you got a fag?"

"I don't smoke, Linda."

"Mrs Jessop smokes."

"Mrs Jessop is asleep."

"When she wakes up?"

"You can ask her when she wakes up."

"Will she give me a fag?"

"She usually does, doesn't she?"

"She always does."

A giggle. The ghost of a giggle.

"She always gives me a fag to make me go away."

Linda is not averse to exploiting the unnerving effect she has on people, and Mrs Jessop is easily unnerved. So is Sioned. Linda changes tack. She knows the answer before she asks the question but she wants a reaction. She wants to see those dark eyes close, that pale skull shake its negative.

"You don't smoke, do you Sioned?"

Sioned is pretending not to be here. She does it well. She is now so thin she hardly makes a ripple under the blankets. She is disappearing. Tonic insulin seems not to have had the desired effect. She is seventeen, always tiny, admittedly, but now she weighs just four stone.

Mrs Jessop sputters into consciousness. Stretches, yawns, sits bolt upright.

"Oh."

"Good morning Mrs Jessop. For this relief much thanks."

Nurse Sandra walks up to the bed.

"How are we this morning?"

Mrs Jessop can't remember how she is. Bleary still from night sedation, she blinks, owl-like, registers Linda's looming presence and makes an instinctive move for her handbag, proffering the packet.

Linda beams.

"Ta, Mrs Jessop. You're alright, you are. You'll be going home soon."

She slouches off to the top of the ward again.

"If you're going to smoke you go to the sitting room, Linda."

"Aw, just this once, Sandra."

"Sitting room."

"Can I go in the wheelchair, then?"

"You know I can't push you. I can't leave the ward."

"There's only Mrs Jessop and Sioned, Sandra. Nothing's going to happen while you push me that little way. It's not far."

"If you want to smoke you go to the sitting room and if you want to go to the sitting room you have to walk."

"You're a tight bitch, Sandra."

"Yeah, I'm a real hard case."

"Can I have a light, Mrs Jessop?"

"Not on the ward, Linda."

"I wasn't talking to you. I was talking to Mrs Jessop."

There is an edge in Linda's voice but she no longer has the energy to put that edge into action. Nurse Sandra gives her a look. Now it's a battle of wills and Sandra will win because she has the will to win and Linda has not. The girl's efforts have already exhausted her. She wants her cigarette but she does not want to haul herself down the corridor to smoke it. In the end the cigarette wins. It always does. She starts to move down the ward again, painfully slowly for Sandra's benefit, holding on to the beds.

"Can I borrow your lighter, Mrs Jessop?"

"Get a light from someone down there."

"There won't be anyone down there. They've gone to OT."

"Get a light from Sister Annie, then."

"Where?"

"In the office."

"Is that where she is?"

"Yes."

"Are you sure? Is she on her own?"

"It's not time for the doctors to make their round yet, Linda if that's what you're worried about."

"Is Dr Patel on today?"

"I don't know."

"She's on holiday," says Mrs Jessop.

"Is she? How do you know?"

"She told me."

Linda looks sulky. She likes to think she has a special relationship with Dr Patel, that she is her confidante. To compensate for not having received this piece of information she makes an extravagant balletic swoop towards Mrs Jessop, hands moulded into a parodic impression of an Indian dancer's.

"She's promised me one of her old saris, Dr Patel has. She said I could have one. She likes me."

"You've been pestering her again, haven't you?" Nurse Sandra cuts in, wishing Linda would really get off the ward and go for her smoke. Linda glowers.

"I like Dr Patel. She's alright."

In a moment of rare humour Mrs Jessop chuckles to herself. "She'll be going home soon."

Nurse Sandra smiles. "She's got a long way to go."

Just then the scream.

A vehicle must have drawn up, but they didn't hear it. The front doors have opened and the scream has come in, has forced itself in, breaking through their innocuous recitative. This is the aria, a full blooded aria.

They hear the office door click shut. But they couldn't have heard it above the scream. They must have just sensed it. They are, after all, alive to the relevance of all the building's distinctive vibrations. Nurse Sandra finds herself standing at attention. It's that kind of scream. Joyce the cleaner emerges from the toilets, mop akimbo.

"Christ," she says. "What's this?"

This is Mrs Jenkins. This is Mrs Jenkins' scream. The scream is on a stretcher. Sister Annie is standing by, keys jingling, along with two ambulancemen and a small fair nurse who looks no more than a child.

"Hello, Mrs Jenkins," says Sister Annie. They seem to have met. Curtains are whisked round a bed. The scream seems to fill the world. It changes pitch, it warbles, it fluctuates, it recedes, but it never stops. Sister Annie knows this scream, consequently it holds fewer fears for her. Mrs Jessop is sat bolt upright again, clutching her capacious handbag. Linda hovers, cigarette forgotten. Even Sioned is suddenly transformed into an unusually animated skeleton. She grabs her housecoat from the bed-rail behind her and the emaciated aims disappear into an incongruous protective blur of pink frills. Her mouth falls agape. More arrivals. Dr Merton (nobody likes Dr Merton) and Dr Patel, who is not on holiday after all. They disappear behind the curtain. Blending into the scream are the soft cooing sounds of Sister Annie, Dr Patel's staccato, the young nurse's uncertain burble and Dr Merton's stentorian boom. It is a virtuoso performance. Now the ambulancemen retreat. Now Dr Merton and the young nurse retreat. Only Sister Annie and Dr Patel remain behind the curtain, as the scream breaks the sound barrier and Sioned starts to cry. Nurse Sandra rushes up the ward, reassuring the pink mist until it sinks again beneath the candlewick. Joyce the Cleaner, ever reliable, appears with the tea trolley, basking in virtue since This Is Not Really Her Job but we're so short staffed this morning, what with Nurse Margaret on ECT and Nurse Meira called to take that awful Mrs Prendergast for another EEG last minute. Joyce pours tea copiously, wearing her Very Dependable Face. And still the scream, the scream. Perhaps the ambulancemen have left the doors open, though there seemed to be no wind. Now there's a Force Nine Gale. The curtains around the vexed bed billow, and the curtains at the windows float in a strange leeward drift, the lampshades swing. Very Dependable Joyce proffers tea to all, with the exception of Mrs Jenkins who can't be expected to scream and drink tea at the same time.

It's as if the scream slowly inhabits them all, slowly expresses them all. It's as if the terror slowly seeps out of it, while another nameless quality enters. What does it consist of, this blend of dark voices beyond Mrs Jenkins' own, far beyond, ungovernable, timeless voices without meaning or order, but shot through with a rhythm they recognise, a substance they have felt themselves, all of them, the Hell's Angel and the nursing sister, the anorexic girl who won't grow up and the Indian doctor who has torn up her roots and crossed the world to do just that, the cleaner who is pompous and kind and commonsensical and the wife of the managing director who is childless and bereft, a loss for which no amount of jewels and furs and foreign holidays can compensate? Perhaps most of all it is Nurse Sandra's scream, since she's been walking on the edge for weeks now, though no one would ever know. She swims with the scream as it ripples and bellows, rises and falls. It is a medley of voices, the cry of aftermath, of battle and birth, of sap and sinew. Mrs Jenkins cannot know that her scream is a benificence, that she takes from all of them their fears, relaying them back, transformed, intensified and finally transcended, that the ward's bland pastels fuse into whirling primary shades, a vortex of richness, of wildness, of courage. It takes courage, this truth, this scream.

Dr Patel and Sister Annie have decided on their course of action. The curtains are whisked back from the bed. Propped up against pillows lies a wizened face, but you can't really tell it's a wizened face at the moment because all you can see at the moment is the mouth. It is so wide open it seems to have taken over, engulfing all. Sioned, huddled under the covers, still cushions her ears with her hands. Nurse Sandra has turned quite white. Linda stands by the bed, unlit cigarette in hand. Mrs Jessop makes strange popping noises like a frog.

Mrs Jenkins comes from a farm, a farm in the middle of nowhere. A farm so old it's like a great fungus, an excrescence of the land, breeding barns and byres full of rusting threshing machines and ancient harrows and flails. Enough to fill a museum with fascinating glimpses of our agricultural past. But this isn't the past. It's the present. Little has changed at Sgubor Fawr since Owain Glyndŵr rode by, swelling his army with sons of the farm, only one of whom returned, an ancestor of Mrs Jenkins' lawful wedded spouse. She was a Jenkins too, before her marriage, since there were only Jenkinses to be found for miles around. But this is the end of the line. The very end. This is the scream of the last of the Jenkinses of Sgubor Fawr, this is.

It's unforgettable.

There's an hour and ten minutes to go till the others come back from OT. Dr Patel and Sister Annie will let her scream till then. She's screamed solid since half-past-seven last night, according to Mr Jenkins who is usually reliable in these matters. She's screamed in the ambulance for thirty-seven miles by green lane and new road. (Mrs Jenkins never leaves Sgubor Fawr except to come here. It is rumoured she went to Shrewsbury in Coronation Year, but that tale might well be apocryphal.) Who knows, by dinner time it may all be over. She might have done with screaming. Till the next time.

Very Dependable Joyce is handing out a second cup of tea to those that want. All drink. Even Sioned, submerged in her pink haze, drinks, but it's the eating she won't do, isn't it? She's in such a state of shock she almost accepts a Nice biscuit from Joyce's Own Personal Packet. But then she remembers she's anorexic and politely refuses. The scream keeps going, keeps flowing. Dr Merton makes a grim appearance at the ward door, shrugs and disappears. Nurse Sandra stands by. Sister Annie and Dr Patel sit and wait and listen. Is that a diminuendo? Surely ... yes ... no. The scream has risen again but it's definitely less screamy, this scream. It's on the wane. It wobbles, it fades, it flickers, it stops. It finally stops.

Mrs Jenkins does not look sheepish. She is not in the least embarrassed. She has the most ferret-like face you've ever seen. A swarthy ferret with black pebble eyes. In her high bird-like voice she asks Joyce if she can go home now. Very Dependable Joyce explains that as she is the Cleaner it's not really up to her to say. But tea she does have to offer.

"It'll be a bit stewed by now. I'll make you fresh if you like."

"No lovey," says Mrs Jenkins who is invariably easy to please. "I'm sure it will taste fine. I like my tea strong."

I bet you do, thinks Nurse Sandra.

It's still on the ward. Now there's not even the faint hum of a mechanical mower. It's an extraordinary stillness. Not a silence as such, more a resonant absence. How wonderful it is to hear the scream has gone. Never has any silence felt this peaceful, more like velvet, more gentle, more deep. Goodness is singing in the ward. Without making a sound.

Dr Patel winks conspiratorially at Sister Annie. Dr Merton was wrong, wasn't he? He wanted to give her morphine. They said leave her alone.

And they did.

And it worked.

It has happened before, of course. Every three years since 1953, the year of the Coronation, the year Mrs Jenkins went to Shrewsbury. If she did.

She will be going home in a day or two. She'll be chatting away to those two nice ambulancemen who brought her in this morning, sirens blaring. Well, it's all in a day's work.

Linda is now *en route* to the sitting room. Sioned lies quietly, thinking. Mrs Jessop is rooting anxiously in her handbag. Strange, she seems to have mislaid her lighter. The electrician comes in to change the dud bulb over Mrs Jenkins' bed.

At Sgubor Fawr the sun has filtered briefly through the trees. Mr Jenkins is feeding the hens.

ALUN RICHARDS

Fly Half

Your drinking!" she said. "My God...."

"Oh, for goodness sake, I just met some people."

"Have you seen what you look like this morning? Your eyes? Well, you should have seen yourself when you came in last night. A man your age. You weren't just squiffy, you were paralytic. Simply dreadful. It took the Under-Manager and a porter to carry you up the stairs."

"It *didn't*?" He was small and chubby, run to fat now, pear-shaped and pink, and his sharp, pale little eyes narrowed with concern as he looked at her, immaculate in white shorts and tennis shirt, her rather severe face and pointed features browned by the sun, her hair still thick and lustrous, her shape good, still youthful, that detached, untouchable air of the well-groomed woman remaining with her even in the casual clothes which she wore on holiday. She remained a Miss Muffet in appearance even though they had been married for seven years. There was still something pristine about her, and trying to alter her had exhausted him. If it could have been done at all, it should have been a younger man, he thought. The seven years between them was too much. And now she was getting waspish. It wouldn't be long until she did it before other people like the other one. Neither of his marriages had quite worked out as he'd hoped, but perhaps that was because he hadn't enough to give them. He wasn't blaming anyone and he wasn't complaining. The fact was, he'd had his moment and his time, and he'd doubted if she'd understand either. He never spoke about it anymore. He'd have to say something though, if she went on in that vein. Her voice ... God save him from ageing head prefects.

But in the event, he controlled himself.

'Steady.... Play it close to the chest now, boys. Keep it tight first half.' What a hell of a night it had been though! *Sospan Fach* in Portuguese.... What about that?

"They had to carry you up the stairs," she continued. "The lift wasn't working and they had to manhandle you. Where were you? You weren't in that place again? Not with that disgusting lecher, the dirty joke person? Not him? Not in that bar?"

"It came on to rain," he said. He didn't seem to have the energy to make up good excuses any more.

"Can't you understand that they're just hangers-on in that bar? I'll bet you paid for every drink."

"I didn't, I..." but he'd really filled his boots, he remembered, and now a pain like a marble seemed to roll down his intestine.

"Every drink! Only you haven't got the sense to see it. I'm sure they laugh at you behind your back anyway. They take one look at what's coming, and just know they're on a good thing. Well, be your age. There are fifty-two weeks in the year and we're just over here for two."

"They're rugby men."

"Rugby men?" That again, she thought. "They're any kind of men you want them to be, provided you're paying."

"Where's the Alka-Seltzer?"

"By your bed."

"Have you got a spoon?"

"Can't you do anything for yourself?"

"There's no need to be like that," he said.

But there was every need, she thought. It was more than just another night out with the boys this time, it was their annual holiday, and she hadn't come abroad just to have a repetition of what went on at home, his finding exactly the same kind of places and people as those with whom he normally cavorted on his night out. It was absurd to think of having a night out on your own when you were on holiday with your wife anyway. What was wrong with wives as part of the human species? But to be fair, it hadn't begun like that this time. She'd wanted to see some pottery in a display they were putting on in the hotel, and then she'd taken coffee with some women who were staying there and he'd said he was going to take a stroll down to the village. But the stroll meant another visit to a tavern and a session, and he was on the tiles again, her husband.

That was how it started, a little thing like that, but the trouble was, as she well knew, she was the second wife, and being the second wife, she had to cope with the impossible as far as she was concerned, his memory of the first wife who as the years had slipped by had become a hallowed figure in his mind, she was sure. He had that capacity for romanticizing the past and although he checked himself from actually mentioning her name now, in his private thoughts it was still Lil this, Lit that, Esme was sure. Even the difference between their two names was chalk and cheese. Lil was valleys and Esme was Cardiff, a Tory Lord Mayor's daughter and that again was part of the problem, one of the many things which stood between them. The other was that she had not known him in his heyday, for he was something very special then, she was given to understand, and indeed, people who had known him, men now in their late forties, spoke of him as a special being whose darting heels and will-of-the-wisp figure had made him the idol of the crowds. For he was that rarest of beings, a much capped Welsh fly half, one of the greatest according to journalists who kept bringing up his name in their columns, a man to be put amongst the immortals, Trew, Willie Davies, the two Cliffs, and head and shoulders above the recent crop, even 'King' John who did other things better, but could not beat a man off either foot and shirked a physical game. He sneaked through anyway like a thief in the night, but her husband could beat a man openly and make him look a fool. It was this beating a man off either foot which was apparently important. In thirty years only two men could do that, one was Bleddyn, and the other was her husband and that was something according to the connoisseur. He had an eye for an opening, and more important than anything else, absolute confidence, a wicked acceleration over twenty yards, and a wonderful pair of hands. He had once sold a dummy which deceived even the referee who blew up for a forward pass and could not then reverse the decision, or so the legend ran.

People who knew went on for hours and hours in this vein, and at first, she was not averse to listening. She had played games at school herself, and she thought physical elegance an excellent thing in itself.

But that was in school. She did not think it reasonable that a prowess at games should haunt you all your life, but rugby was not a game where they lived, it was a religion, and a Calvinist religion at that. She went with him occasionally to internationals, and listening to the roar at the Arms Park and watching the seething faces beside her, she had felt rather sorry for the All Blacks until they started a little bit of this and that, to use the phrase, but that only made them more like the others, in her book. But for their jerseys they were indistinguishable from the Welsh side as human beings, and if people looked at her as if she had committed treason when she said things like that, she did not care. It was no longer a joke and it had got past the point of irritation. The game, the past, his continual wallowing in it, aided and abetted by everybody he seemed to meet even here in Portugal, added up to a kind of cancer which she wished she could exorcize.

But she couldn't. And she couldn't remove his first wife from his mind either, it seemed. The famous Lil. This going out on his own when they were going on holiday had to be stamped on, however. That was one thing she could do.

But she hesitated for a moment, opening the shuttered door which led out from their bedroom to the balcony, and crossed out into the early morning sunlight. It was a beautiful day again, the wind from Spain which blew nobody any good as the legend said, had died down and she felt pleasantly warm. Down below her, past the hotel swimming pool and the terra cotta roofs of the houses, she could see the sea in the distance and a picturesque line of sardine boats chugging their way homewards into the little harbour. It was a perfect little spot. It was relatively undiscovered. The food was splendid, the service superb. In the nights you could hear that savage *fado* singing drifting up from a club nearby and last year, he had liked it as much as she had. That was the thing. They did enjoy things together. She was right to have married him. He had some splendid qualities. He was generous and kind and quite successful at what he did, even though her father had helped him considerably, putting business his way, and one thing and another, but then that was what fathers were for.

Esme's husband was an estate agent by profession, inasmuch as men who gave as much time to football as he did, could be said to have a profession, but they were quite comfortably off with what he earned and what her father had left her, and there shouldn't have been a care in the world, unless it was not having children. She was in her thirties when she got married, he was forty-three, and they hadn't really expected to start a family, and he hadn't any children by his previous marriage either, so he couldn't blame her on that score. But he would drink, would go off into this male world of his, and even when she took him away from it, he recreated it with total strangers. At first, she said, well, good for him, he was a man's man, small, but one of the boys, jovial, jokey, clubbable, something tweedy about him that made you think of cheese and beer, mellow tobacco and the smell of old leather. Wearing his sporty cloth cap, he looked like a prosperous little pork butcher, she often said, but it was said good humouredly. Before she married him, she did not think of going to bed with him. He was not the sort. He was someone you saw doing accounts, dealing with workmen, telling off the gardener, or giving the vicar a glass of punch and an elbow-jogging story as a bonus, and she did not mind that either.

After forty, if you wanted anything in a man, it was comfort. She'd had the other sort. She supposed he suspected but he'd never said anything, although at one time, there were quite a few stories going around about her because she'd been just a little unstable after her mother'd died and her father married again, but that was old, old stuff now. She looked pristine but she wasn't pristine, and she'd never married previously because, after her earlier playing around – hole in the corner stuff in borrowed flats – she felt an aversion to men her own age, preferring the company of women. Not that she didn't know they could be bitches and dreadfully possessive at that, like the County Club and that dreadful Bridge League which had swallowed up her mother. But nothing was simple, nothing was clear before her marriage, although she hadn't worried about it, busying herself with business interests, charity and political committees, only to meet him in the Squash Club in one of his vain attempts to get fit again.

And then he was so unlike her! It was extraordinary that they had a single word to say to each other. She knew he thought her rather a toff, which she was by his standards, but he also thought her more attractive than she did herself. She was very honest about that, and believed she had a capacity for objectivity. The truth was that apart from her father's money, she was rather unattractive she knew. By the norm, that is. Her features were too severe, her nose too large, and unless she was very careful with what she wore, she could be thought angular since she had a long body and short legs. She compensated by being immaculately turned out always, paid special attention to her weight and complexion, but all this she could cope with. She had settled for what she was, and she could even accept him as he was, apart from this football thing, the bar-bonhomie syndrome, and of course, the famous Lil. It always got back to that.

The cardinal fact was, Esme had now decided, that in his two marriages, her husband had done two opposite things, just the sort of things a man would do who was unsure of himself with women. He had married above him – that was her, and he'd married beneath him – that was Lil, and being the sentimentalist he was, now all his affections extended glueily like chewing gum to the past, and his old stamping ground in the Welsh valleys where he'd met Lil, probably wearing jersey and boots in bed, for all Esme knew. He had once confessed that Lil was the daughter of a fish-and-chip shop proprietor who made a habit of bathing three times a day in order to remove the cloying odour of the product. It was apparently something that seriously worried her, kept her awake at night, and as an adolescent, she'd even had to take sedatives because she got quite hysterical about it, refused to work in the shop and actually stopped eating until her father had been persuaded to leave the flat above it. He'd told Esme that, but shaking his head affectionately on recall as if it was some precious detail and part of the mythology which surrounded a person who later became distinguished, rising above rather squalid circumstances.

Hence the 'famous' Lil. She'd once asked him outright what she was really like. (The other information had come in bits and pieces.) "Oh, she was just a Ponty girl," he said dismissively, as if that said anything.

Well, what was Esme supposed to do about it? Fish and chips, typical of the valleys, she thought. But the information she had received upon the subject in roundabout ways was considerable. Lil made grammatical mistakes, couldn't count, was terrified of thunderstorms when she hid under the stairs, wouldn't answer the door in a pinafore, always made tart for Sundays and let it stand over-night on a cold stone, gave money to gipsies, loved male-voice choirs, actually cried when they sang unpronounceable songs, and once threatened to run on the field brandishing an umbrella when he was being trampled in the Neath match. It was difficult enough to compete with any first wife, but when the first wife was as common as dirt, a kind of rugby adjunct who probably vaselined her ears and wore shinguards before divesting herself of her chapel black! – Well, Esme's private sarcasm knew no bounds.

It was laughable to think about it all. And yet, in moments of uncertainty, it preyed on her mind. There was only one consolation. From what she could gather from other people, the impression he gave of Lil was markedly different from theirs. Mother Earth in embryo on the one hand, was an insignificant and rather sickly little mouse of a thing on the other. Not that Esme was going to say anything about the eventual illness which was tragic, but if a man is not a complete man, then it is some woman's fault. That's what her mother would have said, and the thing was, to make a diagnosis about their marriage now, and then do the necessary. It was no good dwelling on the past. No good at all. Absolutely not.

What then, was the diagnosis?

His lack of physical fitness for a start, she thought, beginning to itemize the details. If he was a pound overweight, he was three stone. You looked at photographs of him in the old days and you saw features, actual features, like cheekbones and a chin which had long vanished. He had to diet then, and rigorously, that was the first thing. He took no exercise, had not for at least thee years, and although he still went to clubs, golf clubs, squash clubs, the Athletic, it was only to bend his elbow. His golf things had mildew on them and he didn't possess a pair of shorts he could step into.

Well, she could do something in that direction. They might go to Champneys, that health clinic in Tring as her mother and father had. Hertfordshire would be a relief after Cardiff and its grubby hinterland. Sitz baths and massage, she thought. Not altogether unpleasant. But what else?

His drinking. That was another conundrum and something which she felt to be a criticism of her. Before they were married she did not realize just how much he drank. It was very difficult to know at the time, and while he pretended an interest in the things which amused her and they went to the theatre, concerts and all the gymkhanas and point to points which particularly interested her, he never seemed to drink excessively. Of course he liked his glass, but never gave any indication of serious drinking or even drunkenness. What she hadn't realized was that the moment he left her, raising his cap like a jockey after doing his bit of middle aged courting, he must have gone straight home to his bottle. When they were actually married, it wasn't long before she noticed his nightly tipple. He had a very large way of dismissing all he'd drunk before dinner, including what he'd had all the afternoon in the Spanish Club or the Exchange, by insisting that it could be discounted by what he'd just managed to get into his mouth while they ate. Ironically, they'd inherited a cellar from her father and he'd soon side-stepped his way through that like a will o' the wisp, all right. To be fair, he wasn't an alcoholic, there weren't sinister overtones, he didn't normally make scenes or smash things, but what he did do was fall asleep more often than he should. He was an Olympic sleeper, she'd once remarked. Nothing disturbed him. Like a bat, he could practically sleep upside down. Then he could sleep in trains, on aircraft, in boats, at the dinner table, even squatting at stool on the lavatory pan. It would have been rather amusing if it had been somebody else's husband, and that was another thing, he did look rather amusing, a jolly little man, and he was normally jolly, she was forced to admit.

When he wasn't asleep, when he wasn't escaping her with his fellows, when he wasn't being himself, in short.

So what was she to do? She knew she was the kind of woman who always made decisions, made them and stuck to them, and there were three short vertical lines above her nose giving her face a frowning intensity when she was not relaxed. But there was precious little chance of relaxation when he carried on as he did, without paying the slightest attention to what she called her inner needs. Very well then, she would bring matters to a head. But should she? Was it dangerous? Questions, questions, she said to herself and continued to frown.

She had gone out on to the balcony to think, but now she returned to the bedroom. He remained in bed, in exactly the same position as when she had left him, but he condescended to open first one eye, then the other. As usual, every inactivity on his part set her off. She forgot her doubts for the moment.

He said, "The thing was ..."

"I don't want to know."

"Some of the people we met last year ..."

"I said, 'I don't want to know'."

"... were there, and we had a bit of a ... well, a sing song actually."

She sat calmly and deliberately in the chair facing him. Must not shriek. Must be objective.

But she said, "Have you ever thought what it's like to grow up?"

"Just a bit of a sing song. What's the harm in that?"

"You said you were going for a stroll?"

"It er ... came on to rain."

"You could have got a taxi?"

"I didn't think. I thought you were on your pottery lark."

"The truth is, you'd rather be with them than me?"

"Not at all."

"It's true."

"Really, no. You're making an issue out of it."

"Don't you understand, it's a pattern, your leaving me, always for men, always your grubby acquaintances."

"Oh, come on. I haven't got any grubby acquaintances. Not here anyway."

He was making it good humoured, a domestic argument, but she was not going to have that.

"I never realized you were such a soak."

"Soak? Steady on." He raised his thick little eyebrows and pursed his lips as if a mild protest was justifiable at that remark, but for her sake, he wasn't going to make it.

"I know what you are, you see? I've read about it."

"Read about it?" he looked puzzled.

"You're a problematic heavy drinker," she said. She had actually read that, and it fitted, but she felt foolish saying it. And she was keeping none of her resolutions. She not only sounded like a shrew, but a dreadful blue stocking shrew. She bit her lip.

He was silent, looking away reprovingly. Again his face indicated he was saying nothing for her sake. He had no idea of the seriousness of the problem. Try again.

"I'll tell you – you can lie there, you can do nothing – you can say nothing, but the way you live, your life is dribbling away. Can't you understand? You're making yourself less than a human being."

"Oh, come..."

"Yes!" she said.

"I admit I had a bit too much."

"You were incapable."

"Indigestion. Olives," he said regretfully. "I like them, they don't like me."

Nothing she said seemed to get through to him. His one-dimensional conversation. He still had the quilt pulled up around his neck and there was something almost comic about him lying there like a dazed little pig tucked up in an expensive pram.

"I wonder sometimes what you want of me. Why you ever married me at all? I don't know what you think – ever. You never discuss anything. I don't even know what you think at any given moment. On any topic."

"Listen," he said. "I haven't got any complaints."

"What do you want then?"

"To do? Now?"

"No!" she said, but paused. He didn't understand. Or if he did understand, he was saying nothing. And his refusal to come to terms with her was an act of stubbornness for she knew he was basically a shrewd man. Nobody took him for a fool except her, and it was only on this domestic level that he put up a front. His mind was like wool when he wanted it to be, and that had come as a shock to her, because she came from a quite outspoken family. They weren't as Welsh as he was though, and they certainly weren't valley Welsh, who could, in her experience, be like Africans saying only what they thought you wanted to hear.

They had that capacity for living life on two levels, public and private, and it was this private self of his which she wanted to penetrate. Not that it was a Welsh problem, the two of them were so different as people, she quite realized.

But she would have to do something, she knew. Immediately! She would have to get through to him. But how?

He continued in his sog like a long-term hospital patient, not even looking at her when she had finished speaking. That was Welsh again. If you ignored a thing, it went away. But she must be reasonable. "Cool head!" she repeated to herself. But now his eyes closed again and she could have screamed. It was all she could do to stand up and return to the balcony where she continued to probe. She knew she had to be careful. She could go too far. But if only she could answer that one question. Why had he married her? And what had changed since he had? She meant from his point of view. Therein lay the crux of the matter she was sure.

She determined to make one last attempt. She'd dealt with his obesity, his drinking and the famous Lil. The only thing that remained reflected more on her. It couldn't be that he'd married her for her money. Vulgar as it sounded, one of the problems earlier in her life was just this, and of the three men who'd actively pursued her, two had their eye on the main chance, she was sure. If only parents realized what harm their money did, she thought. She remembered the casual inquiries about the number of cars they ran at home with a shudder. But she couldn't say that about him. One of the endearing things about him was that he'd done rather well, like almost everybody who'd been in property since the war. And Welsh or not, like most Estate Agents, he was a frightful snob when it came to the women he had working for him. The girls in the front office always had to come from a good school. Diamond Lil would have been no good to him dealing with the county families, the Butes, or the Lord Lieutenant, she thought maliciously, and she knew well enough that he always took care to have her with him when he did his country-house prospecting in the Vale. So that was one relief, she was sure. She was everything he wanted socially. It followed without saying, but it was reassuring to say it. Of course, he'd once said that nobody would see a Welsh outside half in the gutter, but that was a joke. It had to be, or where was her father's toryism then?

She sighed. If only she could have shared jokes like this with him. It was so sad, his retreat from her. But she mustn't digress. It was marriage-mending day, she said to herself with an attempt at gaiety.

There remained only one avenue which she had not explored – herself. Suppose she were lying in there, seeing things from his point of view, but looking out at herself? Perhaps that was the crucial thing. There was no point in keeping up with things or being well informed unless you were prepared to turn your mind inwards, spotlighting your own deficiencies, and, of course, as she well knew, she was not perfect. Not by any means. But if there was one thing she would have liked people to say about her, it was that she had character and was honest. Very well.... What was the picture of her which could be seen from the outside? It was a rather intelligent question to ask when she came to think of it, but having asked it, her jealousy returned once more like a sharp stabbing pain.

It was the old problem, the other one again, and no matter how furiously her mind worked, laying one idea on top of another like slices of crispbread, she always reached the same point, the moment when she hesitated and there came, floating into her consciousness like a sail around a headland, that face from the discarded wedding photograph, Lil, Lil, Lil. It was small and whimsical, chin tilted as she looked trustingly up at him, the soft parted lips, that clinging hand, the adoring eyes, that dated, page-boy hairstyle that must have been thought so *chic* in some backstreet hairdresser's. There was a dependent helplessness about it that Esme had never possessed and it was always in the same pose, always striking the same unobtainable note. She was the sort of *little* girl that men felt guilty about leaving, whereas Esme knew that she was the sort who was punished, and at times, she felt there was no escape from the role which her personality had cast for her.

Despairingly, Esme stuck to her train of thought, however. If she had any quality, it was grit, and while it was absurd to be sitting here in Portugal worrying about some trollop from a fish-and-chip shop in Dan y Graig Street, or wherever it was, if there was something which she could learn, she would learn it. And perhaps she was on the right track after all. There was one quality which she did lack and which was manifestly apparent in that photograph. She was never clinging, Esme realized, and never openly dependent. Worse – and she had had trouble with this before – she was very often thought too clever by far. People went off you when you were always right. They found it so formidable. Cleversticks, she thought. She did feel guilty because she had taken pains to disguise it during their courtship, but no doubt, like his drinking, it must have showed afterwards. She was just as much to blame then, in this one respect. Well, if she had to come all the way to Portugal to find out, it was worth it. Now she knew what to do. It was her business, her very feminine business to be the flyer half. She was jolly lucky she'd given her mind so ruthlessly to the situation in time.

Right! Decision – action!

She went back inside the room. Of course, he was pretending to be asleep now. He lay back on the pillows, his eyes closed, looking strangely boyish in his sleep. His hair, once fair, was grey, but still curly and she was delighted he still kept it short. Say what you like, he was a rugger man, a famous rugger man, and that was something, she supposed. She really was proud to believe that he was the best of them all. Her thoughts had turned the full circle. That was what insight did for you. And she did care for him. Now that her father was dead, he was really all she had.

"Darling," she said, "I've got a confession to make. Really ... I want to apologize." She put one hand on his shoulder.

He opened his eyes and blinked. The Alka-Seltzer had done some of its work. He scrambled up on one elbow and leant against the bed-head.

"I want to talk to you," she said in a much gentler voice. "Really talk to you."

"Of course."

"I've been thinking ..."

"Just let me get dressed. I'll take you out to lunch."

"Will you?"

"Yes. And I'm very sorry about last night. Will have to cut down."

"That's just what I was going to suggest."

"Good then," he gave her a friendly grin.

"And if I'm a bit bossy," she said shyly, "sorry, I sounded like a shrew just now."

"Not at all," His famous hand seemed lost for something to do, but he patted her affectionately.

"We have to make adjustments all through life," she said. She suddenly felt rather grand. "Especially at our age." It was very nice of her to include her age with his, she thought.

"Of course, dear," he manoeuvred himself out of bed slyly, first an arm, then a leg, then both legs. It was a controlled slide, edging discreetly away from her. "But I don't want to hear another word. My fault entirely."

There, she thought. It had worked. Just like that.

But in the bathroom, he stuck his tongue out at the mirror, his mind returning immediately to an argument of the previous night that had driven him to apoplexy. Neither husband, nor estate agent, nor clubman was recognisable.

"Barry John," he said to himself. "Barry-bloody-John!" Dear God, under the old rules he wouldn't have lasted until they got the oranges out! And as for this All Black lot, why didn't they strip 'em to the waist, give 'em knives and have done with it! He'd thought he was going to have a coronary every game they played – and won. God blast them, and damn them to hell! Thank God for Llanelli anyway.

"Scarlets forever!" he said, and later: "Now then, darling, where would you like to go?"

LESLIE NORRIS

Sing It Again, Wordsworth

Last night I woke with a troubled mind. It seemed to me that I had no roots, that there was no place, however distant, to which I could return at so desolate a moment. Despite its familiarity, the years I've had of touching and using its furniture, its known sounds, I awoke lost in my own room. The house seemed to hang alone in space. I got out of bed and walked to the window, heavily, groaning a little, my feet turned out like those of an old man. The moon was high. There was enough light to show deep shadows under the bushes and to make sharp the angles of walls, but I recognised nothing. The world stopped at the boundaries of the garden. To imagine the solid lane which passes my gate, its hedges of elder and hawthorn, its green ditch, was an impossible act of the will. I tried in an agony of memory to recall the faces of the men who would soon be cycling in the dawn light along the lane to work. I could not remember one of them, though they are men I've known for years.

This house was built for me twenty years ago. I made its garden from the untouched meadow; the shrubs and trees grow where I planted them. I marked the new course of the little stream at the boundary, dug it out by hand, plank by plank bridged it. It is my home. Yet I went back to bed unable to imagine the feel of the spade in my hand, unable to think of the colour of the roses already abundant in the borders. I turned on my side knowing I would not sleep again.

The weathers and scenes of childhood remain long in a man's mind, and I tried to remember them; but when I searched among the images of the past I found myself too far away. I have travelled away from those places for half a lifetime. Their summers are thin and cold, their voices inaudible. It was then that I realized there is no place mine without the asking for it, no place where I belong by clear right. Sitting in the late afternoon sun, lounging, relaxed, I can smile at that fear in the night. I know that if I had to choose at this moment a place to be native to, I would be unable to decide. I think of the Dysynni Valley, the loveliest in Wales. I see the Dysynni River winding inland from its salt lagoon through the soft, coastal fiats above Tywyn, past the village of Llanegryn where the squat little church, a holy place for over a thousand years, lies under a buffeting wind. Then the river cuts directly into the heart of Cader Idris, the high, wild moorland. Round-shouldered cormorants fly in from the sea until they reach Bird Rock and they sit there, on the harsh cliff above the river, alert for migratory sea trout. I would travel farther, the austerity of the mountains each side of me; I would climb to Castell-y-Bere, aloof on its long rock, its great walls fallen. When I was sixteen I stood one night near this castle, on the lip of a stone ridge high above the Dysynni, and I saw another river, one invisible by day, run straight and flat over the meadows and into the eye of the moon. I could not believe what I saw. I climbed down the steep face, leaped the fence, ran into the visionary water. It was quite dry. I ran in the brittle stubble and dusty grass of a harvested field. What I had thought a river was the light of the moon reflected in the webs of millions of ground-covering spiders, each filament luminous with borrowed moonlight. I stood in the middle of the glittering track and looked the moon in the face.

Or I could be a man of Dorset, that secretive, beautiful county. We used to live there, near Sherborne. We rented a cottage in a lane between Yetminster and Thornford. In a place of beautiful stone houses ours was ugly.

It was over a hundred years old but time had done nothing to soften the raw brick of its walls. It had been a labourer's cottage, built for a man who would spend all daylight in the fields. It was not meant to be attractive; it was meant for poverty. Its rooms were mean and damp, its windows narrow, fires burned reluctantly in its niggardly grates. In summer a climbing rose, the good old noisette Gloire de Dijon, ramped over the south wall and reached the roof, filling the air with nostalgic perfume. Its buff flowers lasted through June and occasional faded blooms hung on bravely into September. It was as old as the cottage and its only decorative element. We had no neighbours, but old Mr Ayling, who farmed nearby, sometimes spoke to us. He let us walk in his pastures, showed us where the horse mushrooms grew, enormous, flat, creamy, over an inch thick. We'd put one in the pan and fry it as if it were a steak.

One Saturday I walked away from the house, past Beer Hackett church and up Knighton Hill. The year had begun to turn into spring and fat buds were waiting on the trees. A cold sun shone, windflowers were growing, frail and white, in sheltered places. I marched through Lillington and up into hilly country near Bishop's Caundle. Leaning on a field gate I looked down into the valley, imagining it turned greener as I watched. Then, from the narrow head of the top field, the hounds ran. Sixteen couples streaming in freedom together, the full, beautiful pack, certain of their line, unstoppable in their galloping. Behind them, riding hard, came the boldest members of the hunt. I could see old Mr Ayling. He had lost his hat and his long white hair was shining in the sun. Too far away to hear the sounds of the chase, I watched their brilliant, silent charge through the valley. It was exhilarating, heartwarming. I stood on a bar of the gate and almost cheered.

A movement among the fists of the new green ferns close by distracted me. It was a small dog fox, hardly more than a cub. I could see his wedge-shaped head. He came out of the hedge, grinning, measuring me with a quizzical little eye, and sat down, settling himself carefully on his thin hams. Vaguely embarrassed, I stepped off the gate and stood near him. He didn't move. Together we watched the disappearing hunt, together we watched the stragglers vanish awkwardly into the bottom wood. The little fox was panting lightly, but he was not distressed. He got up, gave me a sardonic glance, and trotted jauntily down the lane, his brush swinging. It was a revelation to me. I saw that I was on the side of the fox. Such experiences make a man native to a place; I could live in Dorset.

Or in Seattle, I could live there. To think of that Pacific city, ringed by conical hills and filled with the sounds of water, makes me homesick. I liked Seattle from the day I flew in. When I'd been there about a week I went into a tackle shop to buy a fishing licence.

"Are you an alien?" asked the sad, middle-aged lady as she opened her book of licences.

I was astonished and then ashamed. I had to admit I was an alien. "It's more when you're an alien," she said. "That will be seven dollars seventy-five."

I gave her the money.

"Don't be sore," she said; "I've been an alien fifty years. Ever since my parents brought me over from Huddersfield."

I got in the Volkswagen and drove out to Quillayute, a little place on the Olympic Peninsula, and the next morning I took three jack salmon out of the Bogachiel before breakfast. The sun was not up, and I stood on a rock in midstream and threw my spinner into the margin of a fast current and the fish came to me. I went all over Washington State and I took steelhead from the Skagit River and the Stillaguamish River and cutthroat from Chopaka Lake and Jameson Lake and the Hood Canal. And later, sailing out of Aberdeen, I took a big salmon from the ocean, but I was still an alien. Oh, I could live out there, just as I could live at Summer Cove, County Cork, a mile from Kinsale, on the north shore of Kinsale Harbour.

I'm deceiving myself, I know that. The little Dorset fox and the lady in the tackle shop were right; I'm an outsider and an alien. I have this insatiable thirst for other places. I cannot remain at peace for long in one place. I've known this for some time, I see it plain. I work alone, travelling haphazardly the length of the country, shake hands with people I'll never see again, come home. Sometimes I travel by train or plane, but mostly I drive.

Next week I shall drive to Birmingham, knowing every yard of the way. Once I'd have got out my maps and guides, plotted the journey with care, set off early so that I could see every ancient landmark, fine church, old house on the way. For a happy morning I'd have balanced the attractions of one route against those of another. But that's all done now. Next week I'll drive to Birmingham taking the fast roads and the journey will take just over two hours. I shan't stop anywhere.

I went to college in Birmingham. I knew the place well when I was young.

My homeward journeys, often late at night, are nearly always unplanned and instinctive. Last year I was working on the North Wales coast, near Prestatyn. I finished in the early evening and decided not to stay for dinner. I paid my hotel bill and carried my bags to the car. I wiped the midges from the windscreen, sat in the car, fastened the safety belt, and went. I was going to make a fast run. It had been raining earlier, but the evening was brilliantly dry and sharp, the air washed clear. A few clouds moved out at sea, low on the skyline. I sat upright and relaxed, utterly at peace, knowing the extremities of the car as I knew my own skin, driving with the fingertips. I came down the Ruthin road, the A525, neatly and circumspectly, with an amused caution, knowing I could put the car wherever I liked, sensitive even to the grain of the road.

At Ruthin I turned off for Corwen and Llangollen. It was dusk, and a cold, erratic wind began to get up. Soon, before I reached Oswestry, I switched on the headlights. The road was empty. I went straight down the marches through Welshpool and Newtown before hitting the A44 at Crossgates. It was raining hard when I got to Kington. I stopped there and found a little coffeehouse still open, spoke a while with the sleepy young Italian waiter, and drifted gently out of town, the roads dark and wet. It was past midnight when I drove through Hereford. The heavy rain stopped as I was leaving the city. A policeman came out of a shop doorway, took off his wet coat, and shook it.

I knew where I was in general terms, but the darkness and the rain were making things difficult to recognise. I wanted to head for Gloucester through Peterstow and Ross-on-Wye, a road I've driven many times, but when I ran on to a long stretch of dual carriageway I knew I was lost. I wasn't worried. I knew I'd meet familiar roads soon enough. I pushed hard down the wide road, the car dipping gently as it met small pools of water at the edge of the drying surfaces. Two coaches passed, travelling in the opposite direction, their interior lights bright. I saw people asleep in their seats, their heads lolling against windows. The dual carriageway ended and with it the sodium lights overhead. I began to swing down the bends of a narrower road, the weight of sudden darkness oppressive. It was raining again. The car rocked like a boat through the washing gutters and I hunched my shoulders against the hills I felt were steep and close on either side. One or two houses, unlit and blank, stood at the sides of the road. Then I saw the river. I'm a sucker for rivers. I stopped the car and got out. Wind lashed the end of my coat, the rain stung in its gusts. It was a lovely river; swollen by storm, ominous, full to the lips of its grass banks, its loud, black thunder rolled in the channels of my ears.

I got the big torch out of the car and walked down the road. The one street of a village slept under the whipped rain and I walked right through, to the far end. Then, on the left hand, a marvellous abbey pushed its ruined walls into the darkness, very Gothic, very romantic. I let the straight beam of the torch climb on its stones and arches. I knew where I was. I was in Tintern, on the banks of the Wye, looking at Tintern Abbey. A miracle of the night had brought me there. A single light came from a distant hill farm, hanging in the darkness a long way up. I watched it for a long time, wondering what emergency had called its people awake at two in the morning. It went out and I was left alone, listening to the loud river and the swift noise of the rain, I danced a little soft-shoe shuffle at the side of the road, in honour of William Wordsworth.

Laughing, I ran back to the car, took off my soaked coat, and drove down to Chepstow. Soon I was sidling cautiously on to the M4, heavy at that hour with groaning trucks out of Newport and Cardiff, and two hours later I was in bed.

Next week I shall drive straight up to Birmingham and straight back, unless I visit Arthur Marshalsea.

When I first went to college in Birmingham I lived in one of the hostels and Arthur Marshalsea had the room next to mine. His parents lived out at Sutton Coldfield, only a few miles away. Arthur could have travelled each day, but he wanted to live in college. He came into my room the first morning of term; I was making my bed. He wanted to borrow a book, a dictionary. I could see that was an excuse. Arthur stood just inside the door, dressed in a dark track suit with red flashes. He was not tall, but very powerfully made, long-armed, deep-chested. He spoke slowly, using a deep, cultured voice. It wasn't the way he normally spoke, I could tell that. He was trying out one of the many personalities a young man adopts before he accepts the mask that best fits him, or, if he's lucky, presents his own face to the world. He didn't open the dictionary I gave him.

"Coming over to the dining hall?" he asked.

We walked over together and after that we did most things together. Arthur had more pure energy than any other person I've known. Most mornings I'd be the first to get up in our building. I'd potter about for half an hour, relishing the slow quiet of the early day, sit in my armchair and read, make a pot of tea for myself and perhaps for Billy Notley, who came from Worcester and took the same courses I did. I'd shave slowly, feeling the pleasure of a long day stretching out in front of me. I liked that morning silence, I liked my footsteps to echo through the empty halls and corridors.

But when Arthur got up it was like an electric storm. At once the place vibrated. Arthur would be singing, laughing out of his window at friends on their way to breakfast; he would be washing and shaving, surrounded by lather and steam, his towels spinning and flapping; he would be out and off at a run, springing over the ground. He ran everywhere. His knowledge of the city and the countryside around was immense. Most free afternoons we'd get out and Arthur would show me some strange area, streets of small factories, full of old men skilled in dying crafts; a long stretch of black canal, still, very quiet, only a few yards from the city centre; old markets where you could buy cheeses, lengths of cloth, brass candlesticks black with grime and age. I learned a lot about the city from Arthur. In return I talked to him about plays and novels, went to the theatre with him, wrote most of his essays. We played for the college soccer team, Arthur and I, he our one player of true quality and I a competent midfield player. We played other teams around the Midlands, sometimes on Saturdays, often on Thursday afternoons.

One Saturday morning we played at Dudley, a Black Country town near Wolverhampton. It was in early March, and a week of rain had made the ground heavy and difficult, but that day I was possessed by something like inspiration. I ran as if fatigue were a myth, I passed and tackled with a perfect stylish accuracy, I went around opponents as if they were insubstantial as mist. I scored two goals in the first twenty minutes, one with a precise lob from a long way out. It seemed to me that I knew every bounce of the ball. Near the end of the game

Arthur took the ball in our opponents' half, turned inside the fullback, and ran, huge leaping strides carrying him over the mud. I ran inside him, a couple of yards behind. Reaching the penalty area, he checked the ball and pushed it delicately into my path. It was a perfect pass, perfect in weight and speed. I hit the ball with a full swing of the right foot and I saw, as I fell, how it flew into the top corner of the net. It was there, a complete goal, before the goalkeeper had begun to make his leap. I can still recapture every moment of that thirty-year-old game. Afterward I took a bus into the city centre and Arthur came with me.

The municipal art gallery was showing a visiting exhibition of paintings by Van Gogh. For the first time, all the great oils had been brought together, and suddenly I knew I wanted to see them, it was essential for me to see them. We climbed the steps and went in. I could see all the famous paintings I'd known only in reproductions and the sight of those intense and passionate statements set me eloquent. Moving from canvas to canvas I told Arthur of the splendour and individuality of Van Gogh's vision, of the unity of his composition, of the values he gave to the sun in this picture and that, of a thousand things I'd never thought of before but which were suddenly both simple and novel. It seemed to me then that I knew the purpose behind every stroke of the man's brush. In a few minutes I had collected a small respectful audience. This didn't deter me. Aware of the farcical nature of the situation, I explored even wilder flights of invention and rhetoric, but while I was amused I thought that what I said was right and necessary, that there was little about art and life and Van Gogh which was unknown to me at that moment. It was an hour of serious and absurd playacting. At the end I was exhausted. Arthur stepped up to me and shook my hand warmly.

"Young man," he said, "that was a privilege and a pleasure. You have given us all a rare insight into the workings of a creative mind. I hope you will not be offended if I give you this as a sign of my appreciation." He gave me a coin. I started to laugh, but Arthur held up his hand firmly, smiled at me as if he were some polite and well-intentioned stranger, and walked away. My other listeners pressed forward, murmured their gratitude, pushed their offerings into my hand. I held a solid fistful of currency there. When I got outside Arthur was waiting for me, leaning over the balustrade, laughing. We had enough money to visit the cinema and eat a generous dinner at a restaurant normally well out of our reach. Content and leisurely aristocrats, patrons and lovers of the arts, we arrived back late that night at our hostel.

Most evenings we sat in our rooms, working away with the thin plaster walls between us. Conversation was easy. Sometimes we sang. The singing was Arthur's idea. His voice was smooth and pleasant and he knew all the hits, but his great gift was for infallible harmony. However badly I carried the tune, Arthur could so accept and modulate my errors that we always sounded good, a partnership of deliberate melodies. And as our time passed by, we got better. Arthur began to speak almost daily of his wild ambition for us to become a professional act, to stand in the dim and changing lights, dressed in tuxedoes, singing 'How Deep is the Ocean', 'Blue Moon', 'My Funny Valentine', 'Stardust', other standards from our long repertoire. I used to listen to him, but I knew it was fantasy.

He was my friend; we shared our money, our time, our work; we supported each other through the little communal storms which blew up occasionally. At the end we shook hands and parted. I went off to Taunton, Arthur stayed in Birmingham and became a teacher of physical education. He was a fine athlete, the fastest sprinter in the Midland counties.

A year later I went back up to Arthur's wedding. He married Sally, a slim, elegant girl, taller than he. When it was time for Arthur to make his speech, he stood up, smiled, raised his glass to the guests, to his bridesmaids, and with a serious, touchingly humble gesture, to his wife. He didn't say a word; and then he sat down. Later, we watched them drive off to the airport. I haven't seen them since. We wrote to each other, Arthur and I, but the letters dribbled to a halt as time gave us other things. The Christmas cards came to an end. I never thought of Arthur Marshalsea. Five weeks ago, when I knew I was to visit Birmingham, I asked the education people to put me in touch with him. It would be good, I thought, to see what the years had done for Arthur Marshalsea. Sometimes I remembered with a smile his escapades, could almost see him running, hunched, muscular, concentrating every yard of the way. Last night a girl who said she was Arthur's daughter telephoned me from Birmingham. I listened to the young voice, realizing that this was a girl I had not known existed. She had been born and grown into her responsibilities without my knowing she was in the world.

"Great," I said. "Nice of you to telephone. I'll be in Birmingham next week, and I'd like to see Arthur."

She told me that Arthur had been very ill. I could call, but I must not be shocked when I saw him. Unusually strong and active, playing football regularly until he was nearly fifty, Arthur had set off last Easter to walk through the Lake District and come back the length of the Pennine Way. He had planned it for months, his journeys were marked, his climbs plotted, each piece of equipment tested. The girl and her mother had watched him leave the house with his backpack and his ashplant and tramp sturdily down the road. Ten minutes later he was carried home unconscious.

"It's his heart," I said. "He's had a heart attack."

Not at all. An insidious virus, attacking his brain, had brought him down. For nine weeks he had lain in hospital, unconscious in his white bed. His return to the world was slow and painful. For a long time he had been deaf and blind. Even now, although improving, he cannot walk unaided, he cannot feed himself. Slowly he is learning to read again. His voice is often uncontrolled and often says the wrong words, which angers him. It was shocking to think of Arthur helpless. I wrote down the address as the girl gave it to me. They live just outside Knowle, on the way into Birmingham from Warwick. I know the place. I've walked along the canal bank at Knowle and watched the wild geese sit in the fields, spoken to the patient, laconic anglers waiting for small roach to bite. It won't be difficult to find Arthur's house.

After I spoke to the girl I took a glass of whisky and water and thought about Arthur. I went to bed, but sleep was not restful and afterward I awoke with a heavy mind.

I've been thinking of what I shall say to Arthur when I see him. I can hear already the falsely cheerful voice I shall use, the loud memories. Almost anything I say to him will remind him that he cannot walk, that his speech is guttural and false. How can I talk to him of the game at Dudley when he pushed the ball to me and I hit it sweetly even as I was falling? Or speak of the going-down dinner when we sang 'That Old Black Magic'? Frankie Smedley, too drunk to see the keys, had played for us, and the next morning he had had no memory of it at all.

The days are gone when nobody in the Midlands could run as fast as Arthur, when his voice was young and strong and he could hit any note he wanted with easy accuracy, and I'll not talk of them. I'll tell him about the Dysynni Valley, how the river begins up there in Cader Idris. I'll tell him of my time in Washington State, how the waves hit the beaches at La Push and Grayland, rolling in behind the cold fling of the Pacific spray. I'll invent Summer Cove for him, describe the silken passage of the seals, tell him of my dark, unintentional journey to Tintern.

But all the time I'm thinking of Arthur lying nine weeks in a coma, his body in its clean linen being turned at the appointed times by the brisk, compassionate nurses, being fed through sterile tubes. Where was he then? He must have been away somewhere in some solitary darkness, weightless, without senses. I imagine him moving on some dark beach, so lightly he does not disturb a grain of the sand. He can feel nothing. I should like to know where he was then; I am consumed with a curious pity for Arthur Marshalsea, his useless legs, his halting speech. I see in him a terrible general fate about which we shall know very little. The still, sad music of humanity ... wasn't it? Sing it again, Wordsworth.

JACI STEPHEN

The Other Side of Summer

For three summers Julia had been building the wall. There was some contractual clause stating that Grange Cottage should not be visible from The Dell, which faced it, and the new neighbours were adamant that a barrier be constructed between the two houses. Julia could not be bothered to argue. She began searching for large grey stones, bought two bags of sand and cement, and started work.

Grange Cottage was three miles from 'civilization' and was surrounded by only four other houses. Regular trips were made into town throughout the day – a forgotten comic for Stephanie, meat for the dog, extra bottles of milk – yet the family never seemed disorganized. I would 'call in for coffee' and invariably become involved with the tasks at hand; so if Julia went into town for extras, I went along too. Julia liked to make her visitors part of the family and when she started the wall our trips became regular. At first, Adrian went to collect the enormous bags of sand and cement, until his back gave way. "It always happens during the holidays," said Julia, and laughed, proud of her own physical immunity. So we went together and I feigned interest, discussing prices in relation to weights. I agreed with her every time that we had certainly made a bargain purchase.

It was a warm July day when we began. When I say 'we' I mean that I filled buckets with water from the kitchen and made regular cups of tea and coffee, waitressing to both invalid and builder. Sometimes I attempted to smash the larger stones with a hammer, but usually gave up in exasperation when I was able to chip only atoms of dust from their surface, though I was convinced I put heart and soul into the effort. Julia would laugh and mimic my action before bringing the hammer down again, splitting the stone into four or five substantial chunks.

Most of the time, I sat and watched. It was the pattern of three summers. On that first day, Julia was like a child on Christmas morning, having so many toys and not knowing which to play with first. She stood contemplatively and then moved slowly around a huge pile of stones, gathered from the nearby quarry during the week; observed them from different angles, unable to decide upon which to handle first. I have never seen anyone become so involved with physical work as did Julia that summer. It preoccupied her totally. She was possessed. Oblivious to her daughter, her husband, and to me. Only when she successfully picked the 'right' stone from the pile of hundreds, and fitted it perfectly into position, did her eyes resume their usual childish sparkle and smile. Then she stepped back, admiring it balanced in position and asked me what I thought.

"It looks fine."

"But don't you *see?*" she asked. She didn't require an answer. What I was never able to see was something that should obviously have been perceived. I continued, in my ignorance, filling buckets.

Julia's mortar had to be exactly the right texture and her frustration showed in thin red veins under her eyes if the consistency did not obey the demands of her trowel. She pushed the dry ingredients into a pointed heap in a wide, shallow bucket, and dug out the middle to make an 'island'. She said that was what Adrian said when he poured milk into the middle of Stephanie's scooped-out dish of dry Ready Brek flakes. Julia frowned. "But it's not an island," she said, pouring water into the hollow, "it's an oasis."

She pushed the slope of sand and powder gradually into the water, willing the concoction to meet the right texture. The movement of her arm stiffened as the mixture became thick and she added a little more powder, a drop more water until, again, the satisfied glow of success lit up her face and summoned her body back into action.

She carried the bucket to where the stone lay balanced and checked it again for its weight and general appearance in the wall as a whole.

"You don't think I ought to put it at the front, do you?"

"Yes, why not?" I answered.

"But it's a bit big really. I think I'd better leave it at the back."

"Yes, I think it'll be better there, too." My answers were mechanical, in agreement with everything she said: firstly because she never listened and, secondly, because the stones obeyed only her. The foundation stones were laid in a double row, to give more body, Julia said, and as she intended the 'best' side to face her own house, the positioning of the 'good' and 'bad' was an important issue.

"Definitely one for the back," she said, picking out a motley-coloured shape. Satisfied with her decision, she scooped cement into the space. She picked up the stone reverently, as if about to carry a sacrifice to the throne of God. She laid it carefully on the cement, as if afraid to wake it, and made adjustments – small firm twists between her dusty hands – until it sank into position, as if it had been designed specifically for that space alone. I never spoke. Words would have been blasphemous. Then Julia took a smaller instrument than the one she used to lay the cement. It was like a small pallet-knife and she filled in the crevices around the stone until it merged like an extension of the previous day's sculpture.

"There, look!" She brought the loose cement from the sides into one upward scraping movement, as if scooping dribbled food from around a baby's mouth.

"Mmm, marvellous, wonderful, great." I ran out of adjectives. I had no idea what to say to her. It was a stone in a wall. Hardly an object of aesthetic wonder. Julia never suspected my bemusement, she was too wrapped up in the whole thing.

As the wall grew, our relationship changed. In some ways, we moved further apart: the conversations we had enjoyed indoors were gone, the eating and drinking through the long hours of Wimbledon. I missed all of it. Julia, on the other hand, went on living day by day, stone by stone. Sometimes I felt guilty because I couldn't see life through her eyes. Cheerful, satisfied eyes. Now, I don't think it was happiness. I was probably far happier than she. But she was contented. The kind of joy that comes with acceptance: acceptance of suffering, evil, the knowledge that there's very little you can do about it; joy in man's very capacity to hold on. But there was a sadness in it, too: most of all during those summer afternoons and early evenings, when her shadow lengthened along the greyness of the wall. What did she see in those few seconds when the stone first clung to the cement, the cracks were secured, and another part of the wall was completed? They were brief revelations. Moments of transparency.

I was used to silence at the wall. It was as if the words knew by instinct which were the wrong moments to speak. We talked less and less. Sometimes we came close. Understanding nothing but the knowledge that we were each searching. Waiting. Hoping. A sense of silence, more peaceful than the absence of movement and sound. We waited for it. An expectant silence, though nothing occurred. Then our relationship was beyond reach. But close. Closer than during the hours we had spent telling each other about ourselves. Knowing about, and knowing. The point at which you pass beyond knowing an accumulation of facts about someone, to simply knowing.

Julia would tell me to listen to the silence: pinecones splitting their stiff winter scales, a continual crackle of life in the forest. She recognised the different birds' cries and, like a frightened animal, heard footsteps long before they became audible to me. Everything was so green. So still. Stephanie played on the lawn, hunting for four-leaf clovers. She tried to find one for each of her parents and for me. Once she found two and asked if her father would be unlucky because she hadn't been able to find a third.

"He can share mine," said Julia. "I'm lucky enough for two." Stephanie smiled.

The second summer was a particularly bad one and Julia did very little work on the wall. It put her in bad spirits. She stood in the kitchen and gazed out through the window to the dark, wet stones. She moved noisily about the house, as if in the belief that the rain had been sent to taunt only her. I was glad of it. I sat indoors, hoping to resume something of our former relationship, pick up in the middle of an old conversation. It was impossible. Everything we said seemed to have been uttered so many times before. Our words were stale and we wearied of each other's company. We sat in the kitchen waiting for silences that never came. Only the incessant tapping, followed by the sudden gushing of the rain; lightning illuminating the silhouette of black trees, thunder rocking the air, wind shaking the cones from their branches.

THE OTHER SIDE OF SUMMER

"I hate this country," said Julia. She never amplified the statement. As she stood again at the window, mentally building the next stage of the wall, I knew she could never leave – the country or the house. They would have to carry her away by force. The wall had taken a part of her it would never let go. Behind the melting rainwater glass they were like separated lovers, unable to communicate because of unforeseen circumstances arising since they made their original plans.

Occasionally the sun broke through, but for the most part the rain kept the surface too wet to allow for further construction.

"I must finish it," Julia would say, "the neighbours say it's in the contract. It has to be finished." She became obsessive about its completion, as if sensing that something would stop her. To compensate for her lack of activity, she talked about it. Incessantly. How she had dug the foundation, measured it, arranged the position of stones so that they curved almost in a full semi-circle, two arms welcoming her as she came from the house. It was her only topic of conversation. My sympathies transferred to her family. How did Adrian communicate with her? Perhaps he had fantasies about burying her in it. I certainly did. Sometimes, holding the sharp pallet-knife, I imagined stabbing her. I built up a mental picture in which, after killing her, I laid her neatly across the top of the wall in a bed of wet cement; watched her sink slowly, inch by inch between the two layers of stones, her body thickly consumed with the rise of concrete on either side. A grey coffin. When I smashed the stones with the hammer I thought of creeping up behind her crouched body when she was working meticulously between the cracks, and slamming it down with as much force as I could on her skull. Watching the white bone fly into millions of pieces, set into the wet cement like broken glass.

I didn't return to the cottage that rainy season. I had nothing more to say on the subject of walls. Also, Julia had bought two goldfish to amuse her when she was unable to work. She sat and watched them with the same concrete euphoria, ignoring me sometimes for half an hour at a time.

The following year was one of the hottest summers on record. During the fourth week of unbroken sun, I cycled over the Julia's one afternoon. She had made considerable progress with the wall and it stood well over four feet most of the way along. I leant my bicycle against the side of the house and went in at the back door, which was open. Julia was nowhere to be seen in the garden and I hoped, on entering the house, that she would be sitting in her usual seat, occupied by some other task. She was not.

"Hello!" I called. There was no answer. I called again. Stephanie came into the room.

"Mummy's outside," she said, and disappeared. I returned outside. I heard scraping and knew that Julia must be near the wall.

"Hello!" I called again. Her head appeared briefly over the top from the other side. She had caught the sun on her face and looked healthy and happy.

"Hi," she said. "Take a seat." She indicated a small stool on the opposite side of the wall from which she was working. I sat down.

"How are things?" she asked. "I haven't seen you for ages." A feeling of insecurity, speaking to an unseen figure, a voice set in concrete, made me pause.

"I said, how are you?"

"I'm fine," I answered at last. "And you?"

"Great. I've been working really hard."

"I can see," I felt ridiculous, perched on the tiny milking-stool, addressing the air. I looked around, embarrassed, and hoped no one was watching this first sign of madness. I was not invited around to the other side and felt it would be wrong to ask.

"How's Adrian?" I had the awful suspicion she was just tucking the last of his little finger into a wet crack.

"He's fine. I think. We're all fine." We were getting nowhere. The small, precise chippings and scrapings alienated me further from my friend. Suddenly, she broke the awkward silence between us. The scraping stopped.

"Do you know, I've been thinking ..." I prepared myself – the most recent cement on the market, the newest acquisition of stones....

"I don't think I'm an atheist in the same way as Adrian. I mean, he doesn't believe in anything." I remained seated on the other side of our strange confessional, surprised at hearing Julia talk about anything that didn't have its roots in concrete. I was the anonymous priest.

"... and there must be *something*." She paused. We had often talked about religion and it had always ended up the same: Julia criticized the church and the hypocrites attending it, and cruelly ridiculed many of my own beliefs and feelings. I had learnt not to expose myself.

"It would be wonderful to think, to know, that somewhere there was something greater than all this." I assumed she was making a wide gesture with her arms by the rise in her voice that sent the words more clearly to me. I conjectured how the blind form pictures by voices; yet, the more Julia talked, the less I was able to remember her face, as if with each word she were talking herself away. I felt that if I looked behind the wall her physical presence would have disappeared, yet her voice be continuing soulfully on.

"I've always felt that I didn't need God. He was for people who didn't have much, people who couldn't cope. I've always had everything I've wanted. I can honestly say I've been happy. But I think I'd just like to test Him. Know, once and for all. Give Him a litmus test like we did with acids and alkalis at school. Take this – whoever, whatever you are. Red, I'll believe. Blue, I'll know I've been right all along." There was a scraping sound of one continuous movement from left to right along the wall; then the spongy slice of the pallet-knife tapping on a cushion of cement. "I'd just like to know, that's all."

I was lost. From my confessional seat, I felt I ought to recommend six Hail Marys, tell her to beg forgiveness, go forth and not sin again. But I remained silent. I wondered what she had seen – again in the final shifting of a stone into place. I made coffee and returned to the stool while Julia worked, more quickly, it seemed, than ever before.

"This summer it will be finished," she said. "It will," she repeated, as if doubting my belief in her integrity and assurance. She spoke with the force of will, urging herself into the state of mind she knew its completion required. During that one afternoon the confessional rose between us by another layer of thick, grey stones. When I stood up, it topped my head by two inches. Julia had disappeared. I imagined her dark head close against the wall, intimate and secretive, sharing something to which I was an outsider. Our farewells met in the grey silence of confession. She would go on blindly, building stone on stone, layer upon layer, until she came to the God of her strange acquaintance.

It was my last meeting with Julia. Towards the middle of the summer I received a letter in which she told me that the wall was almost finished. The tone was one of urgency, as if she were writing under pressure. A week later I heard from Adrian. Julia had been rushed to hospital with a suspected tumour. Three days later she was dead.

At first I remembered our times together before she had started on the wall. I recalled whole conversations, the tiniest detail of insignificant events. And then, as suddenly as these images came, they disappeared. When I thought of the past three summers, it was as if Julia had never been at all. I tried to bring into focus the features of her face; I saw only the stony stare of the wall; the sound of her voice – the rough, rhythmical movement of her tools.

I returned to the cottage, hoping to stir the hard, grey memories back to life. It was an early evening in late August. Adrian and Stephanie were not at home. I stood outside and stretched my back against the cool wall. I listened. The evening was as I remembered it. Warm, green, the early evening sun resting on the red stone of the cottage, pine trees thick against the pink sky. The wall had grown higher, but it was unfinished, its serrated top exposed and uneven. I pressed the curve of my spine into it; the stones on either side wrapped their horseshoe arms around me. I felt the drawing of that grey strength that had dissolved Julia. Now it claimed my memory of her. The garden was totally silent: a silence not of peace, but a silence that is the consciousness of absent sounds: pine cones waking from their sticky winter sleep; the soft scraping of a knife; the slow, perfect sinking of a stone in wet cement.

DUNCAN BUSH

Boss

The woman angled open the door of the white wardrobe. Then, standing back, looked in its mirror at her now naked body – critically, even professionally, and with something of a grimace at the mouth.

The woman was tall, and perhaps too thin. But these were doubts to which she'd almost ceased to give credibility. Height was important for a model. And as for thinness, well, thinness was the only grace there was. Her hands and feet and head all looked, as usual, too large. But this was something she'd once been assured could only turn out well in photographs. All in all, she'd no anxieties about herself. No new ones, anyway. She'd learnt by now at least to live in her own skin.

She turned away and sat down on the red fur-fabric of the dressing-table stool, opposite the tilted mirror. She lifted one ankle onto her knee. Absently her fingers found and began picking at a snag of hard skin under her foot.

Then, putting down her foot, and with a sense of morose and irritated duty, she took the already half-used stick of theatrical greasepaint from the cardboard box beside the stool. She turned back the silver foil at the used end and began applying the stick to the inside of her left thigh, rubbing it over her skin in a broad, chocolate-coloured streak. Then, with the heel of the same hand, she smeared the trace into a uniform, smudged patch.

Methodically, patiently, she did the one leg, then the other: thigh and underside of thigh, knee and back of knee, calf and shaven shin, then ankle, instep ... finally, the ten toes and the space between them. She left only the soles of her feet undone. He said it was more authentic with the soles and palms left pink.

Then, with both legs darkened to the crease where the upper thigh joins the trunk, she dropped the greasepaint back in the box, looked at the watch laid out on the glass-topped dressing table behind her, and lit a cigarette.

She sat there, smoking and examining, in turn, the long, glossy brown legs: lifting and displaying each at various angles in the light, occasionally rubbing at a certain spot with her fingers. It was hard to get the colouring even all over.

At one point she took the coarse, close-curled Afro wig out of the box and – cigarette in mouth, squinting against the smoke – fitted it carefully over her skull, turning her head from side to side to judge the effect in the dressing-table mirror.

Finally, she crushed out the cigarette in the glass ashtray, pulled off the wig and tossed it on the floor. She looked at her watch, and bent to pick up the stick of greasepaint. One hand opened, in the lean creases of her belly, the sallow rose of her navel. With the other hand, she introduced the sloped, worn end of the umber greasepaint in its sleeve of silverfoil.

Her belly was tanned, and downed with tiny golden hairs. She hunched over it, working outwards and then downwards from the navel, rubbing the dark stain over the prominent hipbones and white loins, then in among the black roots at the upper margin of the pubic bush.

Next – by now weary of the whole lengthy procedure – she did her buttocks: standing to rub the soft stick into the cleft and spreading the colouring evenly across the cheeks with each massaging hand in turn – pivoting on the ball of each foot and looking backwards, over first one shoulder then the other, to gauge the effect in the long wardrobe mirror.

She did her back, as well as she could: reaching back over her shoulders or doubling up each arm behind her, until it ached.

Then she did the narrow, bony shoulders and the pale breasts. Finally each hand did the other, and that arm.

She lit a cigarette. She stood up and slipped the dark body into the cool dressing-gown of gold silk. Loosely knotting the tasselled cord at the waist, she went to stand by the folds of net curtain at the window.

She stared down from the third floor at the blue street, at streetlights, lit pavements and parked cars.

She made a short call on the red phone.

At a little after 9.30 she sat down again and began painting her toenails: lifting each heel in turn onto the edge of the stool, tucking the doubled knee in tight under her chin and, with almost childlike absorption, retouching each tiny crescent of nail with the thick, shell-pink varnish from the brush-stoppered bottle. The varnish gave off a strong odour, like almond essence (or, as she remembered reading in some thriller or other, cyanide).

Next she did the nails on each brown hand. They were oval, and as long and beautifully-kept as a guitarist's. The addictive scent of bitter almonds mingled with the faint, insidious smell of greasepaint.

"Mamma," he'd told her once – a light of gleeful delight in his pale eyes, wrinkling his nose disgustedly an inch from her dark thigh – "you even smell like one."

Cautiously she lit a cigarette and, examining them from time to time, sat waiting for her fingernails to harden.

When they were dry, she picked up the stub of greasepaint again and, throwing her chin up, began darkening the stretched skin at her throat.

She did her face last, and the most carefully: cheek, cheekbone, eye-socket, forehead, nose.... Intently she watched the result in the pivoted magnifying mirror she'd drawn towards her on the dressing-table. She was absorbed and, now, excited even – change is renewal.

She put on the Afro wig and adjusted it to conceal her short, fashionably razor-cut – and now shocking – blonde hair.

Then, standing, and slipping the gold dressing-gown from her shoulders and arms – it fell in a pool at her feet – she offered herself up in the wardrobe mirror: naked, gleaming, black.

"Mamma," she told her own reflected image, "you look gorgeous."

She displayed, more critically, the long black limbs. She smiled the surprising white teeth. Satisfied she looked convincing in the little light, she put on the slithery silk dressing-gown again and took off the wig, which made her skull itch.

It was almost ten. She lit another cigarette and, while it smouldered in the glass ashtray, put on the accoutrements: the narrow, tight gold chain at the base of the throat; the sliding cluster of silver bangles at the left wrist; the square leather thong wound tightly several times, then knotted, about the right ankle. He was very particular about the jewellery. The jewellery was his trigger.

She looked at her watch again: barely gone ten.

She mooned for a while in the window, behind the haze of net. She was suddenly restless, almost impatient: after the hour or so of simply getting ready, now she had time to kill. But then, sometimes they came too soon. You could never tell.

She looked up at the apartments opposite: yellow squares, or dark unlit windows in the pale wall. You could see in through net curtains when the light was on inside a room, and sometimes she had the feeling that someone over there was watching her – someone she couldn't see, of course, because his room, his window, was one of those that were still dark. It was only a feeling. But perhaps she'd better remember to let the blind down when he came.

She went to the dressing table, picked up her tipped cigarette – which had been transformed intact into a column of grey ash in the bowl – and crushed it out. One thing was, usually he didn't stay long.

Of course, getting started took a little time. That was normal. It took them all a little while to suspend disbelief in the rituals they insisted on. But, with this one, it was never easy. He'd just sit there, gulping gin and watching her, and he always gave the slightly furtive impression of being suffocatingly conscious of the very thing they were pretending at first not to have on their minds. The trouble was, let's face it, he had no class. No style. Sometimes, they literally came in through the door in role, and then it was always simple because you never had to think about the person underneath. But this one always wanted her to make the first move, which meant that she had to judge the moment, and his mood, which was always a tricky thing. Usually, she'd get him his gin, then wait a minute or two, or until she saw him lean right back into the sofa, and close his eyes. Then she'd slide in beside him and start stroking his temples and face. Everything had to be 'sinuous', that was the word he used, and she had to remember to keep the thin slide and rattle of the silver bangles going as she moved her hand about his head. Then, after a while, she'd ask him sympathetically:

"You had a hard day out there today, Boss?"

He'd shrug, and sigh heavily, with weariness.

"Hard enough."

He'd open his eyes to stare up at the ceiling. He had a blond, florid face, and in his watery blue eyes there stirred a self-conscious and evasive light: the sly, watchful child that the bluff, heavy, important man would never outgrow or successfully conceal.

Then, finally, he'd start talking – desultorily at first, and keeping his eyes turned upwards, as if to avoid hers. Often, though, his voice would start to gain some kind of conviction through his account, or even a wonderment at it. It was, perhaps, only through his own self-credulity that the expression of his face became one of openness.

As for the stories themselves, though – well, they were straight out of the comics, or those old Tarzan films they kept repeating on TV. He trapped black panthers with a tethered goat. He shot the heads clean off deadly snakes. He brought down a rampaging rhino with a single shot, placed neatly just behind the ear. Once, unarmed, he scared away a maneating lioness by repeatedly dazzling it with a small hand-mirror. In other words, he lived out in some preternatural bush from which at evening, worn out, he returned – a place teeming like a film-poster, with a different danger or adventure in each corner of the layout.

Sometimes, though, he'd just talk mundanely about a crop, some problem he was having with a blight, the laziness of his boys, or a day of quotidian duties such as putting up chain-link or barbed-wire fencing.

"I built this whole place up with my own bare hands," he'd tell her then.

And then, as if to show the incontrovertible truth of this remark, he'd show her, tragically upturned, both unused fleshy palms.

Yet occasionally the odd detail was convincing – as if the story, even if only hearsay, might have once been true. Like that time, say, when he'd told her about someone who'd accidentally run down a baboon which had suddenly scampered out in front of his Land Rover up some dirt road or other. Instinctively, the driver had pulled up thirty yards or so further on, and gone back to see if the animal was still alive. The other baboons in the pack, he'd told her, had come out of the bush and torn the man to pieces before he could get back to the vehicle. He himself had found the body "strewn all over the murrum road", with the Land Rover parked twenty yards away, the off-side door still open and the gearstick quivering.

He'd shrugged at her grimace of horror.

"This is a tough country," he'd told her. "He ought to have known better."

Then after a moment, he'd said:

"Anyway, you've done worse things to men."

"Not to you, though, Boss," she'd answered quickly. "I've always been good to you."

"Not me," he'd said at last. "But other men."

"Other men," she'd said, "aren't men, to me."

And he had laughed at that, and nodded.

Finally too, though, would come the point when his monologue had talked itself to a standstill, or simply petered out. He'd fall silent and again just sit there. Sometimes his silence would prolong itself for an awkward couple of minutes in which she would feel a slightly hectic false glamour come into her eyes and words and gestures as she kept things going and awaited him.

But then, at odd times, she experienced the same fear with other men. Every occupation had its risks. That furtive, bated look was no more than a vestigial embarrassment, a hesitancy to instruct her.

She stood up and laid the just-lit cigarette in the furrow of the glass ashtray. It was now well after ten. He might show up any minute now. She turned the tilted shade of the table-lamp more fully towards the wall, to shed a dimmer glow of light.

Then she crossed to the stereo system. She found the cassette of drums and tribal chants, and inserted it in readiness. It always reminded her of – what was it called? – the *Missa Luba*. One day, of course, he'd simply stop coming and she would inherit it. They always left the equipment.

She smeared her palm over a paler streak on the outside of her right thigh. She would never have passed in daylight, of course. But in that light it was a good enough job. She went back to the window and, holding aside the edge of net curtain, stared down into the street. A white-topped car cruised for a space, parked. A man not him got out of the car. She strolled back to the watch on the dressing-table. 10.15.

At twenty past, she lit another cigarette. That was the third packet today. She smoked too much. It was the waiting. When she was waiting, she always smoked. Killing time, and killing yourself while you were at it. It was like smoking cigarettes on the beach – you never really wanted them or enjoyed them. It was just something to do in the long boredom of the heat and getting a tan. Out of doors, under a blue sky, cigarettes somehow always tasted dead and dry.

Carrying the half-smoked cigarette carefully upright, she crossed to the ashtray and laid the little column of ash gently in it. She went to the window again and hung there, looking vaguely out in restive impatience – unsettled, anxious as if awaiting a lover. Turning away, she considered herself once more in the long wardrobe mirror, adjusting the accessories at throat and wrist.

Startling her, the electric doorbell jangled its double chime.

With a suddenly harried sense of relief she went quickly to stub her cigarette out and empty the ashtray into the woven straw basket beneath the glass-topped table. Stooping to the magnifying mirror, which she'd angled up at herself, she fitted the black Afro wig over her hair, straightening it carefully. She suddenly remembered to take out of the box – before toeing it out of sight beneath the bed – the buckled leather collar and the leather manacles and anklets with their loops of plated chain. She took a last look at herself, full-length, in the wardrobe mirror.

Reknotting the cord of the dressing-gown more tightly at the waist, she breathed in deeply, and consciously grew calmer, more deliberate, poised – the worst thing you can do is look flustered in front of a client. It scares them.

Just slow everything down a moment.

Take your time.

By now she was actually almost surprised that he'd come. Last time, she remembered, there had been that moment of ugliness which she must try to make up for, tonight. Misjudging his mood, or without really thinking – though at least, thank God, in that arch, possessive, teasing manner which, she'd learned, made even clumsy or prying questions pass as a form of flattery she'd asked him afterwards:

"Boss, why don't you really get yourself a nice strong black girl to do all this for you?"

He'd given her a look of astonishment. Then sat there for some moments in bitter and incredulous silence, before he got up, with the jacket in his hand, to leave.

"As far as I know, that," he told her with contempt, "is still illegal in this bloody country."

She smiled provocatively. Then closed the mirror on the hangered rows of clothes. Her watch showed twenty-five past. Probably she'd be through with everything by twelve. She switched the tape of jungle music on and sauntered, loose-hipped, to the chained and spy-holed door.

CLARE MORGAN

Losing

B ut what is it like?" she had asked her Mother a long time ago, when she was about eight and a half, the middle of the first year in the new school.

"Really. What is it *like*?"

"Oh. It is nothing. It is just a lot of heavy breathing, really. That is all."

She had been very much older than her years, even then. Distant relatives who came occasionally and went, wondered among themselves if she had ever really been a child.

"Such a dark, serious girl. And a great pity, when you think of it. But there."

And this one would smooth the multi-coloured feather at the side of her felt hat, that one would dust off the brim of his trilby with clean, thin fingers going the same way as the nap, and they would move on to other more important issues, the rising cost of living, the encroachment of Socialism, the perils of this (for so they were beginning to think of it) permissive age.

Being very much older than her years even then, she had not made the kind of quick, instinctive reply you might usually get from a child. She waited, saying nothing, watching the nervous movement of her Mother's hands straightening and straightening a pair of thick-knitted and unmistakably male socks.

"These came from Aunt Evelyn," her Mother said irrelevantly. "I don't think she knows his size."

How she had watched, after, for him to put on the socks for the first time, wondering would they fit, watching as he sat down with them in his hand, the lamp light casting the shadow of the kitchen table partly on him as he pulled off his slippers and lined up his boots, troops to pit against the raw morning with ice edging the pond like an ageing eye, and snow clouds massing like great grey packs on the back of Aran Fawddwy.

His bare foot shone in the firelight, bronze and pink mixed in together, like sunset was sometimes, very rarely towards the end of summer when the dew comes down by about eight o'clock and you take in your things quickly and close your front door against the rising silence. She could see in the firelight the hairs growing below the cuffs of his long-legged winter underpants and down onto his instep, black and wiry as briar. Black and bronze and pink and then the sudden sharp detachment of shadow under the muscley arch.

His foot slipped easily into the thick, knitted sock. First the tensed toes into the precise gap held open by his thumbs. Then quickly over instep and arch, stretched round the hard bulb of his heel, then up over the ankle bones he unrolled the rough knitted stuff until it met the edges of his underpants, engulfed them, drove on smoothly another two inches, and he tidied it with a satisfied pat and drew the trouser bottoms down over it all like a blind.

"What are you staring at?"

She stepped back into the longish shadow which his body cast.

"Nothing."

"They fit, then," said her Mother from the corner by the stove, peevishly, as if somehow aggrieved.

He put on his coat and went out without answering. Not until nearly an hour later, when it was entirely light, could the kitchen quite rid itself of the cold blast his opening and closing of the door had let enter.

Winter. Spring. Summer. Autumn. Four arcs on a slowly rolling wheel. When you are nine, or ten, or eleven, the length of each is inordinate. The days seemed endless, yet afterwards resemble no more than flakes you could scrape off with the edge of your nail from a healing graze.

When she was nine, she liked winter best. Everything seemed to have stopped. She liked existing in limbo, everything in a state of waiting, with the force of it filling up inside, the growing sense of pressure until things gather, and give.

When she was ten it was spring the young lady (for so her Mother began to try to tell her she had become) now favoured. "I like spring because it is beginning," she had written for an English composition and been marked down because it was, so Miss Bristow who did English said, bad grammar. She did not understand. Spring was beginning – transitive and intransitive, verb, noun, adjective, all of it. "*Spring is beginning.*" She couldn't put it into any other words than those. Any other way she tried to describe it sounded flat and lifeless, or else sounded as if someone else was saying it, not her.

"*Summer is icumen in*" was the start of a verse she learned sometime during the dusty season at the centre of her eleventh year. Rainless days turned into weeks. A fine dry summer developed into something called drought. *Drouth. Drowt.* She tried out the word over and over, balanced it on the tip of her tongue, dribbled it into the succulent parts of her inner gum, slipped the unfamiliar edges of it painlessly past the supple cordings of her throat. *Drouth. Drowt.*

"*Dammit!*"

The shout in the middle of the night, squeezing up through the floorboards as though the parlour were not big enough to contain it. But coming suddenly awake like that, in the middle of the night, with the moon very white on you, it is sometimes difficult to decide whether it was just a dream.

Her Mother saying, "I do pray for rain." And the sympathetic, superior look of the man who delivered the paraffin as he tilted his head a little to listen and took the funnel out of the ten gallon tank and shook the last few pink drops from it and screwed down the top.

The stream was not a stream any more but a sickly trickle. The stones which the water usually flowed over looked dull and lumpish. You could only just hear the movement of it, a little lurking sound, only just audible at the edge of your head. Everywhere was very dusty. As you walked up the track from the road, your heels kicked up fussy little whorls of dust which hung there for quite a while after you had passed. The ground was hard and began cracking. Everyday, cracks you had discovered the previous day widened and deepened. The chickens looked thin and stopped squabbling among themselves over who was to take the first dust bath in the corner of the yard.

At night the downstairs light stayed on a long time.

"Dammit!"

The dust settled in the creases that lay like straight drains from both his nostrils to the corners of his mouth. When the dust mixed with his sweat, it pasted his hair together in ugly clumps. His hands were black, the collar of his shirt dirty. He began to resemble in part the carelessly constructed thing she and the others humped from farm to farm at the beginning of each November, to the reedy and discordant chorus.

"A penny for the guy! *Ceiniog. Ceiniog.*"

In her eleventh year, she certainly liked summer best. Short, hot nights. Blurred moons which cast the pointed shadow of the pine across her as she lay in bed. The dusty, acrid smell of the grass. The thin chickens drawing out sore sounds from the backs of their throats like slowly stretched strings.

It was inevitable that when she was twelve, autumn would have its turn as her favourite. She was such a sullen and capricious thing.

"What child can like autumn best?" demanded the departing relatives of themselves, casting the memory of the place firmly over a turned shoulder, shuddering a little as though a sliver of something had insinuated itself at the root of the heart, and was levering it loose.

Autumn was melancholy. That was why she liked it best.

"*I am of a melancholic humour,*" she said to herself, draining Shakespeare at a sitting, waking to some ancient clash of harnesses and kingdoms, falling asleep under the eyeless invigilation of a Lear, dreaming, perhaps, of Cordelia.

"*I like leaves that are yellow and red, and the frosted pattern of fern.*"

There was no stillness that could match the stillness of things when there was absolutely no wind. It was quite different from the stillness of still life, a book you had just put down on the table, a chair that nobody was sitting in, an unattended desk. It was stillness *within* *which* was movement, like Van Gogh's 'Sunflowers', a print she had recently come across in one of her Mother's old books, retrieved from a trunk in the back of the attic. This movement-within-stillness seemed to her to be at its peak in the clear days of early autumn, when the sun took longer and longer to come up and the turning leaves curled round each other at the edges and dropped like sky divers in a suicide pact to lie on the ground till the frost got them, and her own feet, probably, crushed them into brittle bits.

At thirteen and at fourteen no one season seemed better to her than another. Everything was held together with a sameness, as if a grey lens had been slipped into her retina, there to interpose itself between her and the world like the reflection of a grey veil. Daily, man-made rhythms were of more significance to her than natural, seasonal ones. What occurred day by day made sense. The getting up, the half mile walk to the corner, the lift in Mr Bristow's Landrover which occasionally contained Miss Bristow and much less often, Mr Bristow's young and silent wife.

"They keep to themselves," her Mother said, half inquisitive, half critical, as she handed over the carefully counted brown and silver coins which went to pay Mr Bristow for his trouble.

These daily events made sense, and the school routine, the bell every forty minutes, break at eleven-fifteen and whispering among the rows of gabardine mackintoshes in the empty cloakroom. Changing for games, stripped of your blue serge bloomers, the wind hitting your chest through your cellular blouse as though you had absolutely nothing on. Writing in your pink preparation book lists of things you had no intention of doing. Then waiting on another corner half a mile from the school gates where there was an old wall and a new seat and a carved stone which said 'Grammar School Repaired 1857'. The stone with its carving jarred just a little every time you passed it. The carving was so sharp and clear, as though someone had only yesterday taken his hammer and chisel out of his bag, got down on his knees and manufactured this brief piece of meaning.

She tried to imagine how it had been over a hundred years ago. Vague pictures came to her, insinuations. It was as if she were marooned on a tiny island, straining to decipher across a sea of seasons the faint and blurry shape of the shore. A sense of helplessness overcame her. Once when she felt like that Miss Bristow looked at her, but didn't say anything.

At the beginning of the grey time, towards the end of when she was twelve, she was visited by what her Mother said was womanhood.

"But I am b-bleeding," she said with the first trace of that afterwards characteristic stutter.

"It is nothing. You are hardly losing. Here."

The strangeness soon faded among the pink and white appliances her Mother provided. But the revulsion which she felt, a kind of subdued horror at her own fleshiness, kept with her.

"Be sure you don't have anything to do with boys or men," said her Mother, looking at her carefully over a pile of folded clothes.

After that, she steered clear of anything faintly male. The piano master she went to once a week after school, she became even more restrained with. When he bent over to turn the page of his own score to '*Mae Hen Wlad*' she shrank back into herself and her fingers faltered on the keys. She didn't like the smell of his breath. He said,

"Well, *Cariad*," and gave her more scales to practice.

"He breathes very heavy," she said to her Mother, who was mending trousers in the uncertain light of the fire.

"No doubt the poor man has asthma," said her Mother without looking up. "Don't you think so, Brynmor? That the poor man has asthma?"

He sat with his legs stretched out straight, facing the fire, so his toes seemed in danger of roasting and you could already tell that his thick, knitted socks were yellowing in the heat of it, and the scent of scorching mixed with the heavy, yellowy smell of his sweat.

"Ah," he said. "It's likely. That pansy. Playing the pianer."

She felt his sneer was for her, and she protested.

"But you *said* I should learn. You *said* it was for the best."

"Now then." Her Mother's voice hovered above the needle plying silvery tracers along the green seam.

"It's a good thing for a girl, the piano. The piano's a good thing for a girl to learn."

"I hate it. And I hate *him*; and his b-breathin'."

"O-o-o-oww."

Miss Bristow was whimpering like a kitten in the corner. Her legs were folded up under her and her face was hidden by her hands and she looked crushed.

Or was it a dream? She tried to decipher some of the little

differences which delineate dream from reality. It seemed real enough. She was watching through the window a scene in the Bristows' big kitchen. She had seen Mr Bristow shake his young and silent wife as a cat shakes a rat, until she had run out of the room. She had seen Mr Bristow shake Miss Bristow until she had pleaded and gone limp and whimpered. Miss Bristow had not at first screamed or cried. She had only screamed when Mr Bristow hit her in the stomach. His fist made a soft, thudding sound as it met Miss Bristow's stomach, rather like the sound her Mother made, plumping up the pillows when she did the beds.

"Slag!"

Mr Bristow stood over Miss Bristow with his legs apart and his hands hanging down by his sides. He turned to go but as though it were an afterthought, kicked Miss Bristow just where the pelvic girdle hinges with the hard, bony part of the upper thigh. The toe of his boot made a sound like 'slup', but Miss Bristow didn't scream, just twitched like a puppet does when somebody clumsy is trying to manipulate the strings.

She stopped looking in at the window then. She heard a door slam and the sound of his boots as he crossed the yard, a flinty sound, stone against metal stud. She came away from the window as she heard him get nearer, and tried to pretend to herself she had just arrived. His shadow came round the corner before him, flat and black on the stone. Then he appeared like an unnecessary adjunct to the shadow, his very fleshiness somehow unreal, as if you could poke a stick right through it, as if it were matterless.

"Uh?" he said when he saw her.

He seemed the same. Quiet and tidy. You would never have thought there was any harm in him. His hair grew down in a brown wave in front of his ears. She didn't like that. But his hands were clean. He seemed neutral, and his skin, particularly around his mouth and in the middle of his cheeks, was pinkish and neutral. She hadn't really looked at his eyes before, and now that she tried to, they were nondescript.

"Uh?" he said again, but the same as always, nothing friendly or unfriendly.

She held out the packet of twelve bantam's eggs, her Mother's offering for something or other, an extra lift.

He said, "Oh. Ah. *Diolch*" And took them not roughly, as she had supposed, with a great danger of his big thick fingers poking holes through the thin shells, but in his open palms, gently, the effort of gentleness making his fingers quiver, and his arms right up to the elbow as he carried them in.

He gave her a lift back because it was on his way. He didn't say anything as they bumped along, nor did she, just held on to the handle halfway up the door and watched the white light of midday go by them. When you looked outside at the white light and the sky behind it, then inside at Mr Bristow or your feet or the gearstick or the floor, your eyes took time to adjust, and everything seemed black and white like a photograph, but more like a negative, you couldn't really tell who was who, only by outline, and people's hair was white and their faces black and their mouths white so you had to guess their expression.

Mr Bristow's hand looked black. It looked like a black, predatory thing, a giant spider or a great black bat as he moved it around the cab, up to scratch the side of his nose, down to change gear, back onto the steering wheel which bucked and shuddered as they went over the holes in the road.

She hated his great black hand. The cab got smaller and smaller, the hand bigger still, his nose and his jaw seemed to elongate, his body got squatter, and his deep, even breathing deafened her. When she looked out the sky and the mountain around her which rose and fell like a great green sea, hinged and tilted. She thought, "I must stop this. I must get out," but could do nothing to accomplish it.

They went on like this for another mile. Just when she could feel something about to give, he yanked on the handbrake and they stopped. He didn't look at her as she climbed down, just muttered something. As soon as she had slammed the door the Landrover began to move, and before she had walked more than a dozen steps it was out of sight.

The smell of half-burned petrol wafted up into her nose and she shied away from it. She could hear the sound of the engine getting fainter as it went down the hill. She crossed the road and walked towards the gate. A buzzard swung into the edge of her vision and hung there like a mobile over a child's cot. She heard it mewing, a high sound, rather like a child. A raven came grunting over the pink tip of Tir Stent and flapped slowly towards the north. A south-west wind made a sucking sound in an old roll of wire. The wind in the grass went wuush, shuush, and rattled the gate in her hand as she opened and closed it. It was a white, high, blowsy, April day. Everything seemed to be running in front of itself, there was no stillness anywhere, her hair whipped and jiggled about her ears and onto her cheekbones. She felt for the first time a sense of herself in relation to everything else, as if she were part of a single system, a fragment of something hurrying towards its own special destiny. She turned and put her hands on the top bar of the gate and looked out over the long horizon, clean and green and very definite at the edges, and felt almost content.

She turned and began walking up the track. Her skirt lifted and billowed in the wind. She felt a sudden cramp in the lower part of her stomach, right at the front and just above the *mons veneris* whose identity she had looked up in a school biology primer, and which stuck out in trousers. She recognised the symptom and was not surprised when, within a minute, she felt the first tickling in the cotton gusset of her knickers. She fumbled in her pocket and discovered a grubby paper handkerchief which she stuffed in past her knicker elastic under the pretence of bending down to do up her shoe. She felt like crying but didn't, just kept on up the track towards the house which got bigger and bigger, dwarfing the mountain behind and filling up her whole view, She noticed she was clenching and unclenching her hands, first right then left, rhythmically, in time with her steps to which in turn she controlled and slowed her breathing.

As she neared the house she heard the explosive *phut* of the axe settling its head into a block of wood. Then again *phut* every few seconds as the axe split block after block. *Phut* step step step. *Phut* step step step. She felt like a piece of machine, something self-regulating and contained, and the sound of the axe and her steps and her breathing filled her head until she thought she would never hear anything else ever again.

She entered the yard and walked towards the house. As she approached the kitchen door she saw with unrepeatable clarity its every detail, how the paint was peeling a bit down the one side, little green flakes quivering in the wind, how black and shiny the latch was from a recent cleaning, how bright the hinges looked because they had only been replaced the month before, and just as she saw these things, as they fell into her head as notes do in a musical composition, the door opened and her Mother stood back, waiting for her to go in.

NOTES ON CONTRIBUTORS

Ifan Pughe: This is a pseudonymous story. The identity of the author remains unknown.

Dorothy Edwards: (1903-34), born Ogmore Vale, Mid Glamorgan, educated at Howell's School and University College, Cardiff. She published *Rhapsody* (1927) a collection of stories, and a novel, *Winter Sonata* (1928), both influenced by Russian literature. A remote and distant person, she committed suicide in 1934.

Nigel Heseltine: (1916-95). A poet and story writer, and the son of composer Peter Warlock, Heseltine was for some time joint editor of the magazine *Wales*. His *Tales of the Squirearchy* appeared in 1946, at the time he quit Wales to work around the world as an agronomist.

Geraint Goodwin: (1903-41), born in Newtown. A Fleet Street journalist, novelist and story writer, most of whose creative work was written after being diagnosed as tubercular. His novels and stories are largely set in his native mid-Wales.

Caradoc Evans: (1878-1945). Perhaps the most notorious author from Wales. His infamous *My People* created uproar in 1915, and was followed by several collections of stories, novels and polemical writing on Welsh society.

Margiad Evans: (1909-58) the pseudonym of novelist Peggy Whistler, who lived for some years near Ross-on-Wye. She was the author of four novels, a collection of stories, two volumes of poetry and two autobiographical works, including *A Ray of Darkness* (1952) about the onset of her epilepsy.

George Ewart Evans: (1909-86), born Abercynon and educated at University College, Cardiff. After serving in the RAF, Evans became a full-time writer in East Anglia, producing a series of books, now televised, about that region.

Gwyn Jones: (1907-99), born in Blackwood, Gwent. A miner's son he became Professor of English at University College, Aberystwyth, and later at Cardiff. Jones published novels, stories and scholarly books including translations of *The Mabinogion* and Icelandic sagas. He founded *The Welsh Review*, and edited many books and anthologies.

Gwyn Thomas: (1913-81), born at Porth in the Rhondda. Read modern languages at Oxford and taught prior to becoming a successful novelist, playwright, columnist and broadcaster on radio and television. Perhaps best known for his exuberant humour and vivid language.

Glyn Jones: (1905-95), born at Merthyr Tydfil. A poet, story writer and novelist, he also translated Welsh poetry and wrote the definitive account of Anglo-Welsh writing in the early part of the twentieth century, *The Dragon Has Two Tongues*.

Dylan Thomas: (1914-53). Probably the most famous of all English language writers from Wales. His high reputation as a poet sometimes overshadows his skillful short stories.

Siân Evans: (b. 1912). Pseudonym of Nancy Whistler, sister of Peggy (Margiad Evans), with whom she had an almost twinlike relationship. Her stories in *The Welsh Review* and *Welsh Short Stories* (1940).

Alun Lewis: (1915-44), born in Aberdare, Mid Glamorgan. Judged by many as the finest poet of the Second World War (in which he died), Lewis was also the author of some outstanding stories, a novel, *Morlais*, and various unpublished plays.

Richard Hughes: (1900-76). One of the major figures of twentieth century letters. Author of novels such as *A High Wind in Jamaica* (1929) and *The Fox in the Attic* (1961), he also wrote the first play for radio.

Rhys Davies: (1903-78). Novelist and story writer from Clydach Vale who based himself in London as a full-time writer. His early work was much influenced by D.H. Lawrence, whom he knew, but he evolved his own style in his prolific output. Davies has been sadly neglected since his death.

Brenda Chamberlain: (1912-71), born in Bangor, north Wales. Artist and author whose singular life was spent in Snowdonia and on the islands of Bardsey, and Hydra in the Cyclades. Her striking paintings were the subject of a touring retrospective exhibition in 1988-89, and her classic account of life on Bardsey Island, *Tide-race*, was reissued in 1987.

Ron Berry: (1920-97). Novelist and story writer of the Rhondda Valley, who worked as a miner after leaving school at fourteen. He published six novels, and a nature diary, *Peregrine Watching*.

Dannie Abse: (1923-2014), born in Cardiff but lived mostly in London, where he practised medicine. A popular poet, playwright and novelist, he also wrote autobiography and edited many anthologies. He is best known as a poet, especially as a reader in public. *Ask the Moon*, his New and Collected Poems, was published posthumously in 2014.

Emyr Humphreys: (b. 1919). Novelist, poet and dramatist from Prestatyn, Emyr Humphreys has also produced and directed a number of films for television. Wales' outstanding novelist in either language, he is much involved in the cultural politics of the country and is author of *The Taliesin Tradition*, a history of Wales.

Glenda Beagan: (b. 1948). Poet and short story writer now living in Rhuddlan. 'Scream, Scream' first appeared in *Planet*. She is the author of three collections of stories from Seren.

Alun Richards: (1929-2004), born in Pontypridd. A successful novelist, playwright and story writer. Alun Richards was also the author of the television series *Ennal's Point*, and editor of *The Penguin Book of Welsh Short Stories* (1976).

Leslie Norris: (1921-2006). Poet and short story writer born near Merthyr Tydfil. Although widely recognised as a gifted poet, his first book of stories, *Sliding* (1978), won the David Higham Award, and *The Girl from Cardigan* (1988) was published to great acclaim. Also a children's author, Norris was for some years Visiting Professor of Poetry at Brigham Young University, Utah.

Jaci Stephen: (b. 1969). Award-winning print and broadcast journalist from Bridgend who has also published stories and poetry. Her stories have appeared in the Faber Introduction series. She is presently television reviewer for the *Daily Mail*.

Duncan Bush: (1946-2017), born in Cardiff. A prize-winning and much acclaimed poet whose stories have appeared in *The Fiction Magazine* and other periodicals. His work is often concerned with political and social themes, *The Genre of Silence* (1988), for instance, is a mixture of poetry and prose set in twentieth century Russia.

Clare Morgan: Novelist and story writer from rural South Wales. Her story collection, *A Change of Heart* was published in 1996, and 'Losing' won the 1986 Welsh Arts Council Story Competition. She is the founder and director Oxford University's creative writing programme.

The Editor.
Born in 1944, John Davies was brought up in Port Talbot, South Wales, and in Prestatyn where he taught English. He has also taught in Michigan and Washington. He is the author of four collections, one of which, *The Visitor's Book*, was joint winner of Alice Hunt Bartlett Prize.

ACKNOWLEDGEMENTS

The help of the following people and organisations is acknowledged: Mrs Rhoda Goodwin; the Estate of Caradoc Evans; the Estate of George Ewart Evans; Prof. Gwyn Jones; the Estate of Gwyn Thomas; Dr Glyn Jones; David Higham Associates for Dylan Thomas' 'Patricia, Edith and Arnold' from *Portrait of the Artist as a Young Dog*, and for Richard Hughes' 'The Swans' from *A Moment of Time*; Mrs Gweno Lewis; the Estate of Brenda Chamberlain; Ron Berry; Anthony Sheil Associates for Dannie Abse's 'My Father's Red Indian' from *A Strong Dose of Myself*; Emyr Humphreys; Glenda Beagan; Alun Richards for 'Fly Half', first published in *Dai Country* by Hutchinson; Leslie Norris; Jaci Stephen and Faber & Faber; Duncan Bush; Clare Morgan.

Cent 87.04 210